The Idea
of a Modern University

THE
Idea
OF A
Modern University

edited by
Sidney Hook
Paul Kurtz
Miro Todorovich

Prometheus Books
Buffalo, N.Y. 14215

LA
226
.I34

Published by Prometheus Books
923 Kensington Avenue, Buffalo, New York 14215

Library of Congress Catalog Card Number 74-75349
ISBN - 0-87975-032-4

Printed in the United States of America

The Idea
of a Modern University

Contents

Contents

HIGHER EDUCATION UNDER FIRE

THE CRUCIAL PROBLEMS OF THE MODERN UNIVERSITY

Contents

Preface: By Way of History

Miro Todorovich
*City University of New York,
Bronx Community College*

When Sidney Hook, Gerald Pinsky, and I decided late in 1968 that it
was worthwhile trying to organize a faculty group to resist the onslaught of extremist students and their allies against American colleges
and universities, our move was based on a careful analysis of the academic and general cultural scene. Contrary to suggestions from numerous quarters that a state of normalcy would surely follow the 1968
election, our forecast indicated a long period of academic instability
and turmoil.

Tensions that preceded violent disruptions at some great institutions
on the West Coast were already sweeping eastward; Columbia was
only recovering from its worst spring. The administrations of some of
the most prestigious institutions were in palpable disarray. Their organizational structures, geared to normal day-by-day operations and efficient fundraising, were shattered by violent pressures from within and
without. Accustomed to polite discourse, administrators and faculty
were sometimes shocked into inaction by the mere use of foul language. Existing professional and scholarly organizations proved
singularly ill-equipped to cope with the physical, as well as the intellectual, dislocations on campus. While universities were literally burn-
ing, faculty forums deliberated as to whether to establish a new committee to look into the causes and phenomenology of campus events.
It was a one-sided battle between those thinking in terms of resolutions

and possible censure of violent students on the one hand, and militant fanatics, assured of amnesty, who were quite effectively "doing their thing," on the other.

The swiftness of the collapse of so many academic institutions in the late 1960s can be explained to a considerable extent by the lack of educational conviction among the American professoriat. Decades of campus tranquillity had brought about a professional compartmentalization of the academic structure. Physicists, for example, knew and understood fellow physicists from even the most distant institutions better than they knew or understood their own colleagues from other departments. Committee work was generally viewed as a necessary evil; administrative chores were gladly left to professional administrators. Interests were perused from individual or, at most, departmental vantage points with little thought given to the overall educational picture. The balance between research and teaching was decisively tilted in favor of scholarly pursuits. No wonder then that when the tide of violence surged against departmental doorsteps, many American faculties were unwilling or unable to mobilize on their local campuses sufficient forces to stop the disruption of the educational process. In the apt words of Abba Lerner ". . . a technological breakthrough in the art of disruption" became possible when "in Berkeley in 1964, Mario Savio discovered to his own and everybody else's surprise, how easy it was to demoralize the faculty."

Thus the first order of the day for our new faculty organization was to work on strengthening the intellectual and moral stamina of its members and the general conviction of the American professoriat in the validity of its calling. At stake was its purpose as well as its performance. Even the lengthy name of our organization—University Centers for Rational Alternatives (UCRA)—was meant to underscore the urgent need for a search for rational alternative solutions to pressing educational problems, as distinct from doctrinaire and often irrational solutions advocated on all sides. The hope at that time, in December 1968, was to proceed as quickly and vigorously as possible toward the establishment of centers for discussion of needed blueprints of intellectual and educational reconstruction.

Events in quick succession crowded the spring semester of 1969 and forced a reconsideration of these early plans. The confrontations at Harvard, the "guns of Cornell," and hundreds of other incidents across the land seemed to threaten the very existence of institutions of higher learning. All available energies had to be mobilized in support of the most direct and basic actions for the survival of a nonpoliticized, free, and open-minded university. Discussion of the more complex educational problems had to yield to the elementary issues of simple defense against the stratagems and forcible incursions of the "barbarians of virtue" into the academy.

It took almost four years to reestablish a reasonable measure of tranquillity to college and university campuses. It was only late in 1971 that UCRA was able to realize some of its other objectives. One of these was to reexamine the idea of a university in the contemporary cultural and technological context.

As conceived, the symposium "The Idea of a Modern University" had a twofold purpose: to explore the degree to which an educational consensus is possible and to present for discussion some of the most urgent problems in higher education. The organizers of the symposium believed that after the years of violent dislocation, a *diagnostic* assessment of the current status of higher education was clearly in order. For that purpose, of the many possible topics for discussion, they singled out as most fundamental the question of the universality and integrity of higher education, with the associated problems of faculty role, faculty unionization, and government intervention in university affairs.

We gratefully acknowledge our indebtedness to the Hegeler Institute, whose support made the conference possible.

The present volume is the fruit of the conference held at Rockefeller University, New York City, on February 21-22, 1972. Although UCRA is the proud sponsor of these deliberations, the participants speak only for themselves.

Introduction: The Rationale of the Problem

Sidney Hook
New York University

During the nineteenth century Cardinal Newman's *The Idea of a University* expressed the ideal of a secular university in Anglo-American culture, whose institutions of higher education had reflected in many ways the pervasive influence of the religious establishment. With the emergence of the research-oriented German university system, an even clearer differentiation was made between the religious and the secular; the quest for salvation was subordinated to the quest for the truth, especially new truths.

Neither Cardinal Newman's view nor that of the German university model, although influential, was the decisive force in the emerging patterns of American higher education. For their roots lay in the college of the American colonial experience. As the American college shed its essentially religious character, it became subject to a multiplicity of social, economic, and political pressures. Social needs and tasks that in other countries were fulfilled by nonacademic institutions were entrusted to American colleges and universities to meet. So varied were the interests and activities of American higher education by the middle of the twentieth century that it was impossible to find one overall conception that adequately characterized the crowded academic scene. Clark Kerr's concept, the "multiversity," seemed to be a more accurate description than any other characterization.

The unplanned and undirected growth of American colleges and universities and the absence of any coherent educational philosophy in most institutions created a number of campus problems. When student disorders first broke out, the most widely accepted explanations attributed responsibility for them to internal educational features of the university. Although plausible, these explanations turned out to be extremely superficial. No sooner were they advanced, than events gave them the lie. For these disorders occurred in institutions that were small as well as large, rural as well as urban, curricularly well-integrated as well as curricularly heterogeneous, and in ones oriented primarily toward teaching as well as in ones directed toward research. Not a single educational factor or combination of factors could be found that accounted for the widespread student revolts.

I believe it can be taken as established by now that the occasions for, as well as the main causes of, the rash of violent confrontations that erupted in an unprecedented fashion during the decade of the 1960s on hundreds of American university campuses had their origin outside the academic community. Whether it was the Vietnam war or the draft or racial injustice or civil or industrial strife, the issues were not of the university's making, and nothing that the universities could do would alter the fact that in a democracy these political issues could be properly resolved only in the democratic marketplace of public opinion.

University Centers for Rational Alternatives (UCRA) sought to preserve the relative autonomy of the university from attempts to politicalize it, to discourage resorts to violence and threats of violence on the academic scene, and to facilitate the adoption of procedures by which all genuine educational issues could be peacefully and rationally resolved. It was the only organization in the entire country to rally faculties to the defense of academic integrity and freedom against the enemies *within* as well as outside the academy. Despite its many and heroic activities, UCRA gradually began to confront a question to which neither it nor anyone else had a ready answer. Why was it that the universities, which had traditionally conceived themselves to be citadels of reason, disinterestedness, intellectual and moral civility, had failed to prevent or contain the flood of violence—physical, psychological and rhetorical—which in so many cases overwhelmed the campuses, sometimes resulting in arson, assault and death? Why had the universities failed to stem the rout of reason? What had gone wrong?

It became clear that to answer these and related questions we would have to explore the basic issues concerning the nature and function of the modern university. In the nature of the case, these questions were normative. Teachers and scholars would have to take more seriously than ever in the past their role as educators. Having developed a justi-fiable conception of higher education, all the urgent problems and challenges of university life could be clarified and evaluated.

This volume contains the highlights of a conference called in 1972 to consider the topic "The Idea of a Modern University." The hope is that once uncoerced agreement can be won on the nature and goals of the university, the never-ending struggle to preserve academic freedom and integrity will be waged more intelligently and courageously.

Arrangements have been made to convoke another national con-ference on "The Philosophy of the Curriculum" to explore in great depth some of the unresolved issues of higher education in the United States.

PART ONE

UNIVERSAL HIGHER EDUCATION: PROMISE OR ILLUSION?

The Illusion of Universal Higher Education

Fritz Machlup
Princeton University

As I understand the words, "universal higher education" can be neither a promise nor an illusion, for it is simply a contradiction in terms, like a four-month trimester or a geography of the moon or an extensive intensity. I confess that I am a stickler for clean definitions and uncorrupted word meanings, but I believe that educators have special obligations in this respect.

UNIVERSAL EDUCATION?

On an earlier occasion, when I gave my views at an educators' meeting on universal higher education, I was rebuked for assuming that "universal" meant universal. I was told that it did not mean "for all," but only "for many more than now." Then why say "universal"? Because, as a politics-minded pedagogue explained to me, it sounds good, and it connotes the good intention of making higher education available to all who want it. I did not ask him what he meant by "higher education."

If a particular can be transformed into a universal by adding restrictive qualifications, such as "all who want it," the same transformation is achieved by "all who can master it," or "all who are prepared for it," or "all who are selected," or even "all who can afford it." The deceptive, unspecified "universal," does not really tell anything. The real

3

problem, which the word is probably designed to conceal, is *for what portion of all, for how many,* and *for just what kinds of persons* shall the presumably higher education be available or be redesigned. I have added "redesigned" because the question of numbers, proportions, and qualifications will require different answers, depending on the meaning of "higher education."

HIGHER, BROADER, AND REMEDIAL EDUCATION

The definitions of "higher education" are manifold, even if the meaning of "education" is taken for granted and only the definition of "higher" is specified. Generic definitions that take historical examples as a standard refer to quite different models. The education offered at Oxford in the seventeenth or eighteenth century was very different from the education the University of Berlin was established to provide in the nineteenth century, and the education offered by many community colleges in the United States today is something totally different from both. Of course, the general objectives of these three types of institutions were quite dissimilar: old Oxford was chiefly designed to prepare devout Christians for the ministry; the University of Berlin, to prepare scientists and scholars for academic careers (that is, for producing more scientists and scholars); the American community college, to give two additional years of schooling to young high-school graduates.

By talking about the objectives of these institutions of higher education, I have implicitly touched on the question of the appropriate percentage of people that can be served by them. How many clergymen are needed or demanded? Are more than one or two wanted for a thousand people? How many scholars and scientists are needed for research on the frontiers of knowledge? Can we imagine 10 per cent of the population engaged in pure research? On the other hand, it is easy to imagine one-half of all high-school graduates choosing to spend another two years at college if it promises better jobs and peer-group approbation.

Some time ago, I published a paper of which several abridged versions were prepublished in the daily press. To convey a distinction I consider important, I gave it the title "Longer Education: Thinner, Broader, or Higher." I wanted to emphasize the fact that *longer* education—that is, education beyond high school—need not always be, and indeed rarely is, *higher* education. This provocative statement drew angry epithets: elitist, snob. Yet I have been called worse names and survived. I still believe that it makes a difference if a nineteen-year-old studies high-school algebra or matrix algebra or topology. My insistence on such distinctions is not indicative of contempt for remedial education or broader education. As a matter of fact, I am unhesitatingly in favor of both.

If our schools have been so deficient that a large percentage of graduates, after twelve years of elementary and secondary education, have not yet mastered the three Rs, then remedial education ought to be available. I would prefer that it be offered in high schools. If, however, the teachers there cannot cope with this task or if those in need of remedial schooling hate the old high-school building and would be more strongly motivated on a college campus, then let us offer them this favorable environment and different teachers. But I submit that remedial teaching should not be done by instructors in broader or higher education, because standards at higher levels are likely to suffer if the same teachers also teach at lower levels. As far as certification is concerned, to give college credit for remedial work downgrades the college degree—and there are still many who courageously stick to "credentialism," just as they find a usefulness in quality control for industrial products.

I am also a strong supporter of liberal education, of a *studium generale*. Indeed, I would deny the greatest scientist the designation of "educated person" if he were a narrow specialist, lacking broad education. Hence, I have no doubt that most institutions of genuinely higher education should also offer a wide choice of courses that specialists would not consider highly advanced. The faculties of almost all universities recognize differences in levels of post-secondary education by designating courses as undergraduate and graduate. Standards differ, however, among universities and even among departments of the same university. Many of us have participated in heated discussions in graduate committees when some stricter members questioned whether certain courses in other departments deserved graduate credit; similarly, we can recall debates in college committees or even faculty meetings about denying or approving college credit to courses with questionable academic contents or quality. Thus, even if we may not agree on where to draw borderlines, we cannot deny that such lines, however blurred, do exist.

One may have quite clear and firm conceptions of all sorts of things, abstract or concrete, and yet be unable to formulate fitting definitions. I am not sufficiently familiar with the literature to know the criteria determined by educators for elementary, secondary, and tertiary education, but I know that there is rough agreement on what should be taught in elementary school and what should be postponed until secondary school. The agreement is rough, to be sure; there are those, for example, who advocate that a foreign language begin in elementary school, and there is controversy about when to begin teaching grammar. Agreement about the proper borderline between secondary and tertiary school is probably much more precarious; ongoing debate on this matter has occasionally led to reforms. For example, high-school curricula in mathematics have changed in recent years to include certain materials previously taught only in college, and academic high-schools in Europe—Gymnasium and Realgymnasium—have long taught materials that were left to colleges here. The latter fact was officially acknowledged by academic authorities in the United States, who offered up to two years of college credit for Gymnasium graduates. What in several other countries has been successfully taught in secondary school cannot reasonably be called "higher education."

It would obviously be impossible for anybody to absorb in the time normally devoted to secondary school all the subjects and materials that could conceivably be offered there. For example, a student of average ability can easily learn two foreign languages in high school but probably not five, although most languages can be taught at this level and some even in elementary school. Similarly, a high-school student could conceivably be taught several eras of world history in greater detail, but surely not all periods, all countries, and all aspects. The same is true for survey or laboratory courses in the natural sciences, and for all other subjects that could be learned by high-school students. Choices must be made because the body of knowledge hypothetically teachable at the secondary level is enormous and only small portions can be absorbed in the few years of secondary school. Anyone who wants to learn more cannot help postponing it; he has to come back for post-secondary education. But this does not make it "higher education." Education is "higher" only if it builds upon knowledge absorbed in secondary and introductory tertiary education and could not have been absorbed at the earlier stage (except by a few geniuses) because it requires more intelligence, mental discipline, and perseverance than can be expected from most students of high-school age.

Of the thousands of courses that might potentially be offered in secondary schools, and of the hundreds actually offered there (at least in some countries), a high-school student of ordinary diligence and intelligence cannot take more than about sixty—in any case, less than a hundred. No one, therefore, is "broadly educated" when he leaves high school. Moreover, it would be ridiculous to assume that what can be added in another two, three, or four years can amount to much. The thirty to forty courses taken by the typical college undergraduate are still such a minute fraction of the existing body of knowledge that it would be unduly pretentious to call the graduating bachelor of arts or science a "broadly educated" person. What the liberal-arts college can do for its best students is to stimulate in them a *taste* for broad education, a *desire* for continuing education, to be pursued chiefly through a lifetime of reading, but also through discussions, lectures, conferences, theaters, operas, concerts, exhibitions, and museums. Even the broadly educated man or woman—rarely anybody below the age of forty—will have assimilated only a small part of all existing knowledge, but he will know vastly more than a college graduate, let alone the high-school graduate.

I suspect that only a small fraction of college graduates really go on learning—that is, learning for cultural, not practical, purposes—after they begin a career in business, industry, finance, government, law, medicine, engineering, or whatever. This need not mean that their college work was wasted. They may have acquired habits, tastes, and attitudes that can benefit them as well as others. But I shall later argue that for a considerable portion of graduates the time spent at college was in fact wasted.

Undergraduate studies can also lead to an interest in higher education, or at least an understanding of it. By contrasting higher education with broader education, I have already intimated what I now wish to make explicit, namely, that most of the student's time in college is devoted to acquiring broader, not higher, education. Many colleges offer no higher education at all; even in the most prestigious colleges one-fifth or one-fourth, at best, of all courses deserve to be characterized as higher education. While I regret the complete absence of higher education in many colleges, I neither regret nor disparage the high ratio of broader to higher education. Exclusive emphasis on higher education produces narrow specialists; exclusive emphasis on broader education produces superficial dilettantes. Specialization in one or two disciplines is needed for the student to learn that only studies in depth justify his claiming more than surface knowledge in any field. (Alas, even some great scientists have failed to learn this simple precept of humility.) To postpone specialization until graduate school would be injurious to both broader and higher education. I conclude that no college should fail to insist on distribution of the student's time between specialized studies in a field of concentration and a bouquet of other disciplines.

I must no longer withhold my favorite definition of higher education. I define it as the *education of scholars and scientists, and also of practitioners of those few professions that are based on continuing research*. At first, this may appear to be a restrictive definition, one that limits the percentage of people who should engage in higher education to a tiny fraction. On second thought, the limitation is not imposed by any insufficiency of social need or economic demand for research, development, and scholarship; society does not prohibit or exclude anybody from choosing scientific or scholarly research as an avocation. Just as the absence of social need or economic demand does not prevent anybody from studying a musical instrument, painting, or sculpture, so any person seriously interested in higher education can try it. But, ex *hypothesi*, the prerequisites for higher studies are severe, and I believe that the real limiting factor is the supply of qualified students.

Instead of insisting, however, on acceptance of my favorite definition and its implications, I shall look at the problem from several points of view. These include the qualities needed for successful exposition to higher education as it is or as it might be, the need or demand for qualified manpower, the private benefits accruing to and the costs incurred by students and their families, the social benefits and costs. These views will always be connected with present programs or with redesigned ones, and even with such things as the effects of longer education on students' character traits, social attitudes, and world outlook.

SIX QUALITIES

Allow me to start, however, with my own definition of higher education as the education of actual and potential scholars. In my "elitist" address at the 1970 Invitational Conference on Testing Problems, I emphasized that the qualities needed for this kind of education were so scarce that no more than 10 to 15 per cent of the age group would subject themselves, or could be subjected, to the rigorous effort required.[1] I regard six qualities as essential: (1) intelligence, (2) creativity, (3) interest (intellectual curiosity), (4) ambition, (5) diligence, and (6) perseverance.

I shall not quarrel if some of these are considered overlapping or if some are not considered essential. I have been told that creativity is desirable but by no means indispensable for research, indeed, that a large percentage of scholars and scientists and of members of professions based on science and scholarship lack creativity and can do well without it. In every discipline, some tasks have to be performed that do not require people with creativity and intelligence in the ninetieth or eighty-fifth percentile. I do not deny this, but I wonder whether these routine tasks in research actually require all the minimum required studies for advanced academic degrees.

I would concede, moreover, that trade-offs are possible among these essential qualities. Diligence and perseverance are often effective substitutes for intelligence. Some lazy geniuses have made important discoveries, and some highly industrious mediocrities have done sig-

8

nificant research. Thanks to the partial substituting of needed qualities, the cutoff point in eligibility for higher education (in my sense) need not be the same on all scores.

Before I proceed, let me emphasize that I have been dealing here with higher education, not with that part of college that is given to broader education. For the latter, substantial discounts may be given to the first two requirements: no superior intelligence is needed and creativity may be completely lacking, as long as interest, diligence, and perseverance are present in sufficient degrees. Without these qualities, however, the case is hopeless; any pressure on young people to go to college may do them more harm than good.

This statement may seem illogical and inconsistent with some of my earlier contentions. In particular, if the curriculum of secondary schools is so designed that 90 per cent of the age group can handle it (I assume that about 10 per cent are incapable of completing high school because of brain damage and other mental deficiencies) and if broader education at college is just "more of the same," does it not follow that 90 per cent of the age group can manage the broadening part of post-secondary education? It *would* follow if students were still diligent and persevering after ten or twelve years of school, that is, if one could reasonably assume that 90 per cent of all youngsters would persevere for fourteen to sixteen years in school, willing to spend most of their waking hours in the library, laboratory, and classroom. Such an assumption, however, would be far from reasonable, because that willingness decreases for most young people when they reach puberty and sexual maturity. Many of the most studious boys who love school and devour books at age twelve detest school and books at seventeen.

This decline in willingness to study, or at least to submit to formal schooling of the types we know, is only one argument against pressuring high-school graduates to go to college; it is also an argument against compulsory high-school attendance and, in general, against using social pressures and moral suasion to induce unwilling youth to continue school beyond age fourteen. In a book published in 1962, I advocated a system that would start a child's education at least two years earlier and compress the present school curricula from twelve years to ten. Such a system would avoid some of the harmful consequences of our attempts to force adolescents who would prefer gainful employment to sit passively in classes under teachers they dislike. If they drop out, they know what is best for them, as Michael Harrington (if I remember correctly) once said in a discussion on poverty and juvenile delinquency.

This digression on the school-leaving age is for the purpose of reinforcing my contention that, even if college courses made no heavier

9

demands on the intelligence of students than high-school courses have made, we could not expect the percentage of the age group "qualified to go to college" to be anywhere near the percentage of the age group attending high school. Lack of interest, diligence, and perseverance disqualifies most of them. If we want college to include a modicum of higher education besides its staple of broader education—and I believe we should insist on it—an additional number of high-school graduates will be disqualified on grounds of inadequate intelligence.

I admit that I have no empirical evidence to support my guesses about the magnitude of these various disqualifications. I have seen no conclusive tests that would furnish valid clues. Disqualification on grounds of insufficient intelligence is especially difficult to prove because it depends, among other things, on the type of examinations designed to test the achievements of earlier preparation and, especially, on the extent and level of higher education included in college requirements. I must therefore plead guilty of disseminating mere hunches and impressions, but I believe that such boldness is a necessay first step on the route toward more securely warranted beliefs. Let me then repeat my statistically unsupported statement that, with the extent and level of higher education that I want to see required in college, no more than 10 to 15 per cent of the age group would be qualified for it (on the grounds of the personal qualities listed above).

My proposition is, I believe, empirically testable, especially if we first eliminate the requirement of intelligence. This is necessary because the required extent and level of higher education are inevitably arbitrary. For example, if the required work were to include the most advanced courses in higher mathematics that are taught in the best mathematics departments of the country, or the most advanced courses in microeconomics, microbiology, solid-state physics, and so forth, the percentage of the age group eligible for such a curriculum might be less than two or three. If intelligence tests as well as achievement tests based on earlier schooling are eliminated, we may be able to devise a test based on self-selection by high-school seniors, who are given full information on what they can expect at college.

HOW MANY WILL GO TO COLLEGE IF COST AND GAIN ARE NIL?

I shall try to imagine the conditions that might attract the maximum number of full-time college students.

1. No required courses—only electives, including new courses with contents and methods proposed by students or designed with a view to attracting students.

2. No required attendance at lectures, classes, or seminars.

3. No required examinations in individual courses.

4. No required comprehensive examinations, either written or oral.

5. No required term papers or other exercises.

6. No grades, unless requested by the student.

7. No restrictions on private lives of students.

8. No tuition or any other fees.

9. An annual stipend equal to the average wage earned by employed nonstudent members of the same age group.

10. Earnings in later life of college graduates to be neither larger nor smaller than those of nongraduates.

11. No other forms of discrimination, social or economic, in favor of or against college graduates.

(Note: It goes without saying that students, since they are to be paid for enrolling in college, must be barred from accepting outside employment; otherwise the absence of required attendance, examinations, homework, and so on would make it possible for a registered full-time student to hold another full-time job.)

My expectation is that even under these conditions less than 100 per cent of high-school graduates would choose to go on to college. A good many would be thoroughly fed up with going to school. Of course, the possibility of taking many (or only) "fun courses," and being paid for it as much as the average wage-earner, would be quite an attraction; still, I suppose that a good many young men and women would rather go to work and show that they could earn a higher than average wage.

Let us assume, for the sake of argument, that 80 per cent of high-school graduates, or 70 per cent of the entire age group, would elect to go to college under the described conditions. Now we could eliminate, in turn, any one or any combination of the stated conditions, and find out how many high-school seniors would decline the opportunity to spend four additional years in formal education. As long as we merely *speculate* about the effects the various factors would have on the students' decisions (to take or to decline the option), our answers may differ widely. We may, for example, overestimate or underestimate the importance in the students' actual preferences for abolition of required courses and all examinations. Such demands, made by highly vocal student groups, are sometimes backed by a majority of a student body, but we may interpret this as a bandwagon effect, a desire to join "the movement" because of a fear of appearing old-fashioned and a supporter of the establishment. On the other hand, if we take the loud voices as indicative of strong feelings of a real majority, we may be led to give much weight to the various conditions regarding absence or presence of the customary academic requirements. If this is so, maintaining the usual requirements of course examination and comprehensives would seem to reduce drastically the percentage of those choosing to go to college.

The tenth condition deserves special comment. The expectation that it pays to go to college, because the lifetime earnings of a college graduate promise to be much higher than those of persons without a college education, is probably an important factor in students' decisions. On the other hand, this expectation of higher earnings is based on experiences from a time when, at most, 25 per cent of the age group attended college, and it may no longer be valid at a time when the supply of college-educated labor has greatly increased relative to that of non-college-graduates. It is quite possible that such income differentials will disappear or may already have disappeared; moreover, the income differentials of the past applied to college graduates who were presumed to have had not only broader education but also *some* higher education. Very few productively useful skills are developed by broader education alone and, no matter how highly we appreciate the cultural effects, we may no longer expect that the more broadly educated person will command a higher wage or salary. The highest-paid skills sought in the present labor market are not those produced by the liberal arts. For all these and other reasons it would be important to know how many students would demand a college education that does not promise them any pecuniary rewards.

The survey research proposed here might yield useful numerical information about the factors determining the demand for broad college education and, consequently, the possible supply of college graduates. Are no statistical data available that could throw light on any of the issues in question? Do the enrollment figures of recent years carry any message? Between 1967 and 1970 we saw increases that brought the number of high-school graduates registering for a first year of college to over 50 per cent. It will probably be conceded by most observers that this rush to college was largely influenced by pressures or incentives that may not always be present. They included (1) the promise of a draft deferment and, therefore, the hope of escaping from military duty in Vietnam, (2) the fear of not finding a job or of finding only a poor one, without a college degree, and (3) parental and peer-group pressures, including the threat of social "excommunication." I suspect that the genuine demand for a college education, without pressures, threats, or the promise of substantial fringe benefits, may be no more than one-half of actual enrollment.

THE DEMAND FOR QUALIFIED MANPOWER

I now turn from the demand for a college education on the part of interested students to the demand for college-educated manpower by employers or, more generally, by the national economy. It has often been argued that changes in technology employed in production and changes in the type of products demanded have steadily raised the demand for educated and skilled labor. I myself have argued that the employability of largely unskilled and practically illiterate workers has declined and will entirely disappear if such labor is not offered at sufficiently low wages. However, the proposition that persons with reading skills equivalent to less than two or three years of elementary school are hard to place in jobs (at wages normally paid to better-qualified labor) cannot reasonably be equated with the contention that our highly developed economy can only use persons with a minimum of sixteen years of education. To conclude from the low employability of illiterates that our society can employ only college graduates is to make a truly remarkable jump.

In this connection, it may be helpful to consider the large demand for "guest laborers" from poorer countries for all sorts of employment in Germany, France, and Switzerland. These countries are not so very far behind the United States technologically; the guest workers they employ come from Portugal, Spain, Italy, Yugoslavia, Greece, and Turkey and can neither read nor write the language of the host country. They are thus practically illiterate in the language used at the place of employment. The demand for this labor is so brisk—in Switzerland foreign workers number almost one-third of the domestic labor force—because differences in wages make it profitable to employ them. In other words, employability is a function of wage rates. The notion that undereducated, unskilled labor is unemployable is contrary to the economic facts of life.

The advance in computer technology and the increasing use of computers in all sorts of industries, trade, finance, and government have persuaded some manpower experts of the greater need for college-trained personnel adept in the required skills. What these experts have failed to realize is that most of the required skills can best be acquired on the job and that high-school graduates are not one whit less educable in these skills than college graduates. In personal interviews with managers of computing facilities in several large organizations, I have ascertained that for a large variety of tasks non-college-trained employees are preferred. Chiefly because they are more contented than college graduates to perform the necessary routine work, they are less likely to quit their jobs and, as a result, the turnover of personnel is smaller among non-college-graduates and the actual efficiency attained is greater.[2]

I do not want to deny that the demand for some skills that can be more easily acquired by better-educated persons has increased and may increase further. I do deny, however, that this demand can be met only by an increase in the proportion of persons with sixteen years of schooling toward anything like 25, 30, or 40 per cent of the age group. Again, we lack empirical evidence and, in the meantime, have to rely upon largely unsupported hunches. It would not be difficult, however, to devise research on the educational prerequisites for all occupations that employ substantial numbers of workers. It would not be a very difficult task to establish the length of on-the-job training required to bring the efficiency of workers with different years of schooling up to specified standard attainments. My provisional hunch is that a relatively small percentage of jobs require skills that cannot be acquired by persons with only ten or twelve years of schooling—or require skills that can be acquired by these "undereducated" youngsters only through on-the-job training lasting four to six years longer than is needed by persons with fourteen and sixteen years of formal education.

This hunch seems to contradict the results of empirical inquiries into observed differences in earnings associated with, or attributable to, differences in years of school completed. The differences in earnings have been established beyond doubt, and they clearly point to differences in the productivity of those with more years of school. Some of the studies, especially those by Gary Becker, carefully attempted to eliminate the influences of other contributing factors, such as the income and background of the parents, intelligence as tested by customary IQ tests, ambition and industry as evidenced by grades in earlier school years, and so forth. The remaining differences in earnings were particularly high for differences in the number of years of secondary school, but they were also significant for differences between college graduates and persons without college education. Are these findings not sufficiently convincing to force me to give up my doubts about the role college plays in raising the productivity of its graduates?

THE PRODUCTIVITY OF LONGER EDUCATION

My doubts are based on three considerations. Two of these refer to employers' preferences that are not related to physical productivity. First, the "certification function" of the college degree has played an unduly large role. College graduates need not be superior in the work

14

for which they are hired, and masses of equally competent persons without college degrees may be available, but the certified fact that the potential employees have successfully completed college makes them "safer bets" and saves employment officers the time and effort needed for testing and selecting the most-qualified from vast numbers of applicants. Second, the "polishing function" of college may play a role in job discrimination in favor of college graduates. Many employers prefer to work with better-educated employees and, moreover, can make their best employees happier if they find equally well-educated coworkers. This may indirectly contribute to output, because a team of "nice" associates with broader interests will sometimes work together more smoothly and contentedly, with less friction and more stability.

We must not exaggerate the weight given to these two considerations. I do not believe that they account for a major part of the difference in earnings attributed to college education. My third consideration, however, may be of great importance. It refers to the fact that the observed differences in earnings related to college graduates at a time when the ratio of college graduates to non-college-graduates was much smaller than it is now.[3] Observations of a sample of income earners that included only some 10 per cent of college graduates cannot reasonably be taken as valid for groups that include 30, 40, or 50 per cent of college graduates. If the supply of college-educated persons increases drastically—surely faster than the demand—the income differentials in their favor must decline or vanish. The concept of marginal productivity, which underlies all economic reasoning about such things as the productive contribution of education, has been developed for the very reason that productivity per man depends on the number of men employed.

Of course, estimates of the benefits from longer, and especially from higher, education would be sadly incomplete if they were confined to increases in earning capacity. Higher education not only produces higher lifetime earnings for its graduates, compared with those less educated, but it also contributes to the productivity of the entire economy, through its contributions to technological, managerial, and organizational progress. Becker suggested that, if one attributes much of the growth of productivity per man to the discoveries, inventions, and innovations made by the highly educated, the social return to investment in higher education may have been twice the rate that was calculated on the basis of income differentials alone.

This situation, I believe, is justified, but I question its application if the percentage of the age group going to college is disregarded. If, for example, that percentage is increased from 20 to 40 per cent, not only will one have to expect the income differences between college graduates and others to be reduced, but it would be unrealistic to expect the rate of technological, managerial, and organizational progress to be significantly increased. As a by-product of doubling college enrollment, I would expect the mixture of higher, broader, and thinner education to become weaker, with the amount of higher education substantially reduced.

NONPECUNIARY BENEFITS

Attempts to measure or estimate the benefits from longer education only in terms of products and incomes have been harshly criticized and even rejected by some who emphasize the cultural and other intangible, nonpecuniary benefits to the better educated, their families, associates, and society as a whole. The critique is justified: satisfactions other than greater efficiency, larger earnings, and social recognition must be considered. Rejection of cost-and-benefit analysis, however, is not therefore justified; missing items can be evaluated and included in the accounts, although evaluations of nonpecuniary costs and benefits are inevitably highly subjective—not subject to confirmation by objective, let alone scientific, evidence. Still, when I say that I would not give up my association with my well-read or learned friends in exchange for an income increase of $10,000 a year, I am making a perfectly rational statement. Likewise, those in charge of the public purse strings may, in perfect rationality, say that they would be willing to appropriate another fifty billion dollars a year to an expansion of college enrollment, at the expense of appropriations for hospitals and highways, slum clearance and child-care centers, antipollution measures and other desirable things.

Such value judgments, even if they cannot be refuted, can be debated, defended, criticized. Indeed, most of the public discussion of governmental measures is exactly this. Let us then ask what kinds of additional nonpecuniary, intangible benefits society may derive from increasing the proportion of the age group enrolled at college, that is, from extending from twelve to sixteen years the duration of full-time formal education for large numbers of young people. I can see the following benefits.

1. Among the additional recruits to college, a few may be found to have talents, interests, ambition, and perseverance needed for advanced studies. To have discovered these students and steered them into higher education, where they may contribute to the expansion of our knowledge and to the increase of our ethical and aesthetic pleasures, is a definite advantage.

2. A certain number of the additional college students will develop

a taste for broader education and will pursue it for the rest of their lives, to their own enjoyment as well as that of their families and associates.

3. The largest portion of the group will go no further than assimilate some of the broader education to which they are exposed by their teachers and fellow students. They may or may not enjoy "college life," and they may or may not in their later careers get some satisfaction out of their past "learning," out of an education a little broader than that of high-school graduates. The somewhat nostalgic memories of their experiences at college may be the chief (or only) reward for their four-year academic endeavors and for the cost incurred by themselves and society.

4. An undetermined number of the additional college students may develop critical abilities and socially desirable attitudes, including better understanding of social trends, with less prejudice against, and more tolerance for, the opinions of others.

The last of these four possible benefits has been stressed by several psychologists and sociologists. A paper by Keniston and Gerzon, "Human and Social Benefits," is my text and my target.[4] The authors believe that "college attendance yields demonstrable increases in autonomy, openmindedness, cognitive relativism, independence of moral judgments, along with decreases in authoritarianism, dogmatism, ethnocentrism, prejudice, and adherence to traditional values." And they conclude that, unless many more, if not all, attend college, society might not "remain open, pluralistic and democratic."

The two authors admit that not all kinds of college education yield the desired results; only what they call "critical education" can do the job, and there is no guarantee that all colleges can offer this. Indeed, the authors concede that in several countries, and even in the United States at some times, colleges and universities did *not* offer "critical education."

I would also submit that the "demonstrable" liberalizing effects on students cannot be taken for granted when the proportion of the age group that goes to college changes drastically. "Critical education" may work well for a student body that comprises 20 per cent of the age group, but it may not work equally well, or at all, if 40 per cent are exposed to it. The cause for possible malfunction of a system that is doubled in size may lie in the lack of qualified teachers as well as in the lack of qualified students. Incidentally, both these possible deficiencies may disappear over time. Yet I cannot help warning that we should never rely on the availability of enough good teachers. The average teacher will always be a mediocre teacher. (I have never had a good teacher in my education, and I have met very few in my lifetime.)

I not only question some of the benefits that the optimists expect from longer education for larger proportions of the age group, but I actually fear that longer education for more people may do real harm. If every boy or girl were compelled or pressured to sit in school for six-teen years and were barred or dissuaded from starting to work before his or her twenty-second birthday, the injury inflicted on our youth might be very serious. Compelling young people to stay in school for six, seven, or even eight years beyond their puberty and physical maturity would invite anti-intellectual revolts; in trying to make them like school without rebelling, we would have to transform our colleges into rock-and-roll camps. I cannot believe that the effects on the cha-racter, mentality, or psychological makeup of the graduates would be beneficial; indeed, they might be quite harmful.

I have taken the preceding paragraph almost verbatim from a reply I wrote to the paper by Keniston and Gerzon.[5] I should like to conclude my paper with the final paragraph of that reply:

> One of the worst fallacies is to talk or think about the utility and benefit of anything without referring to the quantity in which it is available. If something is good, and more of it is better, the incre-mental benefits derived from additional quantities are never constant, or hardly ever. If eight years of schooling is good and ten years is better, this does not guarantee that twelve years is better still and sixteen years is still grander, and then thirty-two years, and ulti-mately the whole life. Likewise, if sixteen years of formal education is good for 10 per cent of the population, and also for 12 per cent, and perhaps for 15 per cent or even 20 per cent, this does not imply that there would be benefits if 30 per cent, 50, 60, or 90 per cent were exposed to sixteen years of schooling. Economists speak of marginal utility, marginal productivity, and marginal benefits, to indicate that it all depends on the quantities considered. This is not technical economics, which you may or may not accept; it is plain common sense, which no reasonable man can reject.

NOTES

1. The speech was published in the *Proceedings of the 1970 Invitational Con-ference on Testing Problems* (Princeton, N.J.: Educational Testing Service, 1971), pp. 3-13.
2. In an analysis of performance of federal aviation flight controllers it was found that personnel with no college work performed demanding and techni-cally complex duties requiring a high degree of judgment at least as well as did controllers who had attended college. Ivar Berg, *Education and Jobs: The Great*

Training Robbery (New York: Praeger, 1970), pp. 167-175.

3. The study by Gary Becker, *Human Capital* (New York: National Bureau of Economic Research, 1964) is based chiefly on data from the censuses of 1940 and 1950, giving incomes for the years 1939 and 1949. The percentage of all eighteen- to twenty-one-year-olds that were enrolled in college was 15.2 in 1940 and 27.2 in 1950. The reported incomes of older persons were, of course, not those of graduates of the respective years but of earlier years. Thus the incomes of forty-year-olds in 1939 actually referred to those graduating from college in 1918 or from high school in 1914, when students enrolled in college were between 5 and 7 per cent of the age group.

4. Kenneth Keniston and Mark Gerzon, "Human and Social Benefits," in *Universal Higher Education: Costs, Benefits, Options,* ed., Logan Wilson (Washington, D.C.: American Council on Education, 1972), pp. 49-74.

5. "Matters of Measure," *ibid.*, pp. 78-84.

The Promise of Universal Higher Education

Patrick Suppes
Stanford University

It is a pleasure to comment on Fritz Machlup's provocative essay on higher education. Sometimes in arguments about educational matters it is necessary to pull one's punches because the opponent is not used to vigorous intellectual give-and-take. Since this certainly is not the case for Professor Machlup, I shall state my critical arguments about his essay in unvarnished form. In one way or another, I disagree with almost everything he has to say. My task is to try and say *why*, and at the same time to express my conviction of the importance of the issues he raises and the respect I hold for his defense of his position.

My essay is organized under arguments of distinct kinds. I begin with the semantic argument and end with the moral and social argument. When I speak of *the* argument, I do not mean that there is a single argument but rather a cluster of arguments that can be loosely classified together.

THE SEMANTIC ARGUMENT

Machlup begins his essay with attention to the use of the word "universal" and with what he considers to be the corrupt usage found in much of the educational literature. In retort, I find his way with words far from clean or precise. He says in his first paragraph that he is "a stickler for clean definitions and uncorrupted word meanings . . ." Not only am I a stickler, but I am also a theorist of definitions. One of the first theoretical points I make is that the whole discussion is in an area in which we can scarcely expect exact definitions, precise concepts, and pure meanings to carry the day. An important aspect of intellectual discussion is to recognize when it is being conducted on soggy ground and when it is on something as firm as rock. Necessarily, the discussion of universal higher education is on soggy ground, and we shall not be able to begin or end with precise definitions and logically tight concepts.

There is, it seems to me, a commonsense meaning of "universal education." It is not one we have to strain over; it is reflected in our present society by the very large percentage of students who graduate from high school and go on to college. We thus can talk not only about universal elementary education but also about universal secondary education and universal higher education. We do not mean something deep and significant by the phrase "universal higher education" but just that a large percentage of the appropriate age group continues some form of formal education beyond high school. I do not think, for example, that in terms of Machlup's distinctions he would want to say that we do not have universal secondary education in this country because less than 75 per cent of the appropriate age group graduates from high school. I shall pass over the problem of defining "universal." What he has to say about the universal quantifier "all" is easily expanded upon in terms of standard logical usage. The real issue seems to center on what he has to say about the definition of "higher," and not about the definition of "universal," in the phrase "universal higher education."

A little later in his paper he says that he defines higher education as "the education of scholars and scientists . . ." When, a couple of paragraphs after this, he refers to "my own definition of higher education as the education of actual and *potential* scholars" [emphasis added], any sensitive user of words knows that we are on treacherous ground. In the first statement there is no mention of potential scholars, and in the second there is a distinction between actual and potential scholars.

If we take the first definition literally, it is clear that it is a bizarre definition used only by him—or at least by a very small number of people. While I have in mind just the ordinary sense of words, I also have something more in mind than just the vagueness and trickiness of his characterization. Even if we assume that he intends the second definition to apply not just to scholars but also to potential scholars, I think the condition is neither necessary nor sufficient for what he wants to mean. For example, under any definition of potential scholars that does not make the whole matter circular, we can, I am sure, find courses generally regarded as necessary for advanced scholarship or scientific work in a given field; however, these courses may also be taken by students who do not so advance and who at the time of taking the courses have no intention of so advancing. Also, we can find scholars or scientists in the field who did not take all of these courses.

On the other hand, what proportion of students in a course would need to be potential scholars to make it fall properly within the definition of higher education? Let us go along with Machlup's idea but for schematic purposes try to make it more precise. He may disagree with the exact way in which I have made it precise, but the rough and ready assignment of numbers to things is a habit of economists with which he will not be too unsympathetic.

Let us suppose for purposes of illustration that a course given in what we ordinarily call "higher education"—that is, in a college or university—is called a course in *higher education a la Machlup*, if and only if at least 50 per cent of the students in that course go on to some form of graduate or professional school. At Stanford in recent years more than 80 per cent of the men and about 50 to 60 per cent of the women graduates have done just this. Under the definition we have given, this means that a high percentage of the total undergraduate courses at Stanford are courses in *higher education a la Machlup,* because they are taken mainly by potential scholars.

The nonsense of this definition is evident, however, if we consider that a similar course—let us say a course in ordinary differential equations given at a state college—is not a course in *higher education a la Machlup* because, under our definition, the percentage of potential scholars is less than 50 per cent—say 35 per cent. Yet, without any doubt, the top 15 per cent of the students taking the course at the state college are clearly better than the bottom 15 per cent at Stanford.

It is easy to respond that such exact, extensive definitions referring to percentages are not what is meant in talking about potential scholars. But if percentages, or something similar, are not adopted then we are left with a large and woolly area known for its pitfalls and difficulties. Vagaries of definition, verification, and identification involved in the concept of potential are too many to go into here. I must emphasize that there is not a serious characterization of higher education different from the ordinary one in Machlup's paper. He gives a brief and breezy definition that cannot be taken seriously. It is idiosyncratic, but mainly he does not use it. From henceforth it will be quite satisfactory to use "higher education" to mean formal academic education beyond high school, not only at elite private colleges and universities but also at state and community colleges. In view of the fact that more than 80 per cent of students in higher education, as I have defined it, are in public institutions, most of what I have to say will be concerned with publicly financed education and not with the private sector.

These matters of definition, however, are not the end of our semantic difficulties. Immediately after the recast definition, Machlup gives a list of six qualities he regards as essential for scholarship. With the exception of creativity, they read like a Ben Franklin list of qualities needed to get ahead in the world. There seems to be nothing special about them that is different for higher education, especially because intelligence is the one of the six that Machlup is least concerned to push.

My point is that these six qualities are banal; they could easily be defended as essential for most constructive activities. On the other hand, their definition is as difficult as the notion of potential scholar. I do not see how a serious discussion can proceed if we must deal with concepts like those of ambition and diligence. What does it mean, for example, to say that a student is diligent? What empirical studies have been made of this concept? Who is a reliable judge of diligence? Who is to define the term so that it has any operational sense? The same problems arise for the other concepts as well, with the possible exception of intelligence.

The thrust of my semantic remarks is that I find the methodological framework within which Machlup wishes to conduct the discussion unsatisfactory, and the terms of discourse are vague and loose.

THE ARGUMENT ABOUT THE FACTS

Arguments about facts can be as hard as rock or as soft as ground after a spring thaw. The evidence, for example, is decisive that more than one million people live in New York City. The kind of evidence we would expect for the proposition that men are now living on the moon should be just as decisive. Arguments about education or any other major facet of our society are not of this character, so that many arguments about higher education will necessarily revolve around matters of emphasis and selection of facts, as well as problems of inference from agreed-upon evidence to conclusion.

For me, the three most salient features of Western civilization have been the development of (partially) democratic institutions, the development of formal educational institutions, and the development of scientific concepts and theories. Holding such a view of the pervasive quality of education in our civilization, I find it hard to accept any simple summary of the facts in support of it or to agree on the facts that show how it should be limited. Much of the emphasis and selection in Machlup's discussion is unsympathetic to my own view of education, and, therefore, I want to comment upon a number of his particular arguments.

The first cluster of facts I want to deal with concerns who attended universities in the past and why. Machlup's examples of Oxford and the University of Berlin and his remarks about present-day community colleges suggest that widely different clientele attending for quite varied purposes have characterized different institutions at different times. In broad terms, it seems to me that the empirical facts do not support this idea. I think we can agree that until recently—and, by recently, I mean until post-World War II—higher education in the sense of formal academic education beyond high school was education for the sons and daughters, but especially the sons, of the wealthy. This was true in Alexandria in 200 B.C., it was true in Renaissance England at Oxford and Cambridge in the sixteenth century, and, although I do not have explicit data in front of me, I believe it was true at the University of Berlin in 1870. Of course, it is characteristic that the expansion of education downward in society is to be found in broad terms across the centuries. The selectivity at Oxford in the sixteenth century was not the same as the selectivity in terms of wealth in the nineteenth century at the University of Berlin. However, to put it in technical terms—and I would be interested in Machlup's response on this particular point—my conjecture is that if we did a regression analysis on admission or attendance in the cases I have mentioned, and if we introduced as independent variables the intelligence of the student and the income of the father, then income of the father rather than intelligence would be the more important predictor of attendance.

Plato put the matter nicely in Protagoras's discussion of classical education in the dialogue of that name (326v). After describing this education Protagoras says, "This is what is done by those who have the means, and those who have the means are the rich; their children begin to go to school soonest and leave off latest." Consider the description, in a more censorious tone, of university students in William Harrison's *Description of England*, first published in 1577:

> Most of them study little other than histories, tables, dice and trifles.
> . . . Besides this, being for the most part either gentlemen or rich
> men's sons they oft bring the university into much slander. For stand-
> ing upon their reputation and liberty, they ruffle and roist it out, ex-
> ceeding in apparel and hunting riotous company, (which draweth
> them from their books into another trade) and for excuse they are
> charged with breach of one good order think it sufficient to say that
> they be gentlemen which grieveth many not a little. [1]

I am sure that students at the University of Berlin in 1870 were much more serious than Harrison's students of the sixteenth century in England, but selection from families that were not poor was undoubtedly still the case.

I do not mean to suggest by these examples that Machlup advocates the traditional view that institutions of higher learning are mainly meant to educate the children of the wealthy and those who will govern the society, with a small sprinkling of very bright young men (but scarcely any young women) from the other segments of society admitted because of their extraordinary cleverness. Nowhere does he advocate a position of this kind, and I am not suggesting that he does. My point is rather that in describing higher education as something meant for the 10 per cent or 15 per cent of the ablest in the population, he is describing something that has never been and never will be.

Higher education in the past has been extraordinarily selective, mainly in terms of the wealth of parents and the sex of the child. It is one of the best and most important features of our present society that this restrictive selectivity has essentially disappeared. Today, large numbers of young Black men and women are being admitted to college. The most recent figure I have seen is that 6.6 per cent of college enrollment is Black. This compares with an 11 per cent Black population in this age group, which indicates that in recent years remarkable progress has been made.

Still another cluster of Machlup's arguments centers around courses, the teaching of language, survey courses in history, laboratory courses in natural sciences, what could or could not be done during secondary school, what should or should not be done in higher education, and so forth. It seems to me that his whole discussion has entered a morass of ill-thought-out distinctions. On the one hand, he wants to talk about the number of courses and the reasons students need broader education to continue their absorption of knowledge from different domains. On the other hand, he talks about only people over forty being genuinely educated in the broader sense, a proposition that I find a priori incredible and unsupported by facts of any kind I know. Now that I am well over forty myself I wish I could agree with him, but I cannot. In terms of education or culture, I do not think my friends or I know more than we did when we were fifteen years younger. We know different things now, we have a certain kind of experience to lean upon, but it is not at all clear that we are not more narrow, less broadly educated, or less interested in a wide range of topics. I find this whole discussion about courses and broader education unpersuasive.

Another cluster of Machlup's remarks centers around the undesirable, compulsory character of school and the presumed fact that adolescents often would prefer not to be in school. Indeed, it would be better, it is implied, to eliminate compulsory provisions beyond the age of fourteen or so. Machlup's assertions about complicated matters of fact and difficult problems of policy are dogmatic and simple in character. He does not deal at any point with the long history of raising the school-leaving age in the United States, in Europe, and more recently in other parts of the world. He does not present any evidence on the relative satisfaction or dissatisfaction of students with school at different ages. For example, my own conjecture is that college sopho-mores are probably more satisfied with school than thirteen-year-olds are.

Still another kind of fact relevant to the present point is ignored in Machlup's discussion. He writes as if our colleges were mainly popu-lated by older adolescents, but this is far from the case. In the state university system in California, the average age of undergraduates is well above twenty-one. It varies from college to college, but in a school like San Francisco State University the average age is approxi-mately twenty-five or twenty-six. A high proportion of these students have full-time or nearly full-time jobs. Many of them are married with families and certainly are not dependent upon their parents for sup-port. The many remarks about adolescents could not be less apposite to their situation.

Another related set of facts important to the considerations Machlup discusses, or implicitly uses as suppositions, concerns the interest of students in college, their inclination to drop out, their desire to work and not to study, and so forth. The evidence of past studies shows that the pattern of student dropout is very different from our simple ideas about it. A large percentage of college students who drop out at nine-teen or twenty or twenty-two apparently reenter college at a later date and continue their education with an unusually high degree of comple-tion of degree requirements. This drive for education is such a deep part of our society, like the demand for democratic institutions or the thrust of modern science, that it is not easy to turn it aside and restrict education beyond high school to a small segment of the population.

One other cluster of remarks I want to comment upon concerns the pecuniary rewards of college. Machlup makes the important point that the data are now different from those used in the much-cited studies of Becker and others, which dealt with a college population that was a much smaller percentage of the age population.

Again, I find the argument too simple. In 1870, for example, only about 2 per cent of seventeen-year-olds graduated from high school. Using Machlup's line of argument, one could very well say that the pecuniary rewards of graduating from high school have continued to decrease because such a high percentage of students graduate from high school, and therefore, we make a mistake in encouraging such a high portion of the population to complete high school. Of course, this is a mistaken argument. There is fairly good evidence that completion of high school continues to be enormously rewarding in the labor market and for just the opposite kind of reason to that cited by Machlup. Namely, it has become a necessary condition of employment in a wide range of occupations.

It is no longer a positive accomplishment to have graduated from high school; rather, it is a negative factor not to have. Having graduated from high school is not a strong argument for obtaining a given position, because almost all the competition will also have high-school diplomas. It does mean, however, that the argument for graduating from high school is stronger than ever because of the difficulty of obtaining any kind of employment if one has not graduated from high school. In all likelihood something of a similar sort has already begun to happen with a college education. I am not really impressed by Machlup's interviews with the managers of computer centers; I would like to be persuaded, but only by much more explicit data than those available.

A good deal more could be said about this point, but I must pass over Machlup's comments on unskilled labor and its employability and turn to some other arguments I consider important. I cannot resist noting, however, that much of Machlup's central discussion about the pecuniary rewards of higher education is surely meant to be about higher education in my sense of formal academic education beyond high school, and not about higher education in his sense. Since most of the students he writes about are not engaged in higher education in his sense, it is strictly irrelevant to the announced title and definition of his topic, but as I indicated earlier, it is just the unworkability of his definition that forces him back to the simple standard definition I have used. Also, to deepen the analysis, I wish to reiterate that the considerations he raises about the rewards of a college education should be applied also to a high-school education, and even perhaps to functional literacy. All of what he says about a college education in terms of certification and polishing seems to hold for a high-school education—and the same distinctions seem in order—but I find it hard to believe that he is also against universal high-school education.

One final remark about the facts. It seems to me that anyone who wishes to restrict access to something as important as higher education must be doubly sure of his facts, and the arguments must be based on the best detailed evidence that can be found. The thing I find most disturbing in Machlup's whole position is his cavalier way with the facts. In areas where there are facts, either of a psychological kind—as in the case of students' attitudes, beliefs, and habits—or in the case of historical trends and conditions, Machlup makes no discriminating use of what facts are available. We are given rather broad and not very interesting generalities about diligence or perseverance or the character of young people after puberty. In none of these areas do I have any faith that his generalizations are correct. (I apologize for not being able to make my own argument on these matters in proper detail. It is my conviction that it can be done, and I hope to do so on another occasion.)

THE MORAL AND SOCIAL ARGUMENT

One of the most important single changes in the culture and civilization of the world in the past two hundred years is the universal clamor for education. Two hundred years ago, or even a hundred years ago, in most parts of the world only a very small percentage of the population could expect to achieve functional literacy. The poor everywhere had no serious thought of their children's achieving a significant level of education beyond what they themselves had, bad as it was. The change on these matters is one of the most radical things that has happened to the human race in its entire history. Machlup seems to take no account of this, and perhaps we disagree on its profound significance. For me, signs of this significance are to be found everywhere. In the United States today, class distinctions of speech and dress have almost disappeared. Education is certainly one of the prime reasons for this leveling effect. As has been pointed out by many people, a very high percentage of adults in the United States identify themselves as middle class. Only a small number regard themselves as rich and only a very small number, as poor. Not only the sons of lawyers and bankers but also the sons and daughters of plumbers and taxicab drivers expect to go to college, and do so.

According to the *Historical Statistics of the United States*, in 1870 just 57 per cent of the population five to seventeen years old were enrolled in public schools; only 2 per cent of the seventeen-year-olds were high-school graduates; 20 per cent of the population were estimated to be illiterate, and of the nonwhite population 79.9 per cent were. Arguments over the exact numbers and the correct estimates can be mounted, but the basic facts are undeniable. The change from American society in 1870 to the present is a change dominated by one overwhelming fact: the great increase in the education of the majority of the population. The desire, and indeed the demand, for education at all levels of our society is recognized by everyone. The demand is universal; the satisfaction of that demand is approaching universality. I have cited already the remarkable rise in the number of Black students in college, even since 1968. That trend will continue and, in my judgment, certainly should.

I agree with Machlup that it is important to know to what extent the expectation of pecuniary rewards plays a significant role in this phenomenal demand for education, including the unprecedented demand for higher education. Based on the kind of commitments our society has made over the past two decades—independent of any questions of differentiated pecuniary rewards—it seems evident that the utility of higher education is exceedingly high. I do not think the problem of estimating this utility (in the sense of providing an approximate measurement) is at all impossible, even if I do not accept an economic argument about utility as a conclusive argument for or against universal higher education.

We cannot expect over the next hundred years the same percentage changes that occurred between 1870 and the present, but I do think there are two important considerations that argue for a continued expansion of higher education, both in terms of the percentage of the population that it reaches and the number of years that it is offered.

The first argument concerns the viability of an informed and educationally sophisticated body of citizens. It was the despair of John Stuart Mill in the nineteenth century that he did not see how a democratic society could work when the majority of its citizens were badly educated. I am sure that it would be an immeasurable relief to him to find a hundred years later that Britain, as well as this country, has a proportion of citizens educated to a level that was hardly thought possible in his time.

I hope to persuade someone to undertake an empirical study of the content of newspapers a hundred years ago to compare the level of intellectual and scientific sophistication of the facts presented and the data organized for public discussion with the level today. It is my impression that the increase in quantitative information—the presentation of statistical data, the analysis of budgets in quantitative terms, the careful citation of employment rates and gross national products, the percentage of voters inclined in a given direction, and so forth—is increasing sophistication and the political and intellectual horizons of our citizens at a rapid rate. This can happen because we have laid the base in education. If we went back, as Machlup on occasion seems to advocate, to a nation of fourteen-year-old school-leavers we could scarcely expect to continue this development of an informed citizenry. I do not suggest that I am overly sanguine about what the man in the street knows about international trade (a subject, for example, on which Fritz Machlup is an expert), but I do maintain that there is no comparison between the fund of general information on policies and the economy available to American citizens now, compared with that of a hundred years ago.

Education is not required for a *stable* society, but it is required for a stable *democratic* one. The most perfect example perhaps of a stable elitist society is Alexandria from its founding by Alexander the Great in 331 B.C. to its capture by the Arabs in 642. In terms of its contributions to the history of science and culture, Alexandria is the first city of the world. No other city matches its record of dominating the culture, and especially the science, of the world for almost a thousand years. The educated society of Alexandria was elitist with a vengeance. Even the language, Greek, was not spoken by most of the population. The society's intellectual accomplishments, ranging from mathematics to grammar to literary criticism, were of the first order, but it is not the sort of society any of us would want to see today or in the future. To me there is great hope in thinking that we are moving toward a society in which all citizens can understand and appreciate an increasingly greater number of central political and social issues.

Finally, I come to a development that is already of great importance—and surely one that will be of even greater significance—but that is not mentioned by Machlup. This is the subject of population control. It seems inevitable that we will soon be taking drastic measures to control the growth of population, and, as we do so, the effects on education throughout the world will be profound. The immediate effect upon education in this country will be a decrease in the percentage of the population attending schools or colleges as they are now constituted. The population will become older, on the average; the numbers of students moving through educational institutions will not increase but will perhaps show a gradual absolute decrease. The matter of numbers and their impact on the total cost of education is one of the leavening influences in what would otherwise appear to be a pessimistic picture of future educational costs.

A second and more profound consideration, one that will take longer to have an impact, is what effect the control of population growth will have on the average level of education and intellectual attainment. I have already cited the surprisingly high percentage of undergraduates at Stanford who go on to some form of graduate or professional school. I see no reason not to believe that these percentages will continue to increase for all parts of the college population.

I shall indeed be bold and close by saying that in my judgment Fritz Machlup's gravest error is in looking backward rather than forward. I can envision a society, a hundred years from now, the majority of whose citizens are at the level, at least, of its mediocre scholars today. I can imagine a society that, in a hundred years, will be composed mainly of citizens who are the equal of Machlup's "well-read or learned friends." I see a society based not just on equal opportunity but upon equal opportunity realized, a society in which science and culture are held in esteem and made part of a better life by nearly all. To change my vision of what can be—and indeed of what probably will be—will take far stronger arguments than I have yet heard.

NOTES

1. F. J. Furnivall, ed., *William Harrison's Description of England* (New Shakespeare Society, Series VI, Pt. I, 1877), pp. 77-78.

Democracy and Higher Education

Sidney Hook
New York University

Our attitude toward universal higher education depends primarily on how we interpret the key terms in the expression. Professor Machlup's contention that "universal higher education" is a contradiction in terms is mistaken. It is no more logically contradictory than the expression "universal primary education" or "universal secondary education." Education may be physically, pedagogically, financially impossible at any given time or level, but an impossibility is not a contradiction. Even if universal education were possible, it would not necessarily mean that it was desirable. Nor, if it were impossible, would it follow that its pursuit was undesirable. The actual achievement of universal health, wisdom, happiness, and other ideal and material values in our moral economy may be impossible, but the consequences of *pursuing* them may be highly desirable. "May," of course, leaves us open to "may not." The costs, psychological or economic, of pursuing these values beyond a certain point may outweigh the benefits; but equity requires that if the benefits—health, wisdom, happiness, or what not—are truly benefits, then the burden of proof that their pursuit beyond a certain point results in a net loss to the community rests upon those who make the assertion.

How then shall we interpret the expression "universal higher education"? We should ask, in simple fairness, what those who advocate it mean by it. If we do, we find that it does not mean what Professor

Machlup understands by the phrase. I am acquainted with no proponents of universal higher education (although I have heard that some exist) who advocate mandatory universal attendance at institutions of higher education, in the same sense in which pupils are required to attend primary and secondary schools. Such a proposal would necessitate raising the legal school-leaving age to twenty-one. Such a proposal is foolish, but not self-contradictory.[1]

The recommendation of the Gardner Task Force Report of 1964, recently made public at the Lyndon B. Johnson Library, served as the basis of the Higher Eduction Act of 1965. The Report contains what I have found to be the customary sense of the phrase "universal higher education." It recommends that the federal government commit itself to a policy that goes beyond "equal opportunity" for higher education, because "equal opportunity" is compatible with a severely elite system of selection. The recommended policy is based on the view that "a college education is becoming every bit as much a legitimate expectation as a high-school education has been." The Report admits that it is exaggerated to claim that "tomorrow everyone will have to have a college education if society's work is to be done and if it is to progress." Nonetheless, it asserts that, exaggeration aside, it is close enough to the truth to justify concern with the "inadequacies of the present system." Chief among these inadequacies is an antiquated admission or selection procedure that restricts the number of students enrolled. The Report concludes: "We recommend that the federal government take as a conscious objective assuring that all qualified graduates receive post-secondary education." I interpret this to mean that there should be universal access to higher education to all high-school graduates.

If by "universal higher education" we mean universal access to some institution of higher education, I am prepared to defend it. On my view of democracy, I believe that all citizens have a right to that degree of schooling that will help them achieve their full growth as persons and, further, that anyone who can profit from post-secondary instruction should have an opportunity to do so. I also believe that society can benefit by discovering the potential talents of a considerable number of artists and thinkers, of leaders, shakers, and movers of events who otherwise might remain unrecognized. The anticipation of parents that their children will have access to higher education seems part of the revolution of rising expectations of our time. One study shows that 96 per cent of Black parents and 79 per cent of White parents wanted a college education for their children. Although the main reason for parental desire is that college attendance would improve the economic lot of their children—certainly a legitimate desire—undoubtedly the

34

figures also reflect a judgment about the social status of the college-educated. There seems to be more popular regard for schooling and "book-learning" than in pioneer days when higher education was completely subordinate to professional training for the ministry, medicine, and, in lesser measure, law.

The whole idea of universal access to higher education is not novel. Where it has been tried in the past, it has not interfered, despite Professor Machlup's presentiments, with upholding decent standards of achievement. The debasement of the latter is due to certain political factors. There is no educational objection to the open-door policy, provided the doors open not only *in* but *out*. Despite certain difficulties that arise from the physical inaccessibility of some educational institutions for some students, the three-tiered system of higher education in the state of California, which offers a place in some post-secondary school or college to every high-school graduate and provides for transfer of qualified students from community college to state college to the state university, seems to be working reasonably well. Whatever impairment to educational standards has occurred recently is due to tendencies toward politicalization of the curriculum, not to the ideal of open enrollment understood in this way.

This brings us to the nub of the question. What should be the minimum requirements of acceptable achievement at any institution of tertiary education to which there is universal access? More fundamentally, how shall we conceive of liberal-arts education in the modern world? What should be the knowledge, skills, values, intellectual habits, tastes, and attitudes that we should seek to develop? Granting the necessity for diversification of pedagogical approaches, tied to differences in the educational needs of students, what should be the minimum indispensables or requirements in subject matters and skills before students are certified as liberally educated?

It is in the consideration of this cluster of questions that I find Professor Machlup's treatment rather unsatisfactory. He defines higher education as the "education of actual and potential scholars" or, more explicitly, as the "education of scholars and scientists, and also of practitioners of those few professions that are based on continuing research." This makes higher education synonymous with graduate education and some professional education. But in Professor Machlup's own view, such higher education is not of itself a liberal or an intellectually liberating education. Higher education or graduate education is certainly the education of the intellectually elite. That is not an objection to it. There are intellectual elites, as well as musical elites and artistic elites, and they deserve the best education that will bring them to educational fulfillment. Some snobs would scoff at Professor

35

Machlup's assumption that 15 per cent of the college-age group constitutes an elite. They would restrict it to 1 or 2 or, at most, 5 per cent. I am confident that if they did, Professor Machlup would agree that not only the elite, restrictively defined this way, deserve the best education appropriate to their talents but also the not so elite, or superior student. Morally, however, I would argue—leaving aside crisis situations—that non-elite students are just as much entitled to the education best suited to *their* talents and capacities as elite students are.

What Professor Machlup characterizes as "broader" education, in contrast to "higher" education, is closer to what traditionally has been regarded as liberal education. He is not altogether clear about the nature of broader education. He insists that no one can be considered "broadly educated" on the basis of a secondary education. He then adds that "it would be ridiculous to assume that what can be added in another two, three, or four years can amount to much." I believe this pronouncement is extremely dogmatic and is based upon a vague notion of what constitutes a "broadly educated" person; it also assumes that if "much" is not added, the educational value is little or nothing. I question this. How much is "much"? In some fields, even a glimpse of what is excellent, in other fields a sense of the complexity and contingency of events, in still others, some compassionate understanding of the feelings and agonies of the strange, the outcast, and the defeated may justify the effort and cost of what is added.

Actually, not only is higher education, for Professor Machlup, an education for the elite but broader education is too. He claims that "it would be unduly pretentious to call the graduating bachelor of arts or science a 'broadly educated' person." At most, "What the liberal-arts college can do for its best students is to stimulate in them a *taste* for broad education, a *desire* for continuing education . . ." The logical implication is that save for "only a small fraction," a liberal-arts college education—anything beyond secondary schooling—is wasted. It is of no benefit to most students and to society. Actually, Professor Machlup believes that even secondary-school education, as presently constituted, is largely wasted on the unqualified and unwilling. He has the courage of his convictions. He would reduce the compulsory school age to fourteen. If fourteen-year-olds prefer to drop out of school, it is because "they know what is best for them."

I cannot resist observing, before continuing with my main criticism, that these fourteen-year-old dropouts who know what is educationally best for them must be a singularly elite group of students. I have taught fourteen-year-olds and have found them as a whole even less aware of what their educational needs are, and even less qualified rationally to determine what is educationally best for them, than most eighteen-year-olds entering college, who, more often than not, are also unaware of what is educationally best for them. For what it is worth, I can testify after teaching for almost fifty years that I have met many students who regretted dropping out of school when they could have remained; I have never met any students who graduated from college who regretted that they had done so. The regrets of those who have graduated — and I know that this is a common experience of teachers — is not that they attended college but that when they made their choices they studied the wrong things and failed to study the right things in relation to their educational needs. That is why I am skeptical about the educational wisdom of Professor Machlup's fourteen-year-old dropouts.

I have difficulty with Professor Machlup's sharp contrast between courses in higher education and those in broader education. He would *require* that courses in higher education (graduate courses, in effect) be part of the curriculum of the liberal-arts college. "Exclusive emphasis on higher education produces narrow specialists; exclusive emphasis on broader education produces superficial dilettantes." This seems to me too flip. Everyone knows that some courses taught as part of broader education are also offered as courses in higher education and vice versa. Specialization is a matter of degree. It is the student's interest and what he is prepared to do that often determine whether the course is broader or higher. Courses in higher education should be open to qualified students, but I see no necessity for requiring them in the liberal-arts college. Professor Machlup is fearful that without courses on the graduate *level*, if not in the graduate *school*, the result would be "superficial dilettantes." The expression is a pleonasm. Dilettantism is the pursuit of an "art or branch of knowledge desultorily or superficially," as an amateur. I am prepared to settle for a liberal-arts education that not only effectively prepares a small group of scholars and scientists for graduate school but also educates the rest of the students to be amateurs and dilettantes, that is to say, develops in them an abiding "taste for broad education" and a strong "desire for continuing education, to be pursued chiefly through a lifetime of reading, but also through discussions, lectures, conferences, theaters, operas, concerts, exhibitions, and museums."

I do not interpret such a life in a merely belletristic sense. College students and graduates will soon constitute the large majority of voters. The health of a self-governing commonwealth depends upon the intellectual sophistication of its citizens. A liberal-arts education can and should develop not only amateur lovers of the arts and sciences but amateur politicians and amateur students of politics. Such an education should undergird or accompany all education for a vocation. I am not so naive as to believe that what is taught to most of our youth will be of greater weight than the confluence of social, economic, and political forces that are shaping the alternatives of social development in the future. At the same time, it seems to me defeatist to deny the *possibility* of significant impact upon the intelligent choice of these alternatives in consequence of the broader education offered to all who are willing to study.

In the program of liberal-arts studies that should be devised to implement universal access to broader education, the key notion is "offered." As I understand the current educational scene in the United States—which should be the controlling context of our discussion—no serious educator is proposing that, as Dr. Machlup puts it, "every boy or girl [be] compelled or pressured to sit in school for sixteen years and [be] barred or dissuaded from starting to work before his or her twenty-second birthday . . . " What is being proposed is that every boy or girl who has graduated from high school be given the opportunity to enroll not in *any* college that provides tertiary education but in *some* college.

If in some ways Professor Machlup does not go far enough in offering a chance for a longer and broader education to a larger proportion of the age group, in some ways other so-called "innovative educators" go too far. I say this on the assumption that they are really in earnest about accepting the first of the ten conditions which Professor Machlup set up in a seriocomic vein to determine how large a percentage of high-school graduates would choose to avail themselves of the opportunity to attend and remain at college. He proposes: "No required courses [presumably this means subjects or studies too]—only electives, including new courses with contents and methods proposed by students or designed with a view to attracting students."

Under such a condition, even if 100 per cent of students attended college, I would regard the whole business as nothing but an elaborate farce. It would be better to award all students a bachelor of arts degree either at birth or upon graduation from high school than after the bull sessions, poker, and rock-playing interludes at the community's cost.

I am prepared to argue that without some required studies and without some objective tests of proficiency in the knowledge, values, and skills that are minimally involved in any significant conception of a liberal-arts education, we have no way of determining whether the student has authentically earned his degree or acquired a liberal education. These requirements are perfectly compatible with a program of individualized studies determined by expert educational guidance. This presupposes the authority of the faculty, by right of knowledge and experience, to discover and implement the course of study students must follow to achieve broader education or to qualify for higher education.

I would like to make one final point. Professor Machlup enumerates six qualities that he deems essential to higher education: intelligence, creativity, interest, ambition, diligence, perseverance. (Diligence and perseverance are so closely related that we may consider them as one.) He regards these qualities as "so scarce [among students] that no more than 10 to 15 per cent of the age group would subject themselves, or could be subjected, to the rigorous effort required" for higher or graduate training. If the graduate schools are not to debase their standards, I would maintain that 10 to 15 percent of the age group is much too high. But when we are discussing broader or liberal education, it seems to me that the percentages are much too low.

The five traits or qualities are obviously a matter of degree. Granted that intellectual and creative *capacities* are innate, their exercise, as every teacher knows, can be stirred or triggered by the other three traits. Arouse ambition or encourage diligence or fire interest, and intelligence is challenged to move in unaccustomed ways. Of these three traits—ambition, diligence, and interest—interest is psychologically the dynamic factor. But—and this is a crucial point—interest is not synonymous with intellectual curiosity, which is only one way in which interest is expressed. Interest can be motivated by a large variety of appeals—practical and emotional, personal and social. This is the task of the teacher, a fact largely ignored until recently at the college level.

What Professor Machlup seems to have overlooked is the extent to which the interest of students depends upon the pedagogical skills of their teachers and the extent to which the awakening of interest can lead to the exercise of diligence, the birth of ambition, and the activation of the native capacities of intelligence and creativity. We can even grant, as pointed out by Irving Kristol, that the best students will learn and the worst students may not learn, regardless of who teaches them. But most students fall between the best and the worst. It is especially for them that we need good teachers. Their presence can make a tremendous difference to the educational experience of the overwhelming majority of students. I agree with Professor Machlup—but only to this extent—that we cannot "rely" on the availability of enough good teachers.

Therefore, we must do what has never been done systematically before—develop or train good teachers for broader or liberal education and not rely upon chance and the happenstance of personal inclination to produce them. We may never have enough good teachers. But we can certainly have more, many more, than we have today. And if we do, it seems to me that it is not unreasonable to expect a much larger proportion of the college-age population to profit from universal access to a tertiary or liberal-arts college education than is allowed for in Dr. Machlup's scale of expectation.

NOTES

1. These critical comments on Professor Machlup's paper are based upon the text he originally submitted to the symposium's commentators, not upon the text he subsequently revised for publication.

The Travail and Fate of Higher Education

Daniel P. Moynihan
Harvard University

I was a little surprised by some things Professor Suppes had to say. Perhaps his error may have been in not looking back with somewhat more care. There exists a certain self-celebrating quality within us intellectuals; for example, the attitude "if it were not for us, things would not be as they are." There was a time when it was thought to be the ultimate *gaucherie* to repeat the remark of William Buckley that he would rather be governed by the first hundred people in the Boston Telephone Directory than by the faculty of Harvard College; yet you can get a fairly large vote from the faculty of Harvard College in favor of that proposition today!

I believe now that some of the impulse behind some of the events of the recent past is weakening, and I think there is a readjustment going on. Professor Machlup has viewed the subject as an economist, and I would like to view it historically, as a political issue in American life. I will address myself to the postwar period.

My first proposition is that, to a surprising degree, the United States has succeeded in achieving the goals in education it set out to achieve. Over the last twenty-five years, we have arrived at exactly the point where we said we ought to be. The first major pronouncement on educational matters at the federal level was contained in the 1947 Report of the President's Commission on Higher Education. It was stated there that at least 49 per cent of the population would have the intellectual ability to complete fourteen years of schooling, and 32 per cent would have the ability to go beyond that to a four-year liberal-arts college.

The next specific event came in 1964 when the Democratic Party platform addressed itself explicitly to this subject. It was the first time that a political party had done this, the first time that educational planning became part of a party platform. The statement says:

> If our national purpose is identical with the human purpose, then every person shall have the opportunity to become all that he or she is capable of becoming. We believe that knowledge is essential to individual freedom and to the conduct of a free society, and we believe that education is the surest and most profitable investment a nation can make. Regardless of family background or financial status, therefore, education should be open to every boy or girl in America up to the highest level which he or she is able to master.

Since I wrote that part of the platform, I can review a bit of its history. I was an assistant secretary of labor when it was drafted. We had already done a paper for a meeting on universal higher education that was sponsored by the Fund for the Advancement of Education, and we had some very specific notions as to what we meant by going "up to the highest level" of which a student is capable. Working from the general aptitude test battery that the U.S. Employment Service had developed over the years, we estimated that 50 per cent of the population has a capacity to go through two years of college, 31 per cent through four years of college, and 16 per cent through graduate school. I was not then aware of the estimates done for the President's Commission in 1947. One finds a surprising similarity in the data. The figures are only one decimal point apart in each case. Professor Machlup's notion of 10 to 15 per cent of the people engaged in the higher education that he described is close to our 16 per cent. These are surprisingly stable estimates.

Subsequently, the political commitment to accomplish these educational goals *has been met*. There were, of course, many other specific contributing events—the GI Bill, the Sputnik crisis, the onset of minority issues in the 1960s, and the like—but beyond that, there was a sense that the program was something we ought to do.

It was not for nothing that the federal government decided to provide 25 per cent of the cost of higher education in the United States; it is a national commitment. In the 1960s, data from "Project Talent" showed clearly that we had reached the point where virtually all smart youngsters were going to college. Only the stupid or the poor were not going on to college. There has been almost no loss of talent at the higher IQ levels; only as one reaches the middle IQ levels does a lack of income begin to affect who goes to college and who does not. (Incidentally, I wonder where Professor Suppes got the idea that higher education has been for the sons of the wealthy. In the past, it was not so; it has never been so in this country.)

On the other hand, there is hardly any question that from the social and modern economic point of view, higher education has been a privilege in America. It has been something like an advantage, something you are better off with. And it is not just an economic advantage; it is primarily that, but also something more. This is best illustrated by that wonderful remark, "One can always tell a Harvard man, but one can't tell him much." If one has a degree from Harvard, one has autonomy and is not pushed around. A Harvard graduate is somebody; he can be a snob, and that's what certain people would give a lot to be! De Tocqueville described it as a downward diffusion of elite privileges, which is part of what the whole system of American politics is about.

If one looks at the future now, one has to assume that this process of diffusion will continue. On the one hand, we have just about reached the biological limits of where we want to be. Some remaining exceptions can be easily handled one way or the other. On the other hand, there will still be a tendency toward a downward diffusion. There are two reasons this will probably happen. One of the least understood forces behind things like education legislation is that education is a source of employment for educators. This is coupled with the decline in population growth, which—Professor Suppes to the contrary—does not require forceful measures of control. Population growth *has* stopped. We are going to have a very difficult future because of that fact. One need only walk around the Harvard Graduate School of Education and talk to girls with zero-population-growth buttons. Tell them that, as a matter of fact, the population of elementary and secondary schools in the 1970s will not grow, and therefore they might not get a job. "What? That's not what is meant by zero population growth!" Well, if you have an education, what do you do with it? You begin to think about places of employment.

Remember the great thrust for Headstart? There is presently very clear evidence that this kind of education and experience has no educational consequences of any kind, except for the Hunter College graduates who became Headstart teachers. This is a process very similar to what some call "feeding the sparrows by feeding the horses." Similar considerations may constitute the real thrust for day care. Twenty billion dollars have been requested for day care. Now who is going to get the twenty billion dollars? Not the moms and not the kids, but those who are doing the caring!

Another notion that can be sensed but is hard to prove is the growing belief that higher education is a source of socialization into political liberalism. This is valuable to people who would like to see political liberalism increase. Professor Machlup alluded to this in his remark on Kenneth Keniston. The dominant party is liberal and wants to increase its followers. This rejuvenates the pressure for downward diffusion. The Schumpeterian notion that capitalism will delegitimize itself seems to be inexorable at this point.

There exist, nonetheless, forces impeding these last-mentioned developments, which would suggest going much farther than we have gone. First of all there is, I think, Professor Machlup's sense of marginality. One cannot just talk about the utility of a certain quality without knowing its quantity. As it becomes much more common to have a college degree, the advantage of having it may diminish. Secondly, there is a decline in the attractiveness of the universities; this is a consequence of their own internal cultural experience. Presently, most universities are not the free institutions they once were. They are not politicized yet. But they are intimidated. They are not places for free spirits; they are places for prudent men, who, like bankers, for instance, are never taught to be swingers. A professor of political science who is not prudent will be sorry, and if he is prudent his students will be sorry.

All of this may cause a kind of downward movement. A recent article in Science discusses the size at which a college becomes dysfunctional. The authors use a principle of Galileo's that scale itself has functional consequences and they then try to use an intrinsic factor like growth. (It is not accidental that the elephant is the biggest thing you see around.) Using data from the California state college system, the authors suggest that at a population of about 10,000 an institution begins to become dysfunctional in ways that can be summarized simply: the more you put in, the less you get out in satisfaction.

Such pressures will probably continue, and if, in addition, we find that we cannot produce higher education from which people emerge with a relatively stable attachment to the political society that provided it, one can easily imagine that there would be some political demand for less of that kind of education. It is hard to imagine a stable society which will, for prolonged periods, seriously subsidize the kind of totalitarian political behavior on the part of elite students we saw in the 1960s. In the end, it gets through even to the best of liberals that these products of our schools are not liberals, despite what Mr. Keniston may have said!

Gresham's Law in Education

Ernest van den Haag
New School for Social Research

The recent problems of higher education spring from educational inflation. An unprecedentedly high proportion of the college age group—more than 40 per cent—now attend college. This is double the proportion of twenty years ago. The expansion has been incredibly rapid. Faculties, of course, were inflated in the same proportion. The result is that far more professors teach and do research than are competent to do either, and far more students attend than could benefit if they were taught by competent professors.

The prolongation of schooling for four years—more in many cases—for nearly half the age group is not justified by the returns. Only about 25 per cent of the college age group have the 110 IQ required by previous standards to benefit from college education. Fewer still have the disposition to listen to lectures for four more years after being compelled to do so for twelve. (An IQ of roughly 140 was thought necessary for instructors. There is reason to believe that the IQ of most instructors is now below that.) Since more than 40 per cent of the age group attend college and only 25 per cent have the required IQ, a significant number cannot benefit unless the curriculum is adapted to their understanding, that is, is downgraded. This is being done. Whereas the unadapted curriculum teaches much to students who learn little, the adapted curriculum teaches little to students who learn little. There is a psychological advantage to the latter, but in neither case do the returns justify the additional schooling. The students are right then in claiming that college education is often irrelevant to them. It will remain so as long as those who are irrelevant to college education are admitted.

The easiest way to deal with the problem is to hide it—by giving higher grades for lower achievement. This is being done. Another way of dealing with the problem is to institute "relevant" courses—relevant not to cognitive knowledge but to headlines and the often iatrogenic psychological problems from which students suffer. Thus, colleges offer "encounter workshops," in which students try to find the identities of which the attempt to master alien ideas has robbed them.

But encounters and high grades often do not suffice to restore students' identity and prestige in their own eyes. Prestige is too easily lost in unsuccessful attempts to master intellectual disciplines. Students, therefore, are tempted to regain their prestige by playing the role of revolutionaries, rebels against authority, in the psychodrama for which the university has allowed itself to be used as a stage setting.

Whence the educational inflation with its attending evils? Why is it difficult now for even bright students to accept the authority of alma mater or, indeed, any authority?

Colleges and universities are nonprofit organizations. Nonetheless, faculties and administrations earn their livings through them, and that living tends to be better as the total attendance grows greater. Promotion and pay depend largely, if indirectly, on enrollments. This is one reason why colleges and universities attempted, all too successfully, to expand continuously in the last twenty years—with results about which they now wonder. Since their product, knowledge, is irrelevant or not absorbable to many of the consumers they have enticed, colleges had to diversify and offer courses relevant to the students—if not to higher learning.

There is nothing wrong with letting anyone who wishes attend college courses whenever possible. It is wrong, however, to promise a degree when it is not warranted by expected achievement. It is even more wrong to give it—whether or not the nonachievement is disguised by ungraded courses, grade inflation, or courses in education, baking bread, or other subjects which, whatever their importance, cannot be taught profitably because they lack cognitive content and are irrelevant to the activities for which they are supposed to prepare the student.

Yet the demand for a college education is by no means wholly contrived, even if the colleges are guilty of complicity and instigation. We live in a society that believes that (1) opportunity ought to be equal for all; (2) equal opportunity will make for equal results; (3) equal education equalizes opportunity and thus, ultimately, results. However doubtful the validity of these propositions, they are widely accepted, and because they are, the idea is widespread that everybody ought to have a college education and would benefit from it—regardless of his capacity or previous school record. College is thought to equalize capacities. Differences in past records are thought to have been produced by different opportunities—not by different inherent capacities or inclinations. This idea was bound to lead to open admissions, that is, admission for credit of students without specific indications of a capacity to profit from a college education.

One argument in favor of open admissions is that those who prove incapable will be dropped by means of unsatisfactory grades. But instructors hardly ever give failing grades to a majority or even a plurality of students in their classes. They are afraid of being blamed for a student's failure and they don't want to be unpopular. Anyway, it would upset the arrangement. Hence, the result of open admissions is not post facto selection, but grade inflation and lower standards. An open-admissions policy often is justified as an act of corrective justice to disadvantaged minorities—as though the function of colleges were to equalize social advantages rather than to educate. Educating requires learning as well as teaching. If the ability to learn is excluded as an admission criterion, education is not likely to succeed. In the process of attempting to educate the inept, the education of those who might benefit will necessarily be impaired while very little is gained by those supposed to be helped. Instructors are unlikely to present materials from which the gifted can benefit when the rest of the class would be unable to follow. The materials they end up presenting do not amount to a college education.

Sometimes open admissions are justified by stressing that in the past the offspring of the nobility were admitted even when unfit. This was indeed done. It was thought that the students admitted would occupy important and powerful social positions, independently of whether they went to college. Hence it was better to educate them to whatever degree they were capable of being educated. This reasoning does not apply to present open-admissions policy. The students admitted will not occupy positions of leadership automatically and independently of their education. If they do at all, it will be because of their college degrees, which are taken as proof of education. If, on the other hand, the alumnus does not "make it" by virtue of his education, what the college has created is ambition untethered to possibility—an unhappy person who is likely to hold society responsible for his frustration and who, therefore, will be harmful to it.

What can be done? Educational inflation could not occur without the cooperation of colleges and universities. It is, on the whole, within their power to stop it. They could limit admissions and rededicate themselves to cognitive learning at the college level. The best people that can be found should be selected as students and professors, regardless of race, religion, sex, or anything else except for those character traits that make a person capable of living in an intellectual community and benefiting from having lived and learned there. The proportion of the college age group studying for degrees should never exceed 35 per cent, and faculties should be reduced accordingly.

Although colleges have played a decisive role in creating educational inflation, industry, labor, and the government have cooperated. And there have been ideological misapprehensions. Many Americans now believe in education as they used to believe in religion. They are convinced that attending college must be good and can do no harm, as they were once convinced that attending church was helpful and never harmful. But education *can* be harmful if it is transformed into schooling, if it is overextended and imposed on those who are not able to benefit by those not able to educate. The very word "education" here helps to mislead people since it conflates the process of being educated—which may or may not succeed—with its successful accomplishment or product.

Labor has specifically welcomed education because it keeps people out of the labor market as long as possible. "Education" is the cheapest way of doing so. The government has found it easier to yield to this pressure, which industry has not opposed. Education transfers much of the cost of apprenticeship to the taxpayer, even if it is a comparatively inefficient way, in many cases, of preparing for the business at hand. Last, though not least, business has used the degree, however irrelevant to the requirements of a particular job, as a sifting device in hiring. Yet in many cases, the preference for college graduates is irrational. This preference should be regarded as discriminatory when it is irrelevant, for the same reasons that the irrelevant preference for a particular race or religion is. Discrimination in terms of education ought to be interdicted legally when it is irrelevant, just as racial discrimination is. Any selection on any basis other than the merits relevant to the job is discrimination. It matters not at all whether the selective process is meant to irrelevantly exclude or include groups (sexual, racial, religious, educational) in any proportion, including the proportion in which they occur in the total population.

Parents, finally, cannot escape a share of the blame for the present situation. Many students reach higher education without ever having been led to accept the authority of persons or institutions and without having been asked to do anything requiring a major effort. This is why many talented students find it difficult to accept intellectual discipline, and to accept the authority of those who profess and transmit it. Authority can be transferred to those who stand *in loco parentis* only if there is parental authority to be transferred. Many students have never experienced it and therefore find it hard to accept the authority of the law and the university. Rehabilitation will be hard for them, for society, and for the universities. But it is not fostered by refusals to exercise authority and by acceptance of anyone and anything. Universities must become selective in what and how they teach, in hiring and keeping professors, and in admitting students.

Comment

Ernest Nagel
Columbia University

I want to defend Professor Machlup from most of the criticisms to which his paper has been subjected. In my opinion, these criticisms were not relevant to the views he expressed and were, therefore, essentially shadowboxing. He took the trouble to define with some care what he means by "higher education"—namely, a system of formal education that trains students for careers in scholarship and science. Nevertheless, most of the comments on his essay ignored this explanation of his meaning and, in effect, criticized him for not concentrating on the need for, and the great importance of, a universal post-secondary-school education. But as I understand Professor Machlup, he denied neither the need nor importance. On the contrary, he endorsed the idea that everyone should have the opportunity to continue his education.

The issue he did raise is whether colleges and universities are the appropriate institutions for providing this opportunity. It surely cannot be taken for granted that they are the proper instruments to achieve this end. Thus, in view of the changes (reported by preceding professors) in the ages at which young people become physiologically mature, one must ask whether it might not be a mistake to subject individuals currently or prospectively attending colleges and universities to the discipline required for training scholars and scientists, if they are at an age when they are handicapped by their physiological condition.

Accordingly, I do not think that his critics have concerned themselves with the main burden of Professor Machlup's paper: whether or not the future of scholarship and science in this country is threatened because of the heavy stress placed upon educating students for other dimensions of human experience. I do not for a moment believe, any more than does Dr. Machlup, that these other dimensions do not need to be cultivated. But I share his concern that, because education for these other dimensions has been the focus of popular, as well as official, attention, we have been neglecting the basic function of universities, namely, to develop individuals equipped to contribute to scholarship and science. This is the issue that Dr. Machlup has raised for us, but it is an issue to which the critics of his paper have not done adequate justice.

A Reply to My Critics

Fritz Machlup
Princeton University

As Professor Suppes said before he started the attack on my paper, I know how to take it, I enjoy a good fight, and I do not even complain if some of the hits are foul. I was somewhat amazed, though, about hits evidently prompted by a misreading of my statement.

I have been accused of shirking empirical investigation of what motivates students to go to college, and of engaging instead in a worthless mental experiment. What did I actually say? I deplored the non-availability of empirical evidence, and I offered reasons why certain tests were inconclusive. Then I proceeded to "devise a test based on self-selection by high-school seniors," in order to find out which of the options were essential to attract them. (The interrogator would vary the conditions students could expect at or from college.) I formulated eleven such conditions and suggested that they could be eliminated in turn, one at a time and in various combinations. "As long as we merely *speculate* about the effects the various factors would have on the students' decisions," I said, "our answers may differ widely" (p. 11). But I proposed the whole scheme in the hope of empirical tests, and I also said: "The survey research proposed here might yield useful numerical information about the factors determining the demand for broad college education. . ." (p. 12). Could I have been more specific?

One of the conditions in the bag of options for the students was the promise or expectation of higher income for college graduates. I said,

". . . it would be important to know how many students would demand a college education that does not promise them any pecuniary rewards" (p. 12). It is not that I find anything wrong with pecuniary incentives, but we ought to know how many would not choose to go to college if they could not expect that it would pay off through higher incomes. This test question was misread to be my judgment "that there *should* be no income differentials earned in later life by college graduates." The critic went on to inquire whether I meant to say that all college graduates ought to have exactly the same income or that their median income "should be exactly the same as the median income of noncollege graduates" or that their incomes would not be increased as a result of their studies. I meant none of this, of course. My critic suspects that I raised this issue because I want to exclude some students (and some courses) from higher education.

The suspicion that I want to prevent anyone from getting more education has also gripped and griped other participants in our symposium. I can attribute this suspicion only to some sort of hypersensitivity on the part of educational expansionists, who interpret any doubts about the supposed blessings as attempts to "restrict access" to postsecondary education (or perhaps even any kind of education). I was vindicated by the observations of several people, who confirmed that I had not advocated restricted access for any group or person anywhere in my paper.

Perhaps I should explicitly reply to some of the questions raised or to the claims made by Professors Suppes and Hook. Both took me to task on matters of definitions. Suppes wants "universal higher education" to be understood as *post-secondary* education for a *large* percentage of the population. He claims that his is the "commonsense meaning" of the expression, and he states that in this area "we can scarcely expect exact definitions, precise concepts, and pure meanings to carry the day." A little later, however, he chides me for speaking of diligence without having done empirical research on diligence and without having offered an operational definition of the term. Is there no commonsense meaning of "diligence"? And would it not be quite simple to define it operationally in terms of the number of hours a student spends reading and writing papers on the subjects he studies?

Suppes tries to make fun of my attempt to define higher education by criteria other than the age of the students or the number of years of school attendance. He plays with my phrase "education of potential scholars" by supposing that a college course is called a "course *in higher education a la Machlup*, if and only if at least 50 per cent of the students in that course go on to some form of graduate or professional school." This is nonsense, of course, but Suppes' nonsense, not mine. I have struggled hard attempting to define higher education, and I think I came closest to an acceptable formulation when I said in my paper: "Education is 'higher' only if it builds upon knowledge absorbed in secondary and in introductory tertiary education and could not have been absorbed at the earlier stage (except by a few geniuses) because it requires more intelligence, mental discipline, and perseverance than can be expected from most students of high-school age" (p. 6).

I was told (by someone outside UCRA) that this was a stipulative or persuasive definition, designed to impose my own standards upon others. I submit that my definition merely tries to add a little more precision to the traditional dictionary definition of higher education. Both the Oxford and Webster dictionaries, in defining "university," characterize it by its dedication to the "higher branches of learning"; Webster uses "higher branches of knowledge" in one of the definitions of "college." This does not mean that colleges and universities do or should offer higher education exclusively. As I said, this would be neither practical nor desirable. On the other hand, to call all post-secondary education "higher" education would be a waste of terms; there would be no term left to distinguish education in advanced courses from that in introductory courses.

Incidentally, I do not confine higher education to "graduate and professional studies," as Professor Hook suggests. A good portion of undergraduate courses at many institutions qualify as higher education in the sense defined, and, on the other hand, some graduate schools, give "credit" for introductory courses. No doubt, there may be border-line cases, as in nearly all distinctions, but this is not a serious difficulty. Most college catalogues assign lower numbers to introductory courses and higher numbers to intermediate and advanced courses.

Whether Professor John Searle teaches the philosophy of language in a way that qualifies it as higher education is something that he himself ought to judge. He should ask himself whether a class of high-school seniors could take his course and pass his examination. The course in principles of economics that I am now teaching is *not* higher education by my standards, but I hope that the intermediate undergraduate course which I am scheduled to teach next year will be on a higher level. In making these distinctions, I am not contemptuous of broader education. I stressed that "I am also a strong supporter of liberal education, of a *studium generale*" (p. 5), and that "I neither regret nor disparage the high ratio of broader to higher education" (p. 7) at our best colleges. Abraham Flexner was more of an elitist than I am; he regretted the small share of higher education. "It is clear," he wrote in *Universities: American, English, German* (1930), "that of Harvard's total expenditures not more than one-eighth is devoted to the central university disciplines at the level at which a university ought to be conducted." I do recognize that the university has to offer broader education; otherwise broader education would have to be acquired almost entirely by independent reading and in extension classes.

When Professor Suppes tells us that at San Francisco State College the average age of students is between twenty-five and twenty-six and that a large proportion of the students have full-time or nearly full-time jobs, I share his gratification about these adults' ambition to get more education and about their opportunity to get it. Voluntary adult education is a splendid thing, both for those who take it and for society at large. I am cheered by Professor Suppes' report that many early dropouts return later to continue their education. This is exactly what I have been pleading for: voluntary longer education, noncompulsory continuing education without pressure of any sort—either from parents or from peer groups—nor through fear of job discrimination against those without academic degrees nor through fear of being drafted. If Professor Suppes thought that in making these points he was arguing against my position, he was mistaken. Incidentally, he was also mistaken in intimating that I was advocating that we should become "a nation of fourteen-year-old school-leavers." I am an advocate of the *freedom* to leave school at fourteen for those who hate to stay at school and would not benefit from attending; I am also an opponent of *coercing* adolescents to waste years at school, where they cannot be coerced to learn what is being taught.

Professor Suppes explicitly asks for my response to his statement that higher education has always been a privilege of "the sons of the wealthy." Daniel Moynihan answered this question as far as this country and recent times are concerned: the sons of the poor have had little difficulty getting a higher education, at least in places like New York City, where City College was founded in 1846. I have read in German histories of higher education that since the last decades of the nineteenth century no person could claim that poverty prevented him from getting into a university. I cannot, of course, vouch for the historical truth of these statements. But the way Professor Suppes puts it, the proposition is probably correct that family income was (say, until 1940) a "better predictor" of university attendance than a student's intelligence. But what does he want to prove with this statement, except that he has little love for the rich and that his heart goes out to the poor? At a time when far less than 1 per cent of the population went to a university and the bulk of the people had little or no schooling, would anybody expect that the few university students were recruited from the poor? Schooling was a luxury that only the wealthy could afford. The same situation still prevails in very poor countries (except in China and perhaps other socialist countries, where the children of nonmanual workers are excluded from universities). But again, what is the relevance of this to our discussion?

If I have argued that genuinely higher education is too high for all but the best learners in the population—perhaps the top 10 or 15 per cent—and, furthermore, that pressuring as many as 50 per cent of the population into submitting to sixteen years of schooling would not benefit, and may harm, a good many uninterested and unwilling students, in what respect are these arguments contradicted by a statement that in the past only the sons of the rich could get a longer education?

I have emphasized the important role of the liberal-arts college in giving the student (who has had in high school a rather small dose of broader education) another, however modest, dose of it, and in developing in him a taste for still more—a taste that he may satisfy through "continuing education, to be pursued chiefly through a lifetime of reading" (p. 7) and through taking advantage of the cultural institutions of our society. I added: "Even the broadly educated man or woman— rarely anybody below the age of forty—will have assimilated only a small part of all existing knowledge, but he will know vastly more than a college graduate, let alone the high-school graduate" (p. 7). Why should Professor Suppes object to this statement? Yet he does disagree: "In terms of education or culture, I do not think my friends or I know more than we did when we were fifteen years younger." This could be true only if Professor Suppes at a rather early age stopped reading, going to theaters, concerts, and museums, and listening to knowledgeable people, or found his capacity to learn exhausted. I do not believe it. But why did he think it helpful to say so? Merely as a debating point, merely to show that I am an unreliable character, with a "cavalier way with the facts"? Do we really need empirical tests to prove that after thirty-five years of reading most people are more broadly educated than after only twenty years?

After scolding me for not presenting more "detailed evidence" for my arguments and for not supplying "harder sorts of data"—and, of course, all evidence and data are necessarily from records of the past— Professor Suppes ends by saying that my "gravest error is in looking backward rather than forward." I am afraid that I cannot find hard facts and reliable empirical evidence by looking into the future. I am not persuaded that Professor Suppes can either.

PART TWO

HIGHER EDUCATION UNDER FIRE

In Defense of Intellectual Integrity

Arthur Bestor
University of Washington

In his oration "The American Scholar" before the Phi Beta Kappa society at Harvard more than a century and a third ago, Emerson elected to "say something of . . . [the] duties" of the scholar. What Emerson actually said was not what one might have expected him to say. Though the stateliness of the occasion might well have tempted the young man to play Sir Oracle, Emerson refused to traffic in prophetic insights, to pontificate about the verdict of history, to speak knowingly of forces still hidden in the womb of time that the scholar ought to recognize as somehow destined to reshape the world. Quite the opposite was Emerson's conclusion—his profoundly skeptical conclusion—as to the true responsibility of the scholar in time of crisis: "Let him not quit his belief that a popgun is a popgun, though the ancient and honorable of the earth affirm it to be the crack of doom."[1]

During the preceding decade many of the great universities of the world were reduced almost to a state of siege by deliberate disruption, vandalism, and destruction. Ostensibly at least, the blows were struck, not by outsiders, but by insiders: by students who described themselves as militants (or militants who described themselves as students) and by small contingents of faculty members. This betrayal from within was alarming, of course, as in any surrender to unreason. But far more alarming was the myth-making that magnified these events into awesome signs of the apocalypse. Many of the ancient and honorable

61

of today's world—syndicated columnists, television commentators, foundation executives, civil servants with reputations as serious thinkers, authors who specialize in diagnosing the nation's hangups—were quick to proclaim that the campus disorders constituted, for the university as we have known it, the ineluctable crack of doom. And the prevailing view on these Olympian heights was that the university deserved the doom that descended upon it.

According to the argument, the kind of university that persisted into the second half of the twentieth century was a moribund institution, its intellectual concerns irrelevant, its ideal of objectivity a false ideal, its valuing of excellence a corrupt elitism. The corollary, of course, was that the disrupters and wreckers on university campuses were not vandals at all, but the unconscious—and perhaps therefore the sacred—instruments of a future struggling to be born. Their violence was to be seen as the new rationality, their acts of coercion as the new emancipation, their anti-intellectualism as the new science. In short, their homemade bombs were supposedly firing a salute to a brave, new intellectual order, as well as sounding the crack of doom for an old and discredited one.

Confronted by pretentious nonsense like this, we need the saving common sense of Emerson's scholar, quietly pointing out that a popgun is a popgun, whatever the fashionable opinion makers of the moment may say. The physical damage done to universities by bombings, arsons, and "trashings" was costly but nevertheless reparable. The intention of militants to destroy the university as a place of disinterested and unintimidated intellectual inquiry was both real and exceedingly dangerous. Nevertheless the university and its ideals did in fact survive the batterings of the sixties. It should be clear by now that the vicious new forces of unreason will be victorious only if we, through indolence or cowardice, permit them to be so. Having weathered the assaults of a recent past, the university must not be brought down by the defaults of an upcoming future.

The greatest danger the university now faces is that we—the scholars and scientists on university faculties—will suffer a loss of nerve, that we will succumb to a belief that the forces that have battered the university represent an irresistible wave of the future, that we will abdicate our responsibility for keeping the university true to its intellectual purpose and firm in its commitment to intellectual integrity.

At this critical moment, two distinct but interrelated tasks must be undertaken by the responsible leaders of university faculties. In the first place, we must make clear to the public and to educational administrators the self-evident fact that the jejune rationalizations voiced by militant disrupters are not genuine, well-considered, responsible

programs of university reform. In the second place, we must firmly refuse to accept as permanent the alterations in curriculum and governance that administrators and trustees, acting under intimidation and
often in panic, imposed upon the university without genuine faculty
deliberation and unambiguous faculty approval.

The first of these points is so obvious that it is strange that it should
need to be made at all. On the very face of the record, the militant
student movements were not movements of educational reform. They
never purported to be. Their leaders, with fanatical consistency,
defined their purposes in terms of social and political change. To be
sure, militants who propose to use the university to promote their
political or revolutionary aims are necessarily proposing to alter the
university as well as to use it—to alter it *in order to* use it. But to describe this as educational reform would be like describing the bull-
dozing of cropland for an airfield as a form of agricultural
improvement.

The militants have made no secret of what they would like the university to become. The descriptive word is "politicization." The university is to choose sides on the crucial issues of the day. And then—
to use the revealing word that Dr. Kissinger let slip in discussing American policy toward Pakistan[2]—the university is to "tilt" its offerings
toward the favored side.

This is hardly a new idea. It is the oldest and scruffiest of all sellouts.
In the bitter religious controversies of post-Reformation times, universities were expected as a matter of course to "tilt" toward Prot-
estantism or toward Catholicism—*cuius regio, eius religio*. In time
of war the university was supposed to "tilt" against the enemy and all
his works—including even his language and his noblest cultural
achievements. Where economic and social matters were concerned,
the expected "tilt" was of course toward the views considered orthodox
by those who supported the university and therefore felt entitled to
control it. The "tilt" would be toward laissez-faire under conservative
boards of trustees; it would be toward collectivization if some Marxist
central committee took over. And within the memory of many of us,
the late Senator Joseph McCarthy sought to apply the doctrine of
"politicization" to American universities with the same righteous
fervor as the New Left today, demanding of universities and faculties a
"tilt" that would eliminate all discussion of ideas that he and his co-
horts chose to describe as treasonable.

Academic freedom as we know it today represents a complete repu-
diation of the doctrine of "politicization," or, in more general terms,
the idea that the university should examine the evidence on controver-

sial questions through permanently tinted spectacles. It was primarily the nineteenth-century conflict between theology and science (symbolized by Darwinian evolution) that finally convinced thoughtful men and women that intellectual life would be stultified and stifled if institutions of higher learning attempt to maintain a permanent "tilt" toward some prescribed set of ideas. Such a "tilt" meant weighing evidence in a dishonest balance and closing down the marketplace, whereas, in the words of Mr. Justice Holmes, "the ultimate good . . . is . . . reached by free trade in ideas."[3]

Academic freedom won its way slowly in the nineteenth century, but the achievements were cumulative, so that by the end of World War II university faculties, supported by an alert public opinion, were able to resist and eventually roll back the first major attempt to politicize the American university—the effort usually labeled McCarthyism. The fact that politicization has today become the program of the New Left instead of the Old Right has left many members of university faculties bewildered, with the result that our newly threatened flank has been less promptly defended than it should have been. Many of our colleagues are still fighting the ghost of Joseph McCarthy, when it is now Herbert Marcuse who is masterminding the attack upon the intellectual integrity of the university. But the time has surely come to cease responding with a conditioned reflex; the situation calls instead for serious reflection.

The contention that universities should "tilt" in some predetermined political direction is one we must seriously face. If we do so, we shall find that the argument has been offered countless times in the past and has been essentially the same at every appearance. Tolerance of opposing views, the argument runs, is a fine thing where only routine matters are involved. But on certain issues one position is so incontrovertibly right and the other so infernally wrong that to be tolerant is to become the accomplice of wickedness. Such was the view of Torquemada and the Inquisition, so far as heresy was concerned. Such was the view of Calvin, when he sent the Unitarian, Michael Servetus, to the stake. Such was the view of the Tennessee legislature, when it forbade the teaching of evolution in the public schools. Such have been the views of those who, over the years, have drafted sedition acts designed to ban particular brands of political heterodoxy. And such today are the views of those who urge the "politicization" of the university, by which they invariably mean the establishment of their own particular political and social doctrines as the official standard of truth for the entire institution and all its members.

As a matter of fact, campus militants are remarkably self-deluded if they imagine that the politicization of the university will mean the adoption of their particular views as the determinant of university policy. If the university should abandon its fundamental task of objective inquiry into the problems of mankind and the universe and announce instead that it will adopt a political stance, it would thereby put university policy up for "grabs." Whichever group in the community mustered the greatest political strength would thereafter determine the particular political or economic or social ideology that the university would be required to propagate. It is difficult to imagine anything more unlikely than that the ideology ultimately adopted would be that of the handful of present-day campus militants. Nor is it likely that even the majority faculty opinion would be able to determine the official ideology of the university for long. To politicize the university is to invite outside intervention. If the university ever surrenders its claim to intellectual independence and immunity by abandoning the ideal of objectivity that alone can justify that claim, then the university will be compelled to accept the role of complacent apologist for the status quo, dutifully propagating the ideas favored by the party in power and dutifully shelving any ideas that arouse the misgivings of the surrounding community.

Such a miserable guttering out of a flame that once helped to enlighten the world would be the most probable outcome of a politicization of the university. But the outcome would be at least equally calamitous if, despite all probabilities, politicization should turn out to mean what the campus militants desire and expect it to mean—namely, the harnessing of the university to the social, economic, and political programs advocated by some self-selected radical elite. Among these programs would be many that large numbers of faculty members have been actively supporting as individuals. But the freedom of individual faculty members to take an active part as *private citizens* in the political life of the community is not what politicization means.

To commit a university to a particular political, economic, or social program would not represent an enlargement of the freedom of thought and action of an individual faculty member or an individual student. On the contrary, such an institutional commitment would operate to circumscribe, immediately and sharply, the intellectual and political freedom of every member of the university. Each would be forced to become a participant in the efforts now diverted into political channels. The prestige of the individual professor, which is a basic element in the prestige of the university, would be committed, whether he approved or not, to the advancement of political, not scholarly, ends. Perhaps by vigorous and conspicuous dissent a faculty member might manage to dissociate himself from purposes of which he disapproved. But dissent in a political university would not be the same thing as dissent in one dedicated to academic freedom. A dissenter might well find that he had dissociated himself not only from the policy but also from the payroll of a university that had an exigent political mission to perform.

To become or to remain a faculty member in a politicized university, moreover, would mean buying a pig in a poke. Such a university would be committed not merely to programs that had already been formulated; it would be committed to *staying* committed. In the future it would be called upon to support many as-yet-undreamed-of programs, and it would have surrendered its power to refuse. When objective inquiry and critical discussion ceased to be the means of arriving at conclusions on public policy, the faculty member would have nothing to fall back on but faith—faith in the continuing rightness and righteousness of those charged with mapping out the lines of political action he would be expected to pursue.

Is there anything in the conduct of campus militants that would give us faith in their superior wisdom and probity or that would justify us in entrusting the fate of the university to their hands? It will be said, of course, that recent campus disruptions are upswellings from some deep fountain of youthful idealism and that the pervasive theme is a consuming hatred of war. It is quite true that one important element in campus demonstrations in the United States has been opposition to the war in Vietnam. If this were the whole of the matter, it would be plausible to believe that the only thing being asked of university faculties is to accept a firm commitment to peace. Unfortunately for this argument, universities have been disrupted in nations not only uninvolved in the Vietnam war but overtly hostile to American policy there. And campus disruptions in Egypt, where students have sought to force their government to go to war, ought finally to have shattered the illusion that peace is the worldwide aim of student movements.

There are few beliefs so ill-supported by history as the sentimental belief that the voice of youth is ipso facto the voice of God. To subscribe to such a doctrine one must contrive to forget that Adolf Hitler was thirty-four years old at the time of the Beer Hall Putsch, that Hermann Goering was thirty, and that Heinrich Himmler was only twenty-three. Though Reinhard Heydrich was even younger and was not present on that occasion, he managed at the age of thirty to become deputy chief of the Gestapo; he compressed several lifetimes of cruelty into the years that remained before his assassination at the age of thirty-eight. One could easily defend the proposition that Nazism was the most potent youth movement of modern times. Youth *is* a powerful driving force. That is why it is so important to examine the actual direction in which youthful leaders are driving, consciously or unconsciously.

The rhetoric of the militants has much to say about freedom. Do their actions speak the same langauge? The test, of course, is not whether they demand freedom of speech for those who agree with them. Who in the world has ever done otherwise? The question is whether they accept and act upon the sentiment attributed to Voltaire: "I disapprove of what you say, but I will defend to the death your right to say it."[4] The contrary is suggested by the number of episodes in recent years in which defenders of the status quo have been booed and hissed and sometimes prevented from speaking, both in meetings on campus and in sessions of learned societies. More important than the piling up of such instances, however, is a consideration of the attitude toward freedom of discussion implicit in the actions of those who attempt to enforce their views on university affairs by disruption, by "nonnegotiable demands," and by open threats of violence.

Partisans of the New Left will assert, of course, that they have no intention of making violence a permanent feature of university life and coercion a permanent principle of university governance. These, they will say, are temporary tactics, made necessary by the fact that the university is a repressive institution, working hand-in-glove with a repressive establishment, both being essentially fascist in outlook. Against fascism there is no recourse but violence. Accordingly, the bombing of university buildings (including the murder of any hapless occupant, as at the University of Wisconsin) and the presentation of "nonnegotiable demands" (the fashionable new label for what old-time militarists called an ultimatum) are the justifiable acts of freedom fighters. Once their aim is attained, we are asked to believe, violence will serve no purpose and hence will quietly disappear, just as the state (in old Marxist theory and perhaps even in new) is scheduled to wither away.

Whether such promises are believable is a question that everyone can decide for himself. The important point is to examine the assumptions that creep into an argument like the foregoing and often go unexamined and unchallenged. The most blatant example is the assertion that a cloud of censorship and repression descended upon university campuses in the sixties, stifling discussion of controversial issues, muzzling professors critical of the status quo, and banning every unconventional expression of student opinion. This is a falsehood so breathtaking in its audacity that one cannot avoid a sneaking admiration for the ingenuity of the Baron Munchausen who invented it. In no period in the history of universities have there been so few inhibitions upon student opinion and conduct, so little attempted censorship of books and periodicals and campus speakers, and so few reported instances of administrative surveillance of the ideas expressed by professors in or out of the classroom. Though radical campus editors love to ring changes on the theme of repression, their own files furnish conclusive proof of how free, in fact, they are to discuss—and if they choose, to advocate—anything from Maoism to homosexuality.

Threats to freedom always exist, and vigilance can never be safely relaxed. But vigilance means the precise identification of real dangers, not the hysterical shouting of "Wolf! Wolf!" when a mouse creeps out of the woodwork. The militant rhetoric that equates American government today with the government of Nazi Germany is so grotesquely exaggerated as to create, in the mind of anyone who knows what the Nazi regime was really like, a credibility gap that may lead him to dismiss in contemptuous unbelief even the most responsible and well-considered criticism of current abuses.

Comparisons and analogies are necessary ingredients in any serious discussion of public affairs. But they must be subjected to the most exhaustive critical scrutiny, for a false analogy is a false guideline for action. Indeed, to put the matter more forcefully, it is likely to be the guideline for a false and self-destructive course of action. To propagate a deliberately false analogy is to poison the springs of democratic decision. Precisely such a calculated misrepresentation takes place when the perfectly proper criticism of repressive tendencies in American public life is escalated into the assertion that the United States has become a fascist dictatorship.

There is a fundamental flaw in the reasoning that purports to equate the American establishment with the Nazi regime. The defect is one of historical and sociological analysis. To the extent that the existing American government can be said to manifest repressive tendencies (and any government is likely to do so in time of crisis), its repressiveness is that of an *established* regime seeking to maintain the status quo. However strongly one may condemn such repressiveness, it is *not* fascism. The repressiveness of fascism is that of a *revolutionary* regime which has just *overthrown* the establishment. And the difference is a profound one, even though both forms of repressiveness are hateful.

An historical instance will serve to clarify the distinction. In 1798, as the United States drifted into undeclared war with the France of the Directory, the Federalists pushed through Congress a set of repressive measures known as the Alien and Sedition Acts. These have been almost universally condemned by later generations, and the revulsion against them at the time was such that the Federalist Party went down to defeat at the next presidential election, and never recovered. Though the First Amendment to the Constitution, ratified seven years earlier, had forbidden Congress to make any law "abridging the freedom of speech, or of the press," the Sedition Act of July 14, 1798, prescribed a fine of as much as two thousand dollars and imprisonment for as long as two years for any person who should publish "any false, scandalous and malicious writings against the government," or should "stir up sedition within the United States," or should "excite any lawful combinations . . . for opposing or resisting any law of the United States, or any act of the President."[5] Ten convictions were obtained under the act, and opposition editors served terms in prison. This was repression initiated by the establishment, for the Federalist Party was the party of the establishment.

All too rarely, however, is a comparison made between this repressive legislation, for which an establishment must take blame, and the decrees on the same subject, promulgated in the same period, with the same wartime danger as justification, by a regime that had just *overthrown* an established order. The Declaration of the Rights of Man and the Citizen, adopted by the French National Assembly on August 27, 1789—at the very outset of the French Revolution and just one month before Congress passed the American Bill of Rights—contained the following guarantee, far grander in phrasing than its American counterpart: "The free communication of ideas and opinions is one of the most precious of the rights of man; every citizen then can freely speak, write, and print, subject to responsibility for the abuse of this freedom in the cases determined by law."[6] Three and a half years later war had begun, and on March 29, 1793, the National Convention adopted the following decree on the press: "Whoever shall be convicted of having composed or printed works or writings which incite to the dissolution of the national representation, the reestablishment of monarchy or of any other power which constitutes an attack upon the sovereignty of the people, shall be arraigned before the extraordinary tribunal and punished with death."[7]

The French decree of 1793 and the American Sedition Act of 1798 are comparable documents. Both were wartime measures. Both were directed against the domestic opposition and reflected a fear of subversion or overthrow. But the first was the decree of a revolutionary regime and it carried the death penalty; the second was the statute of an established order, and its penalty was a fine and two years in jail. There is one other important difference. The Sedition Act expired on a fixed date, less than three years after its enactment and has ever since been regarded by public opinion as unjustifiable and unconstitutional. The French decree, on the other hand, set a precedent that was eagerly followed—and expanded—by the leaders of every successful coup d'état for decades thereafter.[8]

Repression is to be condemned wherever it occurs. But to say this, is not to preclude a consideration of the diverse origins of repression and its varying severity. The most atrocious repression we have knowledge of is that which occurred thirty years ago at the hands of the Nazis. In view of what the world went through at that time, we cannot be too vigilant in looking for evidence of any recrudescence of fascism. But we need not be so simple-minded as to look only in the places we are told to look by partisans of the New Left. Their own tactics, after all, should be scrutinized for possible resemblances to those employed by the Nazis in successfully undermining and destroying the Weimar Republic and erecting their totalitarian dictatorship on its ruins.

The historical parallels that the New Left and their militant allies have invented are wide of the mark, and deliberately so. Their allegation is that American society and government are moving, like the Weimar Republic, step by step into a fascist dictatorship comparable to that of Hitler. But the simple and obvious historical fact is that the Weimar Republic did not evolve by slow stages into the Third Reich. The crimes that were committed in the name of the German Reich in the 1930s and 1940s were not acts of the Weimar Republic. They were not abuses of power by an established regime that had grown increasingly repressive. They were the crimes of a revolutionary regime that had deliberately subverted the Weimar Republic and repudiated its institutions, to which they applied the sneering epithet "liberal." More than that, the massive atrocities the Nazis committed once they had seized power were simply magnifications of the acts of terrorism they had employed when, as a disciplined minority, they commenced their career of intimidation and subversion.

These considerations should teach us where we must look if we detect an incipient fascism in the American republic today. Our attention should be focused; not so much upon the spokesmen of the so-called establishment (greatly though we may oppose and even distrust their policies), as upon the various groups (whether they label themselves "left" or "right") that frankly propose to subvert this establishment—by simple disruption if possible, by outright violence if necessary—and to climb to power over its ruins.

What has just been said is not a digression. A totalitarian takeover of the state would threaten the continued existence of a free, open, fair-minded university, just as the politicization of the university would threaten—ultimately if not immediately—the continued existence of a free, open, fair-minded society. Members of the university must be alert to both kinds of threat and must be ready to uphold and defend the ground rules upon which freedom, both in the university and in society, depend. This is *not* politicization, but the opposite.

The distinction will be clear if we shift our attention elsewhere. In a sport an umpire is not supposed to sit idly by while the rules of the game are broken. On the contrary, he is expected to exercise his authority vigorously and to impose the necessary penalties to prevent any contestant from breaking the rules and destroying the game. To do so does not make the umpire a partisan in the contest. His impartiality, indeed, is his only reason for being in the game at all.[9] The umpire has no business deciding that one side is, on the whole, worthier. He betrays his trust completely if he begins to favor one side and to call fouls only on its opponents. Such favoritism is the analogue of politicization.

To be impartial, objective, and fair-minded is not to run away from the contest. The umpire is not an ostrich burying his head in the sand. And the scholar who goes after objective data, who weighs evidence, who listens to arguments on both sides, and who is ready to revise his conclusions when an error is revealed—he is not avoiding the world's problems but facing them squarely and honestly. In doing so he is the genuine activist. Moreover, the university is an activist institution, not on those occasions when it allows classes to be interrupted for mass rallies, but when it makes sure that its own proper work goes steadily forward in classrooms, laboratories, and libraries. As an institution of higher education it has an obligation to send forth its graduates in possession of something more valuable for the world than a headful of secondhand slogans. And, as an institution for the advancement of knowledge, it serves the world best by insisting that its members conduct themselves as scholars, not propagandists. When they are performing as scholars, it must protect them from interference and pressure as they pursue their critical inquiries into the whole range of human concerns and announce their documented, if often controversial, conclusions.

The conclusions, more often than not, *are* controversial. The allegation that universities and their faculties have been timid apologists for American foreign policy or credulous dupes of a military-industrial-labor complex will hardly survive a moment's serious examination. Over the past few decades no professional group in American society has come close to being so fearless, so independent, or so critical as the university community in examining the great issues of foreign affairs and collective security, as well as the domestic problems of racial discrimination, poverty, and environmental pollution. In these highly controversial areas, universities have been able to exercise influence because—and only because—they have enjoyed public respect. And this respect has been given to the extent—and only to the extent—that the impartial and unbiased investigation of issues has been recognized by the public as a genuine commitment of the university. Had the university sacrificed its integrity by succumbing to politicization, it would have exercised no such influence. Pronouncements emanating from a "kept" university would have possessed no more credibility than the nondescript "scientific studies" that hucksters foist upon a television audience.

Objectivity, scientific rigor, and scholarly integrity are important, however, for a far more important reason than that these qualities obtain a respectful hearing for scholars and scientists. These qualities are indispensable safeguards in every situation where the welfare of society or of individual human beings depends in any way upon the accuracy and validity of the findings on which policies will finally be based. To the impatient activist, the meticulous testing of conclusions is so much academic mumbo-jumbo, standing in the way of an immediate and wholesale application of new insights and new ways of doing things—insights and methods that are still untested, to be sure, but that promise benefits too great to be postponed. (The best commentary on this argument is the history of thalidomide. Impatience to put a hopeful new drug to use led to the bypassing of rigorous scientific procedures. Thousands of hopelessly deformed children, with long years of suffering before them, form a living and tortured monument to an irresponsibly activist pharmacology.)

To look at the side effects before rushing pell-mell into action—this could almost stand as a definition of the critical method. It is a method that ought to command increasing respect as we contemplate the frightening ecological damage to our world that has resulted from neglect of this principle.

As an historian, I have a final word. One function of a university is to keep alive and usable the knowledge and ideas of the past. This is not because the past has said the last word, but because it may have said the first. The facts and concepts and insights that are necessary for dealing with the exigent problems of a complicated world cannot all be found in one nearby, convenient cupboard. The scholar must ransack other places and other times. But everything he finds, whether in the past or the present, whether on this continent or another, is to be the object of intense critical examination, not of worship. And the motive, even of the historian, is to enrich and illumine the present, to answer and not to deny its needs, to encourage the expansion of knowledge and not keep the intellectual activity of men within bounds that someone once thought proper to prescribe.

NOTES

1. Ralph Waldo Emerson, *Complete Works*, Concord ed. (Boston, 1903), I, p. 102.

2. Washington Special Action Group (an arm of the National Security Council), meeting on India/Pakistan, Dec. 3, 1971, Memorandum of Record. Made public by columnist Jack Anderson and published in the *New York Times*, Jan. 6, 1972, p. 16, cols. 1-2. Remarks by Henry A. Kissinger: "I am getting hell every half-hour from the President that we are not being tough enough on India . . . He wants to tilt in favor of Pakistan." "It's hard to tilt toward Pakistan if we have to match every Indian step with a Pakistan step." "I remember a letter or memo interpreting our existing treaty with a special India tilt." As Russell Baker pointed out in a caustic commentary, "tilt" is the word that lights up on a pinball machine when the player is cheating.

3. Dissenting opinion in Abrams v. United States, 250 U.S. 616, at 630 (Nov. 10, 1919).

4. The point of view is that of Voltaire, but the actual sentence can be traced no farther back than S. G. Tallentyre's *The Friends of Voltaire* (*1907*).

5. Sedition Act, July 14, 1798, 1 U.S. Statutes at Large, 596-597.

6. Frank Maloy Anderson, *The Constitutions and Other Select Documents Illustrative of the History of France, 1789-1901* (Minneapolis, 1904), p. 60. This Declaration was subsequently incorporated in the Constitution of Sept. 3, 1791, which also included another provision to the same effect in Title I (Anderson, p. 61). This guarantee was reiterated with little change in almost all subsequent French constitutional documents.

7. *Ibid.*, p. 158.

8. See, for example, the press laws of April 16, 1796 (under the Directory), of Jan. 17, 1800 (under the Consulate), of 1810 (under the First Empire), and of March 17, 1822 (under the Bourbon Restoration). *Ibid.*, pp. 254, 282-283, 434-435, 488.

9. The etymology of the word "umpire" tells the story. In Middle English he was a "noumpere," the word having been taken from Old French, where *non-per* simply meant *not* one of the peers or equals or principals in the contest.

The Betrayal of the Citadel

Robert Nisbet
University of Arizona

My agreement with Arthur Bestor's splendid, often moving essay is very nearly total. He has not exaggerated or distorted certain events that came very close to destroying a number of major universities in this country during the 1960s and that had the inevitable effect of weakening the idea of the university in America. Despite the writings of some excellent scholars, suggesting that a degree of violence is ingrained in the history of the American college going back to colonial times, I do not think that the American college and university had ever known, prior to the 1960s, anything like the ferocity of assault, the unremitting attack upon faculty and administration, the nihilistic depredations, and the calculated degradation of the university ideal that we have witnessed.

Having expressed my substantial agreement with Professor Bestor's essay, I would rather leave it at that and turn to certain other aspects of our problem that did not fall within his purview. I should like to consider, not the revolutionary epoch as such, not the kind of nihilism Professor Bestor has described in such rich detail, but, rather, the character of a university that permitted, that in some degree at least generated, this nihilism on the campus.

I do not think it sufficient to refer simply, as many have done, to the ideological nature of the New Left. That this ideology is committed to destruction of what it regards as a hopelessly corrupt civilization, family, church, industry, and state, as well as university, I do not question. That it is, doctrinally and intellectually, substantially below the levels of the other Lefts in Western European history—indeed it is almost at an infantile level—I do not question either. Finally, I am well aware of the fact that the depredations of the 1960s began with the campus mainly as the *setting* of revolutionary planning and foray rather than as the major *object* of ideological thrust. Certainly, extramural issues such as civil rights and Vietnam fueled the depredations.

Still, the question remains: How did it happen—even making allowance for the ferocity and the vandalism of many in the New Left—that the American university was such relatively easy prey for this ferocity and vandalism? How are we to account for the fact that great faculties at Berkeley, Harvard, Wisconsin, and elsewhere often could not even reach agreement on the fact of the vandalism and the university's need to protect itself from enemies within as well as from those outside its walls? Why was there this failure of academic nerve? Why were some of our most distinguished scholars unable to recognize vandalism and nihilistic ferocity for what they were and to respond accordingly, instead of becoming involved in tortuous distinctions, supine indulgences, and a dispensation, in many instances in advance, for further acts of destruction, terror, and intimidation?

If I may digress parenthetically for a moment—little, if anything, analogous to this existed in the 1930s. That decade was a revolution-threatened, ideologically passionate, and profoundly torn decade of American history. Capitalism was the enemy in as real a way as the establishment is today for the radical Left. To my recollection, there were several hundred, at the very least, declared Communists among the students at Berkeley in the 1930s, and I daresay there were at least a few among the faculty; certainly there were a substantial number of what we then called fellow travellers. Issue after issue came up; there were meetings on and off the campus; there was widespread radical determination to destroy capitalism and establish socialism in one form or other. But—and this is the point I wish to stress here—there was really a minimum of *assault on the university*. I have not forgotten that there were issues involving administrators and trustees, issues usually however arising from efforts of this or that misguided president or trustee to inject political considerations into the operations of the university. As Professor Hook has somewhere written, the great objective of liberals and radicals in the 1930s was to keep the university as separated from politics as was humanly possible. Then it was the Left, for the most part, that tended to argue the necessity of the university's relative autonomy from politics and the marketplace. Today the Left argues *for* politicization.

Now this is, I believe, the greatest single difference we have seen in the American university during the twentieth century. Beginning approximately in the late 1940s and gathering momentum in the 1950s, the conception developed that the university must enter politics, must become consecrated, not primarily to pure scholarship and teaching as its own end, but instead to the rebuilding of society, to the general civilizing of the American mind, to humanitarianism on a limitless scale, to the advising of governments, especially liberal ones, and as the instrument of major social change in society. I have a very vivid memory of that state of mind coming over key areas of the faculty and administration at the University of California, beginning foremost at Berkeley. Those who think the notorious loyalty-oath controversy of 1949-1951 was solely the effort of the faculty to repudiate a gratuitous declaration of loyalty to state and nation miss the larger point: it was precisely at this time that the University (especially its faculty) achieved a degree of politicization that it had never known before and that would constantly rise thereafter. It is fair to say that the fifties, far from being the tranquil, politically passive decade it has so often been declared by those insensitive to what was really happening, was the single most political period in the American university's history up to that time.

It is important for us to bear in mind that well before the onset of the hyperpolitical activity of the 1960s on the campus, replete with violence and terror, there had been a significant heightening of political consciousness on the campus, most notably in the faculty. I do not mean, of course, politics as its own end. Such politics is rarely to be seen. I mean, rather, politics as the indispensable technique for achievement of some of the goals I have mentioned: above all, the assertedly humanitarian goals, the goals that would take the faculty to all the privileged and underprivileged parts of the earth, that would indeed bring into the university new, atmosphere-displacing structures called institutes and centers and bureaus, which would be havens for representatives of the world's privileged and underprivileged.

The idea that the university is good became transmuted into the idea that the university is so good that no part of American society should be without the ministrations of its chemists and sociologists, its mathematicians and political scientists, and its historians, philosophers, and philologists as well. Who else, it was arrogantly asked, is as well qualified as university faculty for the work of straightening out the ills of government at all levels and the angularities of the American social ethic, and the work, too, of liberating Americans from their numerous alienations, anguishes, and deprivations? Who else is so well qualified to put ethnic and racial hostilities in history's lumber room forever? Let the university be the keystone of the research establishment, the church of all humanitarian-political intellectuals, and, above all, the temple of Service: social, moral, political service in all the numberless manifestations Service can take in the minds of intellectuals. Thus it was trumpeted by the sophisticated among university presidents, by the elite among faculty members, and also, be it noted, by an increasing number of trustees and legislators, convinced in time by the arguments of the new priesthood that was the American professoriat.

The violence and the terror of the 1960s have generally disappeared. For the time at least, the so-called "revolution" is over. I doubt whether a corporal's guard could be mustered today for the vital work of putting the dean in captivity or of breaking windows or desecrating walls. But what is not by any means terminated is that general thrust of the academic mind—born in the late 1940s at the beginning of the greatest period of affluence the American university has ever known and fully developed by the late 1950s—that had so much to do with nurturing and then giving haven to the student revolutionaries of the 1960s (student and *faculty* revolutionaries, it would be fairer to say).

I wish I could believe that American faculty members, having been burned badly, were once again willing to elect the roles of teacher and scholar, to the exclusion of competing roles that appeared so profusely on the university campus after World War II. For teaching and scholarship are what the university is basically about, what it alone is really well fitted for, what has given it strength and luster over the near-millennium of its existence in the West, and what has enabled it to survive the tempests and earthquakes of modern European history. The structural stability of the university in the 1930s, despite the radicalization of so many of its students and faculty, can only be understood, I believe, in terms of the then widespread belief that the university should remain as far from direct participation in politics as possible, that it should be an enclave for the freest possible investigation, study, analysis, and critical assessment of the culture and society surrounding it. The mission of the university, we believed, was the germination of radical ideas in all areas of knowledge—not radical forays into the marketplace.

As I say, I wish I could believe that this ancient but still fresh and buoyant conception of the university's mission were once again widespread in the American university. But I cannot. There are too many evidences even today to the contrary. What *is* widespread, the lessons of the 1960s notwithstanding, is the belief that the professor is not only teacher and scholar but also political intellectual, man of power in party and government, research enterpriser on a large scale, priest in the religion of individuality, therapist for all student needs, reformer, revolutionary when need be, and humanitarian supreme. And with this concept of himself goes the professor's concept of the university's role as the supreme institution in American life—as privileged aristocracy indeed, owing little, owed much—instead of as the last enclave in our society for a detached, honest, and critical assessment of society, as a setting for the scholarly imagination in all areas.

I can see the American university surviving many things, many blows from its enemies, as it has survived these in the past, but it is difficult to see it surviving the hubris that has been so vivid on the American academic scene for the past quarter of a century.

Historical Factors in the Decline of the University

Oscar Handlin
Harvard University

I associate myself wholly with Professor Bestor's forceful plea for the independence and freedom of the university as we have known it. I am not so sure that I can agree with him on the assessment as to whether it is the sound of a popgun or the crack of doom that we heard in the 1960s. I tend to shy away from either extreme, but I am more inclined, perhaps, than he to view these events as the exposure of a fundamental flaw in the university, the consequences of which will be with us for a long time. The rather optimistic statement that the university and its ideals have survived the batterings of recent years seems to me to require some qualification. Certainly, the university has survived and there is no doubt that it will continue to survive, but I take no consolation from the mere extension of the existence of institutions that will be called universities if, in the process of keeping them alive, we lose the fundamental and enduring qualities that made the university valuable to us—at least to me and my generation. The shock through which we passed raises serious questions. After all, it was not just the battering of a handful of *enragés* that has brought us to the present crisis. Why were these few, relatively unserious people able to bring to the point of crisis an institution that was so deeply entrenched, that seemed so secure?

Professor Bestor himself, I remember, well before 1964 was pointing to problems in education, higher and lower, and I occasionally go back with a kind of wry attempt to understand what it was I was driving at in an article called "Are the Colleges Killing Education?" which I wrote in 1953.

I would like to note a few points of ambiguity and weakness in the university as an institution; these have created its vulnerability and seem likely to endure as problems even after the immediate crisis is over. The university as we know it in the United States is roughly a century old. There were antecedents even in this country and, of course, in Europe, but the establishment of Johns Hopkins and the arrival at Harvard of President Charles W. Eliot just a century ago marked the emergence of the institution that has to its credit enormous contributions both to our culture and to the knowledge of the world. Yet the university contained within it certain ambiguities that were never resolved, that remain with us still, and that lie at the heart of our difficulties.

First is the issue of politicalization and objectivity. It seems to me necessary to recall that the claim to objectivity rested on a premise that was widely held but that may not be so widely shared today. Within the disciplines encompassed in the university there were inner standards of validation and concern already separate from the standards that prevailed in the outer world. These inner standards had sanctions of their own, claims for respect that did not depend upon submission of criteria external to themselves. A proposition in logic or science, a conclusion in history or economics, a judgment in art or literature rested upon criteria that were not necessarily identical with, and might even be contradictory to, what seemed useful, expedient, and helpful in the outer world. These conclusions were pursued by scholars dedicated to the discipline for reasons of their own. The claim to a separate set of standards in turn rested upon the claim that the people who practiced the scholarly disciplines had not only excellence or wisdom but also a kind of scientific competence within their discipline, a competence that had been demonstrated in ways recognized within the discipline itself and that enabled them to make these judgments by the accepted codes and standards, or the canons of criticism, within the discipline. It seems to me that there was always a problem about maintaining this claim, a problem that can be traced to the other function the university performed in educating students who definitely were not committed to scholarly careers; such a problem derived from the relationship of the university to the society at large, which made other kinds of demands upon it.

The assertion of the validity of scholarly standards and the utility of retaining the criteria of scientific competence in meeting all the expected obligations of the university have been largely unchallenged.

But what happens now, when many of those standards have been eroded by forces that are outside the control of the university itself? The simple expansion in numbers over the past two decades is one element in that erosion. The challenge from sources outside the university to all forms of scientific inquiry and to the basic modes of rational organization of knowledge is another. Whatever these sources, I think it is nevertheless profoundly and seriously true that one can no longer expect that claims for the upholding of special competence, of internal standards of validity, will be accepted without a fight. Those who wish to continue to assert and defend these standards have their work cut out for them. They must define them and defend them.

Secondly—and related to these problems—is the ambiguity of the American university in relation to mass education. On the one hand, some have insisted that the university was providing a special kind of training for a special kind of people, a select education for the select; on the other hand, for reasons again largely outside its control, the university was willing to acquiesce in and even vigorously pursue the active expansion of the number of students, the number of institutes, the size of the faculty, and the magnitude of the plant. In retrospect we can see that this was relatively slow until our own generation. It was accelerated in the years between 1930 and 1950 and was further accelerated at a breathtaking rate in the fifties and sixties.

Expansion was a desirable thing, insofar as it brought into the university wider elements of the social and economic system, to the extent that it made the university less a private preserve of elite social groups and subjected the university to the influence of wider pools of talent and ability. To this degree the growth was desirable and manageable. But to the extent that attendance at the university skyrocketed, to the extent that four years of attendance at the university came to be considered a right for the age group as a whole, the university was overwhelmed by the challenge of finding something for all these people to do within the scope of their capacities—or just something to interest them.

Inexorably this led to a dilution of the accepted curriculum, which in itself would not have been a bad thing had it not attenuated and undermined its own peculiar functions, its own internal standards. The irony is that now in the period when the university faces financial constraints of a severe kind, it can no longer safely cut back to what it had once been. It is no longer dealing with a faculty of scores or of a hundred but of thousands, with student bodies of scores of thousands. The choices it must now make are, therefore, far more difficult than those in the past. Simply to say now that the university ought not to have done what it did is no solution, because the situation and elements that brought growing numbers of students into it are not shaped by the university itself but by forces in the society outside it. As long as there is no alternative in our society for some kind of meaningful activity for most individuals in this age group, they will continue to seek admission to the university. The challenge will grow and result in a diversion from genuine scholarly functions; this diversion has already gone very far and is likely to go much further. These external elements are quite general, operating outside the United States as well as within it. They affect the universities of Germany and Japan, just as they have the universities of the United States.

When we consider the factors that are peculiar to the United States, one sees the full dimension of our problem. First is the fact that in the United States universities have always depended upon voluntary support in certain critical aspects of their existence, unlike the universities of Europe, which have had either autonomous endowments or a firm relationship to the state. In the United States there has been a long, durable, and effective tradition of voluntary support for universities, which often stood in the forefront of the effort to maintain and extend the academic enterprise. This support provided some of them with sufficient freedom and independence to maneuver toward goals of their own. No doubt this had offsetting disadvantages, such as the necessity of attracting alumni, trustees, and all of that. We know these disadvantages well enough. Imagine, however, what the situation is likely to be in coming decades if this source of voluntary support dries up and the university becomes totally dependent upon the state. But this would not be the state as it exists ideally either in our minds or in the minds of the students, but as it actually exists—a bundle of compromises and contending forces that operate within fifty state legislatures and the halls of Congress, all making demands of their own upon the university. Under such pressures, the unique and central function of the university (as we view it) is not likely to have great importance.

A second disturbing factor is one that is again special to the United States. It arises from the fact that in the century between 1870 and 1970 the American university was linked in a very intimate and sustaining fashion to the universities of Europe. That meant, first, that the United States had access to a pool of talent that continually improved the American university faculties and kept them growing dramatically in the period after 1930 (although I think this was significant even in the years before 1930). It seems most unlikely that this kind of brain drain will continue in the future. Further, the relation with Europe sustained a universal view of the kind of knowledge that was imparted through and at the university. Not only were the propositions of physics or logic regarded as equally valid in Cambridge or Princeton as in Berlin or Vienna, but also American scholars constantly subjected what they achieved here to the criticism of others and compared their work with what was done in other parts of the world.

I would like to suggest that we are seeing throughout the world provincial, local, and particularistic pressures on the university. These pressures are not only nationalistic. In the United States there are even more narrow pressures than that: the insistence that particular groups of students require exposure to particular forms of knowledge, that the language suitable for one group is not suitable for another, that learning and scholarship are shaped, not by their own universally valid standards, but by the needs and desires of those to whom it is, or is not, relevant.

Finally, in the United States we see a special relationship between what goes on in the universities and what goes on in the rest of the society—in the ways in which information is communicated and diffused outside the society. The university deals with perhaps half of the age group. It has to be aware of how information is supplied to the students who will ultimately enter its classrooms, of what the means of learning are before freshmen become freshmen. Inexorably, it is forced to accommodate itself to what operates outside its halls.

Formerly, those destined to come to the university had at least the beginning of a preparation for study there. In the past century, with all its complexities and difficulties, there was still an emphasis upon rationality, upon the power of analysis, and upon the value of the record and the printed word. These are precisely the qualities that have been devalued in the society outside the university during the past decade. The visual image, the sensate response, and immediate gratification are today more important in the upbringing of young people than the discipline of work and the importance of responsibility and reasoned decisions. These seem to be standing problems. They lay at the roots of the difficulties we had in the sixties. However much the campus may have quieted in recent years, these earlier, long-standing difficulties have not vanished.

I join with Professor Bestor in declaring that our own social loss of nerve is partly responsible for the inability of the scholar to appraise fully the difficulty of his situation. While it is easy enough to say we ought not to accept the alternatives in curriculum and government that have been thrust upon the university, it will be difficult in practice to resist them. That is by no means a reason why the struggle should not be conducted however. It will be a difficult endeavor to continue to find a place in the university for the values of rationality and the pursuit of scholarly truth and freedom that Professor Bestor advocates.

The Need for a Philosophy of Education

Irving Kristol
New York University

Somewhere, John Dewey says (I think in *Art as Experience*): "It is only when we see the consequences of our policy that we begin to understand the premises upon which we acted." And this, I think, is generally true. It is especially true when one's policies lead to disaster. It is therefore always a good idea, when policies have led to disaster, to go back and ask: "What were the premises upon which we acted? Why did it happen this way?"

I associate myself fully with Professor Bestor's statements about the mindlessness of student radicalism and also about the mindlessness of many people who fail to perceive the mindlessness of student radicalism. I am less certain about his "popguns" and "cracks of doom." I have never heard the crack of doom—but for all I know it may sound like a popgun.

I also worry that critiques of student radicalism—perfectly valid critiques in their own terms—may end up as little more than a defense of the status quo in the university today. I think this defense cannot and should not be made. Thus, I am struck by the way in which Professor Bestor refers to the "intellectual integrity of the university." I have no doubt that he is generally concerned about this matter. On the other hand, his remarks were really not about the intellectual integrity of the university; they were about the professional integrity of the university. I submit that these two concepts are not identical, though they are obviously related. I do not think that you can reduce intellectual integrity to professional integrity. "Intellectual integrity" is the larger term. It defines what professional integrity—professional behavior and misbehavior—is for the members of a profession. Intellectual integrity involves a general philosophy, within which professional behavior is prescribed for specific circumstances. Which is to say that, in the university today, the integrity of the academic profession can only be given meaning within a somewhat larger philosophy of education that defines intellectual integrity. It is this philosophy of education that seems to be lacking.

It is certainly true that student radicalism does not flow from the defects of the university, as these defects are defined by student radicals. On the other hand, there is a sense in which an institution is always to blame when its members are so easily moved to subvert it. The times are then clearly out of joint for this institution, and it has to rethink the premises upon which it has been operating. I have been a professor for only two and a half years, but I have been struck during that time by the absence of any significant number of contented and loyal students. Having come from the "outside world," as it is called, I would say that the morale of American university students today, in terms of contentment and loyalty, is somewhat lower than the morale in the Internal Revenue Service. I mean that seriously, and I think it represents a very serious problem.

It is not simply a question of making concessions to student radicals; on this, Dr. Bestor and I are of one mind. There is not much point in making such concessions because student radicals do not always know what they really want and they certainly do not know what they really need. Still, it hardly makes sense for a university to say: "These people have the wrong ideas in their heads and therefore we cannot educate them." It cannot say: "Get rid of these ideas, and then we shall educate you." If the university cannot educate these students, cannot make them contented and loyal members of the academic community, it has to wonder why.

There are many short-term issues to which we might all address ourselves and one very significant long-term issue. I will pick three of the shorter-term issues; they may not be the most significant, but they happen to be the three that have most impressed me during the past few years.

One is the utter state of confusion between the idea of the college and the idea of the university. It is, I think, an undisputed fact that over the past twenty-five years we have witnessed a usurpation of the undergraduate curriculum by the graduate faculties. This has created enormous problems in college education. When the curriculum of the college is shaped in terms of what the graduate faculty defines as prerequisites (to make its own task easier), education indeed becomes "boring." E. M. Forster, in *Aspects of the Novel,* says that a novel ought to be interesting. That is a very important fact about the novel that many novelists forget. I think it is also a very important fact for education that educators forget: education should be interesting. Boredom kills the spirit and, eventually, boredom may incite to revolution.

What is interesting is not necessarily what students say is interesting, just as what is interesting about a novel is not necessarily what the reader, on the basis of his experience with past novels, would assume to be interesting. It is the job of the educator, as it is the job of the novelist, to create interest on his own terms. Still, all educators do have to have a notion of what is genuinely interesting, and it has to be not only something that they think will be interesting for the students—like Afro-American studies, urban studies, or the study of revolutions—but also something that genuinely interests *them*, the educators. If it does not interest them, it is not going to interest students. Students can spot the phoniness of educators who invent courses and curricula in a purely managerial way, hoping that these commodities will "catch on" in the student market. How many of us can look at our colleges and the undergraduate curricula and the state of the campus, and say: "Gee, I wish I were young again so I could go to this college!" Most of us do not say that, and I think when we don't say it, something is wrong. If we do not want to take our own courses, we cannot very well ask other people to take them in good cheer.

My second point is in reference to graduate education. I may be vague, because I am not quite sure *why* we are in the kind of trouble I am *certain* we are in. I would attribute much of that trouble to the domination of a species of decadent scholasticism within many of the disciplines in graduate school. (I refer especially to the social sciences and humanities; I know nothing about the sciences.) Watching the way graduate schools teach, or try to teach, and what they teach, I am reminded of nothing so much as the condition of late Renaissance Aristotelianism. The people who wrote those late Renaissance Aristotelian texts were very, very intelligent. They were very, very learned. But what they wrote was, in the end, utterly trivial, utterly boring—not only from our own perspective but also in terms of the original Aristotelian tradition.

Today we are witnessing in our graduate schools the trivialization, for instance, of the Ph.D. Most advanced degrees, these days, involve purely mechanical "research" into non-problems that interest no one. The human emotion, curiosity, is utterly missing. Graduate work consists, too often, in doing research that is quite meaningless, in asking questions whose answers interest no one, in filling supposed gaps in our knowledge that are not real gaps at all. This being the nature of graduate study as it has developed in recent decades, students are inevitably involved in an experience of agony and shame. Writing a Ph.D. thesis should be *exciting*, but it is definitely not so for most of our graduate students today. It is an ordeal, not only in the sense of being difficult, but because it is an ordeal of conscience. Students are aware of the fact that in most cases the work they are doing is absolutely meaningless and is being done simply to meet demands that are not even taken seriously by the people who make these demands.

Thirdly, one of the things we ought to reflect upon, as we look at the American university today in its troubled condition, is the whole question of faculty government over the academic content of the college and graduate schools and over academic appointments. It is now an accepted idea that the faculty govern these areas of the university. I believe it is time for a reassessment. De Tocqueville referred to the possible tyranny of the majority. There are not many areas in American life where one can point to an actual tyrannizing majority, but the university faculty, I should say, *is* one.

What has happened as a result of faculty self-government over twenty-five years is the homogenization of the American university, so that every department in every university is engaged in one great competition—to become like other departments in every other university. This, too, creates boredom, that deadly sin. In the few fields that I know something about, it is striking how homogenized department after department has become. Analytical philosophy, for example, is the new thing, and one by one each philosophy department becomes dominated by analytical experts. It becomes ever more difficult to find one that is dominated by metaphysicians, one that is interested in classical or medieval thought or Renaissance Neoplatonism. One by one they all ape each other. And this absurd condition somehow seems to flow, as far as I can see, from faculty control. Indeed, I think it is inevitable, given faculty control, because professors, like other people, prefer being fashionable to being unfashionable. I confess I have no idea what to do about this. I certainly do not think that bringing students or trustees into university governments will help in any way. But I do think it is a problem to which we should address ourselves.

The long-term issue is, as I have already suggested, the devising of adequate philosophies of education. Students complain of our universities being bureaucratic. They are probably not bothered by bureaucracy per se. I think that they are discontented to find themselves living in a *soulless* institution, an institution emptied of its ideal content. When an institution lacks some ideal content, all that is left is bureaucracy, the naked skeleton of the structure itself. In a sense, the modern American university—like the modern American polity—is a creature of modern political science. The "multiversity," as it was called, is seen as an equilibrium of academic interests, an equilibrium of countervailing academic powers. This is the way the democratic polity has been developing over the past thirty to forty years, and this is the image in which the university is largely seen. As a result, the university today is suffering exactly the same crisis as the polity.

In human life equilibrium is not enough; the equilibrium has to yield meanings for one's life, not a mere stability and balance. I would suggest that we need to think about these meanings as they apply to a philosophy of education appropriate to the modern university. What the university needs is a structure that is organic and not simply bureaucratic, a structure that constitutes a meaningful whole. Just as it is the soul that contributes such organic meaning to the body, so it is that only a philosophy of education can infuse an educational institution with the requisite organic meaning, thus making it come alive.

The Fragmentation of Knowledge

Samuel Lubell
American University

If our theme were stated as "The Value of Contemporary Higher Education?" and this were clearly a question, my own response would be a clear "No." The complexity of the task makes it impossible for me to give anything like a full bill of particulars on how the universities are flunking out in our society or to balance that overall negative assessment with some of the things of value that higher education still offers. For the sake of discussion I shall concentrate on what I regard as the sorest failure of our universities: their failure as organizers of knowledge in the governing arts.

Above all else, I believe we need to understand the totality of the changes and continuities, being fought for and resisted, that are remaking our society. Yet higher education remains structured to fragment the knowledge, thinking, and teaching of the arts of self-government into separatisms and specialties. As one result, we no longer have an intellectual legacy to pass on to the next generation of students, whether they be numerous or few. In contrast, we are able to pass on quite astonishing technological and vocational skills: moon-landing with split-second accuracy; electronic invasions of privacy; fearsome military weaponry; medicine, engineering, and agricultural production; and, though not really a form of higher education, an awesome, hard-hat, earth-moving capacity.

For our universities the essential problem, I believe, is its *feudal* structure—not academic tenure, not the unionization of teachers, not the proliferating offerings of needless courses, nor the size of the student body. Apart from these and other important problems, there remains the fact that our universities are organized to fragment, rather than unify, the available knowledge of self-government. There are, for example, the varieties of psychological experience being taught: social psychology, clinical psychology, psychology in history, psychology of communications, and sometimes just plain psychology. Economics, government, sociology, political science, foreign-policy institutes—the specialized fragments dominate our campuses; the unifying whole is generally too shadowy to be seen.

Before proceeding further, perhaps I should make clear that I have never served a lifetime sentence in academia. My image of the university largely reflects my stay at the School of Journalism of Columbia University. While there, I was appointed to a committee of five charged with drawing up a university-wide program for dealing with urban-minority problems, for which the Ford Foundation had extended Columbia a ten-million-dollar line of credit. The other four members of the committee were outstanding scholars; I was the only nonacademic in the group. Our instructions from the president of the university were quite clear: to put together a university-wide program. But in the course of the committee's deliberations, the other members patiently taught me—I was a slow and stubborn student—how feudal an institution a university is.

The popular notion, which I shared at the outset, is that the president of a university is important. I learned that the strengths of a university lie, not in the authority of the president, who is often looked upon as a benevolent fundraiser who may come and go (at Columbia he went), but in each of the separate schools. One might scotch the snake, even cut off its head, but the individual schools would survive, operate, and flourish.

My first, quick reaction was to liken the faculties to members of AFL craft unions, each jealously guarding their feudal jurisdictions. Then I came to understand that the spirit animating professors is much more akin to that of the small businessman, spurred to develop his own mom-and-pop-plus-secretary store—his own pet enterprise or foundation project—and quite willing to leave other faculty members alone with their own mom-and-pop-and-secretary projects. There is much to be said on behalf of laissez-faire, although it might be noted ironically that many of the same professors who insist so strongly on being left alone are constantly lecturing elements beyond the academic castle upon the evils of laissez-faire, particularly as practiced by businessmen, television broadcasters, and other devils.

I do want to emphasize my appreciation of the important refuge for thinking and scholarship that universities offer; it *is* vital for the individual scholar to be able to pursue his learning free from outside or campus suppressions. I am also aware of the countless interdisciplinary efforts to cut across the intellectual limitations of any single discipline. Still, all that is being done in this regard falls short of dealing with what I fear is a mortal struggle between technological change and our ability to govern ourselves.

Looking ahead, I do not expect some Joshua-like trumpet to bring down the feudal walls of academia, even by the year 2002, the year many corporations are currently setting as the due date for loans they are now floating. More effective action should be sought beyond symposia like this one, or special lectureships, or varied interdisciplinary efforts.

As a contribution to the idea of a contemporary university, may I advance a specific suggestion: *that each university, able to do so, set up a* Chair of Contemporary Conflict, *to be held by someone, man or ms., who will be charged with trying to think through the totality of effective self-government.*

That suggestion is not made under the illusion that superminds exist who can package and deliver "the truth in the whole." To the contrary, I envision that this chair would be held at different universities by individuals coming from varied intellectual fragments, with each chairholder striving to reach a sense of the whole from a different starting point. There might well be a rotation, with one individual holding the chair for a few years, succeeded by another from another discipline. In short, we should organize a conscious search for a way of minimizing fragmentation. Even if no chairholder succeeds in finding the Holy Grail, the many quests for it should yield a fuller and expanding understanding of the whole.

May I add that my proposal is not advanced with any thought of quieting conflict or without regard to many other aspects of the contemporary university discussed here. Those who have read my political writings will recall that I have always looked on American democracy as an arena, with conflict being essential for the proper functioning of that democracy. The university has been moved into the arena by powerful forces that educators are unable to control and may not even be able to anticipate. My hope is that the conscious thinking about and teaching of contemporary conflict will move us to confront, earlier, many other problems of the university such as the following:

1. the depersonalizing, antipeople effects of some popular behavioristic techniques;
2. the danger that our universities will become factories for bureau-

crats;

3. the importance of the university as a socializing center in a society polarized by conflicts over race and economics, over the clashing demands for defense and needs at home, over drug use and other differences in generational experience;

4. the peril that the university's feudalism will be employed to entrench the "ins" against the millions who must still find entry into our society.

A Plea for Pluralism: A Dissenting Note

Charles Frankel
Columbia University

I thought I might be alone in wishing to introduce a note of mild dissent. I agree with the foregoing comments by and large, and their authors are people I would like to think I could continue to agree with. But I cannot quite, because some of the statements are wonderfully nostalgic; they are statements that seem to me appropriate for a dying guild. Besides, they have a certain metaphysical quality that arouses my philosophical hackles.

Surely, everyone in this symposium must know that there is no such thing as *the* university. Not in America. And surely one should also know that, if one insists on speaking about "*the* university" and introducing a single set of ideals connected with it, the world will go on its own way, creating its own institutions to satisfy a variety of needs, and they will each be called "*the* university." The disparity between ideal and fact will create cynicism, and what is best about our universities will gradually become obscure and eroded.

I do not make the point either to warn or complain, but only to describe. The universities in America rest on public support. In a democratic and egalitarian society of our sort there will be growing demands for something miscalled "universal higher education." To some extent, this is the result of demagogic politics. To some extent, it can and should be avoided—for example, by offering people past seventeen or eighteen (I would prefer to say fourteen) alternatives to classroom education. But the *only* thing that I can find common to the twenty-five hundred higher educational institutions in this country that we have called *the* university is that they are holding institutions for people past seventeen. That is where the society collects these types in large numbers, and that is about the only thing all colleges and universities have in common. For one reason or another, good or bad, we shall probably continue having such institutions in America, and they will go on serving a very large number of·people. (Incidentally, our society and educational premises are different from France's and Japan's, but I know something about those two countries, and they are in for the same thing.)

The real problem, I think, is to talk about diversification, about *types* of institutions. We can only retain the standards that I think *we* wish to represent, we can only retain and restore the kinds of universities most people here work in if we insist that there *is* a special audience, a special public, a special function to be served by certain types of university. In this symposium we can think of them as elite, but let us not call them that outside. Let us maintain our standards but, at the same time, not throw our hands up in despair at the creation in our country of other institutions that exist to serve other legitimate purposes.

The Content of a Liberal Education

Steven M. Cahn
University of Vermont

The welfare of a democratic society depends ultimately upon decisions made by all members of the community, and a proper education is essential to making wise decisions. But what specifically constitutes a proper education for the citizens of a democracy? That is the critical question to which I wish to address myself.

In a democracy each individual's education should be of equal concern, for all adult citizens participate in the decision-making process. A democracy that neglects the education of some of its members will pay a dear price, for the enemies of freedom feed upon ignorance, fear, and prejudice. Thus, if an individual should complain that his democracy is providing too much education for too many people, he thereby reveals his ignorance about the very nature of democracy. There is no such thing as too much education in a democracy; too little education, however, and there may soon be no democracy.

Equal concern for each person's education means providing each person with appropriate educational opportunities, but it does not mean providing each person with exactly the same education. Individuals differ in their capacities and interest; what stimulates one individual may stultify another. A democracy should recognize such individual differences and should show equal consideration for all persons by enabling each to enjoy his own distinctive growth. As John Stuart Mill pointed out: "In proportion to the development to his individuality, each person becomes more valuable to himself, and is therefore capable of being more valuable to others."[1]

But just as it is important to recognize the need for individuality within a democracy, so it is important to recognize the need for all members of a democracy to possess certain characteristics in common. Indeed, an examination of the most important of these characteristics will disclose the essential elements of a proper education for free men in a free society.

Let us begin such an examination by noting the obvious fact that all members of a democracy should be able to read, write, and speak effectively. An individual who is unable either to understand others or to make himself understood not only is hindered in his personal growth but also cannot participate fully in the free exchange of ideas so vital to the democratic process. A command of language is indispensable for such an exchange, and thus it is of vital importance for members of a democracy to acquire linguistic facility.

Also of crucial significance to democratic citizens is an understanding of public issues. How can a citizen participate intelligently in the discussion of an issue he does not understand? Furthermore, how can he intelligently evaluate the decisions of his representatives if he is unable to comprehend the complexities of the questions they are deciding? Public issues in a democracy cover an enormous range of topics. Indeed, every action taken by the government is a subject for public discussion, and such actions typically involve social, political, economic, scientific, and historical factors. Consider, for example, some of the most critical issues that confront the world today: overpopulation, poverty, pollution, racial conflict, ideological conflict, the dangers of nuclear warfare, and the possible benefits of space research. How can these issues even be intelligently discussed by those who are ignorant of the physical structure of the world, the forces that shape society, or the ideas and events that form the background of present crises? Thus, substantial knowledge in the areas of natural science, social science, world history, and national history is required for all those called upon to think about public issues; in a democracy such thinking is required of everyone. For though elected representatives must carry the major burden of formulating and implementing governmental policies, each citizen has both the right and the duty to evaluate and try to influence the decisions of his government.

Knowledge of science requires familiarity with the fundamental concepts and techniques of mathematics; not only do mathematical notions play a crucial role in the natural sciences but also they are playing an ever increasing role in the social sciences. Furthermore, apart from its use in other areas of study, mathematics is itself an invaluable aid in the handling of everyday affairs. As Alfred North Whitehead noted: "Through and through the world is infected with quantity. To talk sense, is to talk in quantities. It is no use saying that the nation is large,—How large? It is no use saying that radium is scarce,—How scarce? You cannot evade quantity." [2]

It is not sufficient, however, to know the results of scientific and historical investigations; one must also understand the methods of inquiry that have produced those results. No amount of knowledge brings intellectual sophistication, unless one also possesses the power of critical thinking. To think critically is to think in accordance with the canons of logic and scientific method. Such thinking provides needed protection against the lure of simplistic dogmas that, while appearing attractive, threaten to cut the lifeline of reason and stifle the intellect. A democratic citizen who cannot spot a fallacious argument or recognize relevant evidence for a hypothesis is defenseless against those who can twist facts to suit their own purposes.

Yet another characteristic should be possessed by all citizens of a democracy: sensitivity to aesthetic experience. Such experience is, to use John Dewey's words, "a manifestation, a record and celebration of the life of a civilization, a means of promoting its development, and is also the ultimate judgment upon the quality of a civilization." [3] An appreciation and understanding of the literature, art, and music of various cultures enriches the imagination, refines the sensibilities, deepens feelings, and provides increased awareness of the world in which we live. It should never be forgotten that in a society of aesthetic illiterates it is not only the quality of art that suffers but also the quality of life.

It should be noted in connection with the study of literature that there is significant value in reading at least some foreign literature in its original language. Not only does great literature lose some of its richness in translation, but learning another language increases linguistic sensitivity and makes one more conscious of the unique potentialities and limitations of any particular language. Such study is also one of the most effective ways to help widen cultural horizons, for understanding another language is a key to understanding another culture.

One further element is requisite to a liberal education; that is a knowledge of human values. Aristotle recognized long ago that virtue is of two kinds: what he termed "moral virtue" and what he termed "intellectual virtue." Moral virtue, which we might call "goodness of character," is formed by habit. One becomes good by doing good. For example, repeated acts of justice and self-control result in a just, self-controlled person. Such a person not only performs just and self-controlled actions but does so, in Aristotle's words, "from a firm and unchangeable character."[4] Thus, moral virtue is not acquired primarily through formal schooling, for a school cannot be expected to instill decent behavior in those whose moral education has been disregarded or mangled by family and community.

Intellectual virtue, on the other hand, is what we might refer to as "wisdom." In a narrow sense of this term, a wise man is one who is a good judge of value. He can distinguish what is of worth from what is merely costly. He possesses discernment, discretion, and an abundance of that most precious of qualities—common sense. Wisdom, in this sense, is acquired partly as a result of habit, partly as a result of informal teaching, and partly perhaps, as the ancient Greeks would have said, as a gift of the gods.

But in a broader sense a wise man is one who possesses intellectual perspective, who is familiar with both the foundations of knowledge and its heights, who can analyze the fundamental principles of thought and action while maintaining a view of the world that encompasses all reality—both what is and what ought to be. Such wisdom is of inestimable value to members of a free society, for it enables them to stand firm in the face of intellectual challenge and to hold fast against those who would first entrap the minds of free men and then enslave their bodies. The path to wisdom, in this sense, lies in the study of those great visions that comprise philosophy.

It should be clear that education within a democracy must not be limited to training individuals in occupational skills. For, no matter what occupation a citizen may choose, he is called upon to take part in decisions of public policy; his education must be broad enough to enable him to make such decisions wisely. Since among the Romans such a broad education was permitted only to freemen (in Latin, *liberi*), this sort of education is appropriately referred to today as a "liberal education."

It would be a serious mistake, however, to assume that liberal education has nothing to do with vocational education. If the members of a democracy are to be not only knowledgeable participants in the political arena but also effective contributors in the social sphere, then each citizen should be provided with the necessary skills, social orientation, and intellectual perspective to succeed in some field of occupational endeavor. But such a vocational education must not be confused with narrow job training. Animals are broken in and trained; human beings ought to be enlightened and educated. An individual who does not understand the aims of his actions is unable to adjust those actions in the face of changing conditions. He is thus stymied by a world in flux. As Sidney Hook has noted, "There is a paradox connected with vocational training. The more vocational it is, the narrower it is; the narrower it is the less likely it is to serve usefully in earning a living . . . [T]here is no reason—except unfamiliarity with the idea—why vocational education should not be liberalized to include the study of social, economic, historical, and ethical questions . . . "[5] For the sake of the future worker as well as for the benefit of his society, such liberalized vocational preparation should be included in the spectrum of a liberal education.

At this point it would be well to consider a question about liberal education that has recently been widely discussed. The question is usually put this way: "Is a liberal education any longer relevant?" The word "relevant" is one of those terms so aptly described by the English philosopher J. L. Austin as "snakes in the linguistic grass." Such a term, according to Austin, is used "without caution or definition or any limit, until it becomes, first perhaps obscurely metaphorical, but ultimately meaningless."[6] Nowadays the word "relevant" seems to wriggle into every conceivable context, although it rarely possesses any clear-cut meaning. The only practical way to deal with a word of this sort is to distinguish its various possible meanings and then consider how each of these different meanings would affect the sense of the question we are examining.

Sometimes the word "relevant" is used to mean "topical." In this sense a study is relevant if it deals with current matters. Thus a course in Greek tragedy or the history of the United States would not be relevant, whereas a course dealing with today's avant-garde dramatists or the current racial conflict in America would be relevant. When we use the word "relevant" in this sense, however, there is no reason why all or most of a liberal education should be relevant. To think otherwise is to confuse what is topical with what is timely. The plays of Sophocles were *topical* only during the golden age of Athens, but they are *timely* in every age, for they never lose their power to enrich human experience and deepen our response to life. Slaves in America were freed by 1865, but an understanding of the sort of lives they lived prior to that time is crucial to an understanding of racial problems in the United States today. To confine a liberal education to what is topical would exclude much material that is of value to all members of a democracy. Therefore, if "relevant" is taken to be synonymous with "topical," relevance should not be a criterion for deciding what ought to be included in a liberal education.

However, the word "relevant" is not always used in this sense. Sometimes the word is used in such a way that any subject of study is relevant as long as it is concerned with the nature, origin, or solution of the fundamental social, political, intellectual, or moral problems of our time. In this sense a liberal education *should* be relevant, for the very purpose of such an education is to enable citizens of a free society to make wise decisions about the problems that confront them. But in order to apply this notion of "relevance" without distortion, it is necessary to clarify its potentially misleading aspects.

First, not every problem of our time is a fundamental problem. An education that fails to analyze the nature of capitalism, concentrating instead upon ways to increase sales in a local store, will not provide the intellectual perspective required to understand economic decisions taken by the government. It might be useful to examine capitalism from the standpoint of a local storeowner, but it is important not to concentrate so heavily upon an individual case as to lose sight of the broader picture that a liberal education ought to provide.

Second, experiencing the actual situation in which a problem arises does not guarantee increased understanding of the problem. Field study can be a valuable tool in learning, but such study should be structured to enable a student to acquire knowledge or skills requisite to a liberal education. Some reasonable means should be employed to determine how well the student has learned what he was supposed to have learned. Insight into fundamental problems is not gained simply by immersion in the stream of experience. Indeed, some experiences may engender laxity or carelessness and do more to impede learning than to foster it.

Third, there are subject matters and skills that, although not directly related to any specific contemporary problems, are nevertheless crucial to a liberal education, since they form the basis for an intelligent approach to all problems. As we have seen, without linguistic and mathematical facility, the power of critical thinking, aesthetic sensitivity, and philosophical perspective, it would not be possible to deal adequately with the fundamental problems of our time.

Fourth, in concentrating upon present issues we may fail to recognize how inextricably the present is tied to the past and how much we can learn about the present through a study of the past. Dewey put this point very well when he noted that "knowledge of the past is the key to understanding the present" and that "the way to get insight into any complex product is to trace the process of its making—to follow it through the successive stages of its growth."[7] The urgencies of present concerns should not make us think it is a waste of time to consider what has occurred in the past, for in order to know where one is going it is advantageous to know where one has been. With these four clarifications in mind—and remembering how the term "relevant" is being used in this context—we can safely say that the liberal education we have described is and should be relevant.

One way to insure that people are interested in what they are taught is to teach them only what they are interested in. If a person is interested in history but not in science, then he is taught history and not science. If he is not interested in all of history but only in the history of the American cowboy, then he is taught that history and nothing else. Such an education would unquestionably be relevant—that is, interesting—but it would not achieve the aim of a liberal education, for it would not properly equip people to carry out their obligations as citizens in a free society. Thus education should not be restricted to what an individual happens to find relevant, for mastery of certain knowledge and skills is indispensable to all members of a democracy, whether or not they find such study interesting.

It would be a serious mistake, however, to assume that, because a student's education should not be restricted to what he finds interesting, it therefore makes no difference to the quality of his education whether he is interested in what he is learning. An interested, attentive learner unquestionably derives far greater benefit from his education than does a bored and inattentive learner. But we have already seen that it would be a major error to interest the learner by teaching him only what he is interested in. How then should the student's interest be aroused and maintained?

There are two possible answers to this critical question. One answer, which is the view of "traditional" education, is that the learner's interest should be engaged by the external pressures of reward and punishment. The other answer, which is the fundamental principle of "progressive" education, is that material should be presented in such a way that it connects with the learner's own experience, with his own aims and purposes; the material itself thereby becomes the learner's personal concern.

To engage the learner's interest through the promise of reward and threat of punishment is obviously dangerous, for, if interest remains dependent upon external factors, when these factors disappear, so may the learner's interest. He may thus fail to develop a most important characteristic—the desire to continue learning. Insofar as possible, therefore, it is advantageous to focus the learner's interest directly on the material itself. But it is not easy to accomplish this goal; finding the means of doing so is one of the most important and difficult challenges facing any teacher. Indeed, this challenge is so demanding that one is tempted to escape it by allowing the learner's interest to dictate the material he is taught. To succumb to this temptation is, as we have seen, a fatal blunder. Every attempt should be made to render a liberal education interesting, but to do so by abandoning the proper content of a liberal education is to repair the ship by sinking it.

Unfortunately, such sinkings have become all too common in our colleges today. Our only hope is that faculties around the country possess the wisdom and courage to preserve the content of a liberal education and thereby make a valuable contribution to the education of our citizens and the welfare of our democracy.

NOTES

1. John Stuart Mill, *On Liberty* (New York: Liberal Arts Press, 1956), p. 76.
2. Alfred North Whitehead, *The Aims of Education and Other Essays* (New York: Free Press, 1967), p. 7.
3. John Dewey, *Art As Experience* (New York: Minton, Balch, 1934), p. 326.
4. Aristotle, *Nicomachean Ethics*, trans., Martin Ostwald (New York: Bobbs-Merrill, 1962), 1105a, 34.
5. Sidney Hook, *Education for Modern Man: A New Perspective* (New York: Knopf, 1963), pp. 203, 207.
6. J. L. Austin, *Sense and Sensibilia* (Oxford: Clarendon Press, 1962), p. 15. For those who are interested in the study of snaky words, a study that might properly be called "verbal ophiology," I suggest the following specimens: objective, subjective, natural, absolute, pragmatic, and existential.
7. John Dewey, *Democracy and Education* (New York: Macmillan, 1963), p. 214.

The Irrelevance of Relevance

Robert Hoffman
*City University of New York,
York College*

I want to advance an unfashionable thesis about higher education—
that relevance is irrelevant—and to draw some of the implications of
this thesis.

What is meant by saying that a college or a university should be
"relevant"? (I shall use the words "college" and "university" synony-
mously, although they are not strictly synonymous.) Two things primarily are meant: first, that one of the college's main tasks should be
to solve the major social problems that beset the nation or the local
community; second, that its other main task should be to respect and
foster its students' uniqueness by teaching them whatever they claim
to want to learn. A college that performs these tasks is "relevant" and
may be sharply contrasted with one that does not, which is often dis-
paragingly called an ivory tower. Members of an ivory-tower college
conceive of themselves as a community of learning, pursuing and
transmitting knowledge in various disciplines independently of any
usefulness in solving social or personal problems. They believe, moreover, that they have an entirely objective responsibility to their subjects and to learning, in contrast to any kind of personal responsibility
to their students.

Even this brief description of an ivory-tower university is enough to
indicate what those who clamor for a relevant university object to. For,
as they see it, a university's indifference to the particular social evils of

the day and to their own students' uniqueness is reprehensible. I do not share their belief. To say this, of course, is not to deny that these social evils exist and should be eliminated or that students' uniqueness should be recognized and developed. Rather, I would deny that it is the university's proper task to eliminate the one or to foster the other. A college is a community of a quite special sort, and its goal should not be relevancy or popularity. It should remain sufficiently detached from what is, so as not to become infected by it. In short, I believe that a university *should* be an ivory tower.

I want to explain and justify my belief. I am thinking of what a university is ideally, recognizing full well that actual universities often fall far short of the ideal. To begin with, it is a community, a relatively permanent union of individual persons in pursuit of a common objective, which they consciously and intentionally join together to pursue, and in willing pursuit of which they recognize their union to be reciprocal. A university is an artificially created society. It is produced and sustained by choice, with a particular structure in order to fulfill certain purposes. It depends upon the mutual expectations of its members. Moreover, it is indefinitely perfectible; in principle, the reciprocity by which it coheres may be indefinitely extended and deepened. Progress in a university community consists either in increasing the number of persons who benefit from membership in it or in improving the quality of the benefit conferred upon its members.

In a university, the common objective is to pursue knowledge. The members of a university community are teachers, students, and administrators. The administrators' function is to create and maintain conditions under which the teachers and students can pursue knowledge. The knowledge that students pursue is new to them but not to the teachers who teach them. By training, skill, experience, and achievement, the teachers have acquired the capacity to do research and produce scholarship that yield new knowledge and create new boundaries for the subjects investigated. The students, on the other hand, do not have this capacity. Their business is to engage in the activities set for them so that they may be initiated into a distinctive form of life—the intellectual life.

In doing research, teachers pursue the truth about their subjects; in teaching, they communicate what they discover, or some of it, to their students. But in teaching, they do not necessarily pursue the truth, pure and simple. Take my field, philosophy, for instance. When I set out to solve a philosophical problem, the works I read and consider differ from those I assign my students, for there are works I can understand that they cannot. What I present in the classroom is a compendium of my work on a problem, not the work itself. To initiate them into the activity of philosophizing about a problem, I give a mock-performance of the way in which I pursue the truth concerning it. When I present material in the classroom, I am never surprised to find what I find.

Inquiry in a university presupposes the inquirer's having certain lower-level knowledge that inheres in a certain conceptual framework. This framework, which can be revised or extended in the light of inquiry, comprises principles that do two things: first, they organize the inquirer's knowledge so that it ceases to be a collection of disconnected facts; second, they determine his intellectual perspective by committing him to certain modes of inquiry and appraisal.

An example of the first, the organizing principle, is the idea that the same presupposition or operative notion is present in very diverse provinces of thought or activity. Thus, the idea that technology is supreme (or supremely important) is present in electronic music, in the growth of behaviorist psychology (with its denial that ideas, motives, or feelings have any part in determining conduct), in the systems approach (input-output) to political theory, in public concern over being computerized by various social institutions, and in the way in which people regard themselves as "turned on" or "turned off" by one thing or another.

An example of the second kind of principle is the principle of inquiry that says one should express putatively factual conclusions in statements that are empirically testable. Thus, the assertion that all men are selfish—meaning that they always try to achieve their own happiness—is often made as though it were a factual statement about human behavior, without admitting the possibility of an unselfish action. Accordingly, it is not a factual statement at all, but a mere verbal truth, like "a biological brother is a male sibling," for its truth is compatible with every possible state of affairs. It is the mark of a genuinely factual proposition that there is some conceivable set of circumstances in which it would be false.

To learn what is taught in a college is not a matter of chance but a function of rational inquiry and responsible judgment. Still less is it a matter of pretending that one is at liberty to fashion the world after one's heart's desire. If a person wants to arrive at a clear and unbiased view of some matter, he has to ignore his heart's desire. In a college, we should subscribe to the ideal of truth. We should regard truth as something independent of our wishes and needs and recognize that what is true is true whether we like it or not. The ideal of truth demands that we try to make clear and definite statements that are amenable to rational appraisal; we subvert the ideal of truth by being obscure or indefinite. But by far and away the greatest subversion of the ideal of truth is intellectual arrogance concerning the method of discovering truth and the proper attitude toward accepted beliefs. Put briefly, the method of discovering truth should be rational inquiry, which includes respect for reasons and for evidence; the right attitude toward accepted beliefs is one of tentativeness, which includes the desire for *rational* criticism of the beliefs, since the weight of evidence may show them to be erroneous. As Peirce remarked, "Living doubt is the life of investigation. When doubt is at rest inquiry must stop . . . "

However, there are people in colleges who have no doubts and to whom inquiry is not something to be pursued rationally or beliefs something to be accepted tentatively. According to these people, they stand in a privileged position with respect to truth, for they have some special insight or attitude or background that vouchsafes it to them, and only their self-proclaimed sincerity is required to guarantee it. In short, they need be no more than self-responsible. Since the degree of influence our wishes and our need for self-esteem have upon our beliefs is well established, it takes only slight insight to perceive that such contentions are romantic illusion or sheer dogmatism and that self-proclaimed self-responsibility is nothing but a studied refusal to recognize anything incompatible with one's prejudices and pretentions. A college cannot reasonably set an a priori limit to the number of ways one can learn the truth about things, but it rightly requires that the putative truth discovered be submitted to the test of rational criticism. One may stumble upon the truth any number of ways, but to *know* that a certain proposition is true, as distinct from merely *believing* that it is, demands being able to defend one's knowledge claim rationally. To claim that one knows something is to put oneself in the position of having to answer the question "How do you know?" by stating the evidence or reasons that *justify* one's belief. To do that is to submit to criticism, and criticism is essentially public. A person has an intellectual right to his opinion only if he can defend it against rational criticism and show that what he believes is more likely than its negation.

What I have said, so far, indicates that a university is a quite special kind of community. It concerns itself with the disciplined pursuit of truth by rational and rigorous methods that presuppose a basic knowledge of certain subject matters. In a college, some people know more about those subjects and the methods of inquiry appropriate to them. They teach. If students were treated as equals, there would be no point in treating them as students. Only someone who has mastered a subject is competent to teach it to those who have not. The activity of a teacher is to be specified by its correlative, the activity of a pupil. And a pupil is not just any learner, but a learner who learns by being taught. Teaching is an intentional and thoughtful initiation of a pupil into a subject or an activity. Every subject and activity has an (historical) achievement—for example, a physical theory, a poem, a piece of literary criticism, a political analysis, a philosophical essay—and every such achievement has an underlying rationale of principles and standards.

If teachers are to advance knowledge and to initiate their students into the activities in which they themselves engage when advancing it, they must preserve the quality of the activities. Ordinarily, a teacher must impart certain information to his students in the process of initiating them into the practice of a subject or the appreciation of its practice. His main tasks in imparting this information are: (1) to organize it so that students can acquire it in an order that maximizes intelligibility; (2) to present it so that students are able to use it as the basis for learning whatever principles bind the facts together in the subject; and (3) to structure the relationship between the imparted facts and the taught principles so that students acquire the capacity to recognize the facts and principles in contexts other than those in which they were first presented.

Whether one is a teacher or a pupil in a college, higher learning is what should be pursued. The knowledge of an educated person, in addition to its organizing power, involves his awareness of its justification, of alternative beliefs, and of the criteria of relevance, evidence, consistency, and proof that are appropriate to various fields of inquiry. Finally, an educated person is not merely someone with a specialized competence but someone who has mastered his own language and has a respectable knowledge of the fundamentals of history, philosophy, literature, the fine arts, mathematics, and the natural and social sciences. The skills, procedures, and understanding that are taught in higher education are governed by rules and involve standards of performance. What is learned brings a student into a position to see or to do things a certain way; he is taught to comprehend better what may have been only implicit previously. That kind of learning requires the discipline of repeated performance and rational criticism according to principles and standards. The business of students is to make mental efforts under such criticism.

I have explained somewhat generally what a college and higher learning are. I want to discuss next some subversions and perversions of them, all of which are expressions of the desire to be "relevant."

First of all, we may ask who should be members of a community of higher learning. Although it may be a sad truth, it is truth, nevertheless, that higher learning is too high for the average intelligence, the average sensibility, the average interest, the average initiative, the average perseverance, the average self-reliance, the average honesty, the average dispassion. It is not the function of a college to educate everyone who wants it to educate him, but it need only educate those who seem reasonably able to enter into the traditions of discourse and inquiry of the college community. If applicants for admission cannot reasonably meet the standards implicit in those traditions, they should be rejected. And once applicants are admitted, if they cannot perform satisfactorily when judged according to those standards, they should be dismissed. To accept or to retain the incompetent lowers the standards governing the discourse and inquiry of the academic community. This is followed by the dishonesty of certifying students as having been educated to do what they are not competent to do. Failure to reach a professionally approved standard of performance should result in being excluded from the community, either by not being admitted in the first place or by being expelled from it. In a college, the faculty should set standards of performance in accordance with the competence necessary to engage in the intellectual activities in which *they* engage professionally.

One way in which the demand for relevance subverts higher education is by opening colleges to high-school graduates independently of the quality of their past academic performance. I do not intend to discuss the degree of reliability of correlations between high-school performance and college performance or between various pre-college tests and college performance. Suffice it to say that when colleges begin remedial reading and mathematics programs for incoming freshmen, these colleges plainly betray their belief that the freshmen cannot enter into the discourse and inquiry of higher learning. For higher education presupposes that teacher and student already have certain basic skills and knowledge. Clearly, the abilities to read and do elementary mathematics are among them. The pretense of educating when one is not educating and the distortion of professional standards to disguise the pretense are equally pernicious. Each is incompatible with and subversive of the honest pursuit of knowledge, to which a college should be committed. To admit, to the community of learning, people who cannot participate in its life or enjoy its benefits and whose presence causes the quality of the benefits to deteriorate either destroys the community or makes it dwindle to insignificance.

Let us consider two things: first, that a college is a specific kind of community that confers certain benefits; second, that colleges have traditionally slighted certain ethnic and racial groups in admitting students. Accordingly, the members of these groups have been disproportionately denied the benefits conferred by those colleges. In short, there has been a specific injustice. Lately, however, colleges have recognized the injustice and have affirmed their moral commitment to remedy it by recruiting qualified students from the slighted groups.

There are two ways to remedy the injustice. First, there is "open enrollment," whereby high-school graduates are admitted into the college irrespective of their achievement or interests or self-reliance. This method requires introducing remedial and pseudointellectual courses into the curriculum and thereby subverts the college. Second, there is the "transitional program," as at Brown University, for instance, whereby the university recruits Black students from academically weak environments who are judged to have the necessary intelligence and motivation to succeed at Brown. They are admitted as regular freshman only after they have completed a seven-week transitional summer program. In this program they are introduced, for example, to long-term assignments with relatively little supervision, since the capacity to do that sort of work is presupposed by the regular course work.

The issue of which program is preferable does not depend upon whether or not the university should remedy the injustice. Whichever program a college chooses presupposes that the injustice should be remedied. But, as with almost any action, there are consequences other than the specific one for which action is taken. In choosing the transitional program, Brown University takes care not to damage the university; whereas, in choosing open enrollment, universities either do not consider that consequence or resolve to ignore or to accept it. The faculty of a university should take great care to preserve the integrity of scholarship and the community of learning against deterioration, whether it comes in the name of justice or not. Open enrollment, far from preserving that integrity, causes it to deteriorate.

In 1969, when the Brown University program was initiated, it served only thirty-one students. Given the magnitude of the injustice to be eliminated, we cannot but recognize the insufficiency of such programs. They are splendid but limited. However, we should also recognize that higher learning is not for everyone. One of our society's grave weaknesses is the lack of variety in the kinds of schooling it offers. Servility, regimentation, and alienation are what its schooling chiefly begets. Our society is dominated by the belief that since education is valuable for everyone, higher education is valuable for everyone. But that is a non sequitur. To be sure, everyone can benefit from some kind of education, but genuinely higher education can be engaged in only by those having exceptional intellectual and imaginative ability and a strong desire to master a subject matter. Our society needs to increase the kinds of schooling it offers, so that the great majority of students (who are not interested in or fit for higher learning) can be guided to realize their potentialities for achieving both private and public good.

113

The respect our society pretends to have for intellect would be amusing were its consequences not pathetic. Our society loves gadgets and ease, but it does not value theoretical inquiry or trained intelligence unless they are directed toward producing the former. Yet it persists in advocating higher education for its young adults, who find, when they have received a degree after four years, that their schooling has little or nothing to do with their lives—whether personally, socially, or vocationally. We should at least offer them the opportunity for schooling that is vocationally useful and as liberal as we can make it, while keeping its humanistic function strictly subservient to its vocational objective. It is axiomatic that education, no matter what its level, is liberating. But different kinds of education liberate different kinds of people, and it is a mistake to believe otherwise.

Not only does a college's choice of students often betray its confusion about higher education but allowing its students to help make decisions concerning curricula does also. There is good reason to consider students' opinions about the courses they take, but that does not mean we should permit them to decide what courses should be given. During the early nineteenth century, romantics proclaimed that children and idiots knew more of what was important to know than adults and normal persons. A college, however, cannot afford this romantic condescension. I have already alluded to the tradition of discourse and inquiry in the university. Recognizing this tradition does not commit us to accepting it uncritically, but it is perfectly compatible with accepting or rejecting or modifying it critically. Tradition not only provides an ordering framework for inquiry and discovery but is also something we can criticize and change. But the only justification for rejecting or modifying it can be its demonstrated inadequacy.

A tradition is grounded in careful and cumulative effort when it achieves well-thought-out objectives in the various subject matters of the university. The knowledge thereby attained can be rationally criticized and emended, and is itself cumulative. Those, and those alone, whose mastery of subject matter makes them part of the tradition are competent to decide upon a college curriculm. For subject matters have histories and developments and are interrelated; they are not mere collections of disconnected statements or discontinuous happenings. They form a stable background for continuing exploration and discovery. A college is a repository of cumulative experience and the knowledge that it yields.

Students who demand curricular revisions (for example, that there be no required courses) base their demand upon their lack of interest in what the college requires or offers. They decide that the college's curriculum is defective, not because they prefer some other curriculum for its intrinsic merit but because the improvisation of taking whatever courses they want is allegedly better. Doing that expresses the students' spontaneity and attacks the stable and therefore sterile determination of a curriculum. What is allegedly needed in this matter, as in others, is the direct and immediate response to circumstances, not the deliberative constancy of reasons.

But that basis for reform is unsound. The worship of spontaneity and immediacy is incompatible with the affirmation of community. It is because the curricula of a college have histories and are interrelated that the people who jointly pursue and master them can form a community. A college cannot be all things to all men. What it is, is determined partly by the interests of its members. An interest is not something that can be compromised; either one has it or one does not.

But interests may conflict, in the sense that those who have them may want to do incompatible things. If some students are not interested in higher learning or in taking particular courses that the faculty thinks are needed for the discourse and inquiry appropriate to higher learning, then those students belong outside the university community. A student who, for instance, does not want to concern himself with science or its history, since he is interested in English literature, does not understand that he cannot master some literature (sometimes not even understand it) without knowing some science and its history. Book Eight of Milton's *Paradise Lost*, for instance, is primarily a discussion of the astronomical theories of Milton's time; Shelley's *The Witch of Atlas* and *Prometheus Unbound* are replete with references to the speculative physics of his time. Accordingly, those who require an English major to study some science and its history in order to better understand his literature are right and he, if he objects, is wrong. This point, of course, is independent of the more general purpose of higher education (discussed above) namely, to develop the student's cognitive perspective. But we do have here a clear instance of a student's inability, due to ignorance, to decide wisely what courses he should take. And because the instance is typical, teachers, who know more, should decide what the curriculum should be.

Consider another instance of the demand for relevance: the demand that a college busy itself with political issues. To be sure, every member of a college community, *as a citizen of a municipality or state or nation,* has the right to engage in political activity without forfeiting his college rights or privileges. But the demand has been that the college, as a *corporate* body, should take an *official* position on political issues. Now, although every teacher and student ought to be concerned about his municipality or state or country, and even *if* teachers and students ought to work together to achieve the political objectives they think worthwhile, no teacher or student may properly be asked to subordinate the scholarly or educational purposes of his college to such concerns. To pursue knowledge and to communicate knowledge, teachers and students alike must forsake their concern with the political issues of the day, unless those issues are the subject of their scholarly inquiry. This is not to say that teachers and students ought not *otherwise* to deal with political issues. But for a college to put aside scholarship and the transmission of culture to concern itself with politics is for it to cease being a community of higher learning.

Moreover, when a college asserts an official position on a political issue, it threatens the academic freedom of its members who oppose its corporate position. Rational discussion of the issue becomes suspect and, gradually, inquiry and debate are foreclosed. If the college is opposed to something on moral grounds, then whoever is not opposed to it is distrusted and whoever favors it is regarded as immoral. To those who would like to view a college as the government's adviser on practical matters or as a social agency by which a governmental decision is to be implemented or in which a social experiment is to be carried on, the very idea of a college as a community devoted to free, rigorous, and dispassionate inquiry into values and the consequences of commitments is unintelligible. Yet that is part of what a college is rightly devoted to.

A college's basic commitment to dispassionate inquiry is not tantamount to an indifference to society's problems but to a *neutrality* with respect to nonscholarly and noneducational issues. In that neutrality lies a college's strength to inquire skeptically into subjects and to discover truth and its strength to conserve and transmit our cultural heritage. Becoming a political association to solve social problems or a service station to eliminate particular evils subverts its proper purpose.

If it is impermissible for a college to become a political association, so too is it impermissible for any of its members to engage in secret research while simultaneously holding college positions. Such research is incompatible with a college's being a community, for the commitment to secrecy undercuts the reciprocity that binds the members together. The commitment to conceal truth conflicts with the commitment to publish and discuss it. A researcher who accepts a grant to do secret research will not be offering his research and discovery for consideration by his colleagues. Because his objective is now a private one, he places himself outside the community, and his colleagues may not discuss his work or benefit from it. If, for example, the Department of Defense, as part of its effort to spot troop movements in a war zone, wants research on photoreconnaissance, it may perfectly well hire college teachers and install them in laboratories outside their colleges.

But contracting with them and demanding secrecy for work done with college facilities is impermissible.

Although I have stated that students who are not interested in higher learning should not be permitted into the college community or, once there, be permitted to transform it in accordance with their own interests, I have not said what should be done about them. The college students I generally teach are neither stupid nor devoid of interests, although they are relatively uninterested in college subjects. They fail to recognize that the great value of some subjects is inseparable from the lack of any immediate practical use. These students, who demand that every subject have a use, have themselves been utensils for so long that they cannot conceive of a subject's not being useful. Their own disinclination to make the effort necessary to engage in intellectual activity causes them to allege the worthlessness of the activity. Whatever the causes, there cannot be any doubt that there is a large proportion of students who do not belong in any community of higher learning, either because they lack the ability to do college work or because they obdurately refuse to cultivate their studentship.

Two main things need to be done. First, business and industry, which today require a college diploma of many of their personnel for no sensible reason whatever, should stop requiring it. The diploma is simply a convenient screening device for business and industry, although what is being screened in or out is not clear. Requiring a college diploma seems to be unthinking obeisance to an era when a college education signified that a student was intelligent to begin with and that his intelligence had been trained and cultivated. Neither may be necessarily true today.

Second, instead of obliterating distinctions and demanding one kind of mediocre education for all, we ought to recognize different degrees of human capacities and interests. People with little capacity for abstract thinking or with little humanistic sensibility may have considerable talent for constructing machinery or working on automobile engines or designing clothing or doing secretarial work. Their contributions to society lie in directions other than scholarship. Yet, despite this, society has made them second-class citizens, and, instead of providing appropriate institutions to train them and develop their talents, it forces them to engage in college work, which is pointless and painful to them. They should be offered an opportunity for the vocational, technical, and professional education that they want and society needs. A post-secondary-school alternative to college should be available to students who have insufficient aptitude or inclination for college but who want and can profit from specialized training beyond the high-school level.

A curriculum designed to train people in the methods of redressing particular social evils should be available in one more kind of post-secondary school. Those teachers and students who want to eliminate particular social injustices would form a separate educational institution, with faculty and students reciprocally committed to practical objectives. Such an institution would offer, for instance, no course in the language or culture of Greece, since neither is directly relevant to any contemporary social ill to be cured. Rather, the languages and cultures of contemporary city ghettos would be studied, because the students would want to better understand and communicate with the people whose problems they want to help solve. Students' desire to solve problems and eliminate recognized evils is commendable, whereas the unwillingness to school them in whatever is necessary to facilitate their objective is censurable. We need to use creative intelligence in devising policies to enhance specific human values and objectives by suggesting ways to liberate diverse talents, without destroying historically significant and socially valuable institutions.

Only a fool will say that since colleges are defective, they ought to be abolished. The ills of society are hardly to be ascribed to an over-abundance of scholarliness or dispassion—the virtues of a college. A wise man knows that imperfection is always part of any institution or community, for these are composed of people, and people, though infinitely corrigible, are not perfectible. The beauty and dignity of the intellectual life of a college are precarious because they depend upon good will and common aspiration. It is not only violence that destroys intellectual life; the warring of self-interested factions or indifference also destroys it. If it is destroyed, we shall lose a great tradition of intellectual responsibility that cultivates excellence and discovers truth. No society can afford to lose that. As a people, we have still to develop a common interest in excellence and truth. Perhaps the choice we must make concerning the future of higher education will persuade us that it is important to develop that interest, and that sacrifice for the sake of excellence and truth is preferable to bitter strife in behalf of misconceived objectives.

Rationality in the Contemporary University

Gray L. Dorsey
Washington University

The future of the university depends upon the future of rationality. If a body of knowledge independent of whim or chance is illusory, then an institution devoted to discovering and transmitting it is not needed. Academic standards would become meaningless. Adherence to procedures for objective verification of facts and mastery of a subject area would not prepare one to perform any sort of task better than persons not similarly "qualified." Certificates and diplomas might as validly be awarded in response to power or money as for compliance with academic requirements.

If the case for rationality is so clear, why have we heard so many voices raised against it? I suggest that a part of the answer is disappointment and that we in the universities are largely responsible. The accomplishments of rationality have been great, but we have encouraged Utopian expectations.

Ever since Plato prescribed the training for a philosopher-king, rationality has carried a pretension to perfection and sovereignty. The professors of medieval universities were shielded somewhat from the hubris of rationality because only God was deemed to be fully rational. The expectation that everything can be put right by reason did not apply to this world, but to the next.

The professors of the Enlightenment were not so lucky. Reason had been secularized and was therefore available to put all things right in

119

this world. Turgot said at the Sorbonne in 1750: "Manners become gentler; the mind becomes more enlightened; nations, hitherto in isolation, draw nearer to one another; trade and political relations link up the various quarters of the globe; and the whole body of mankind, through vicissitudes of calm and tempest, of fair days and foul, continues its onward march, albeit with tardy steps, toward an ever-nearing perfection."[1]

Voltaire's *Candide*, nine years later, made the point that the abstract rationality of the Enlightenment could put right all things in general, but nothing in particular.

I would suggest that the hubris of rationality has shown itself in the contemporary university in the expectations we have encouraged that anything in particular can be put right by making it the subject of a well-funded research project. Do you want to abolish polio or walk on the moon? Establish a research project! The paradigm was organized at the University of Chicago to make an atom bomb. Unfortunately, the particularity of the problem evokes a response that tends to be unconcerned with any effect except the particular one desired. We provide more convenient laundry products and pollute rivers. Are people aggressive? It is proposed that the controlling portion of their brains be removed. Further, we tend to think that any problem, no matter how complex, can be solved if it is restated in terms of a narrower problem that has already been solved. Psychoanalysis relieves the sexually based neuroses of a few thousand persons, and we find world political leaders being psychoanalyzed and world peace being sought by removal of sexual inhibitions.

What point would the satire of a contemporary Voltaire make? Perhaps that with our concrete rationality of science and technology we can put right anything in particular, but not without getting lost in general.

Hopefully, the university of the future will view rationality as indispensable but not sufficient. Hopefully, it will not encourage the intrusion of corrosive reason into areas of personal experience or community life that are stronger and better without conceptualization and analysis. Hopefully, it will help—but only help—men and women to realize their full potentialities.

NOTES

1. Paul Hazard, *European Thought in the Eighteenth Century* (New Haven, Conn.: Yale University Press, 1954), p. 369.

Some Things We Need

Stephen Tonsor
University of Michigan

I was struck by some of the comments Professor Bestor made about the difference between the ethos of intellectuality and the purposes or ends of intellectuality in the university. They are not at all the same. I think, however, that Professor Kristol came much closer to the mark in his consideration of this question. The demand for relevance, the demand for a wide range of investigatory techniques and stances in the university is not out of place. Rather, the demand that these postures be taken witlessly, that they serve the purposes of unreason rather than reason, that they refuse the exploration of all the evidence and exclude any view that is not consonant with their private vision—these are the attitudes that so trouble the university at the present moment.

Nonetheless, I think we would be deluding ourselves if we believed that there was a good, golden past that has only recently come crumbling down around our ears. I do not think that is true. I recall reading, long before the student disturbances began, an inscription in the men's room at the University of Michigan that said, "The University of Michigan is a big fake." "Fake" is a four-letter word too. And there was and is a great deal of truth in that graffiti. The university made claims and held pretensions to debate, to difference, to catholicity that were not present in actuality. The university said it sought the truth, when in fact it all too often sought to protect or create an establishment, when it sought to exclude or hinder the open discussion of issues. My university, for example, for one hundred and fifty years did not have a tenured member of the history department who was a Roman Catholic. That seems to me a remarkable feat.

To demonstrate the correctness of Professor Kristol's remarks, let me point out that it is difficult to find a member of our philosophy department who is not an analytic philosopher and it is difficult to discern any major differences of viewpoint in our economics department. Nonbehavioralists were, until very recently, nearly absent from our political-science department. Moreover, this is not a condition of recent origin. The university has stressed like-mindedness for a long time. There is an enormous homogeneity in our university faculties.

I myself believe that students have come to think that universities are power bases because they *have* been power bases for one-sided political, social, economic, and religious viewpoints in the past. We would delude ourselves were we to assert that this has not been the case. The university of the future must be a much more open university than has been the case in the past. Profesor Kristol's remarks about the necessity of restructuring our appointments and tenure policies must be given the most serious consideration.

An Economist's View

Abba Lerner
City University of New York, Queens

I am an economist, and maybe this makes me want to look at things from a slightly different angle. I too was bothered by the popgun-crack-of-doom proposition. A popgun would hardly be noticed unless there were a situation in which a popgun could do great damage, and there is no need to call on the trumpets that blew down the walls of Jericho.

In this symposium, the word "university" is being used with at least two different meanings. Part of the time people refer to the university as something they would like it to be—essentially a place where people try to discover things, where they do some teaching at the same time; the teaching helps them discover, the involvement in discovery helps them teach. The other meaning of "university" is the kind of institution we have around us. The fact that these two are so different cannot be blamed simply on the existing university; it is the result of the general situation in which we find ourselves with our economic and other problems.

It may be a kind of professional aberration on my part, as a result of my specialization, that whatever problem I meet I find that the trouble is generally due to unemployment. Nevertheless, I think it is so in this case. If there is a high degree of unemployment, every potential employer has too many applicants and he needs some way of choosing the few he can interview. A diploma or a degree of some kind is a marvelous way of saving time. So, a high-school diploma is required to give one even a chance at a job. If there are too many applicants with high-school diplomas, a bachelor of arts or science is required; if there are too many bachelor degrees, one needs a Ph.D. The university then has to invent things for people to do in order to get their degrees.

A further result of this kind of "certification" for jobs, for which college studies are not really necessary, is that high schools do not do their job of teaching, with the result that the colleges have to do the work of the high schools and the graduate schools have to do the work of the colleges.

These are very serious problems, but I do not think they are the fault of universities or their faculties. I don't think we should beat our breasts and say we have been "bad." We are in a mess because of these external forces, and we must recognize that there are limitations to what we can do about them. The danger is that we might be tempted to politicalize ourselves to get something done about the underlying economic and political issues. That, of course, would be the wrong thing to do.

Education and a Free Society

Edward J. Rozek
University of Colorado

The function of education is to shape the intellectual, moral, and spiritual life of an individual and of a nation and to transmit the knowledge and wisdom of the ages from one generation to the next. Professor Werner Jaeger in his *Paideia* reminds us that this transmission is achieved through reason and the conscious will—that is, through training that develops the finest human potentialities in each generation. This is done for a threefold purpose: self-preservation, the achievement of selected goals, and excellence—that is, the deliberate pursuit of an ideal. Thus, education consists of three parts: (1) education for the inner life, (2) vocational education, and (3) education for citizenship.

Educating for the inner life means giving an individual the kind of education that will enable him to become a completely developed human being. To develop to the utmost his potentialities, high standards of excellence must be set for him. Education should aim both at good habits of learning and thinking and at the cultivation of will, desire, and emotion, which are no less necessary in the forming of a good character than in the training of a mature mind. A free human being should have a growing understanding of himself, his fellowman, and the world in which he lives. He should be acquainted with the intellectual and moral achievements of the great masters and architects of Western civilization and have a notion of other great cultures. This will enable him to discover what excellence means and, if possible, to be infected with its appeal. By following the Olympian path that the greatest minds have traveled, the student will gain a certain mental disposition that will remain with him even when he has forgotten much of what he has studied. At the same time, he will be concerned with such indispensable virtues of a good man as courage, temperance, justice, and wisdom, which may guide him and, through him, his society.

The study of greatness will reveal human *potentialities* and *limitations*. The former will show him how to transcend many of his insufficiencies and how to fulfill himself, while the latter will teach him humility, that indispensable virtue for growth and self-control. An awareness of human weaknesses and an appreciation of his advantages will open his soul to the grace of God, which, in turn, will deepen the meaning of his life. These are some of the indispensable ingredients in the development of a rounded and wise personality and a good man.

A skeptic might say that this is too large an order. I would reply that it is ambitious, but today free men everywhere, and those of Western civilization in particular, are facing the most deadly challenge ever cast by ruthless men. If we are to survive and preserve our heritage, we must produce a higher type of man, and he cannot be produced by a mediocre plan.

To be sure, we can hardly expect that this program will produce such a man at the end of the senior year in an American college. Education does not end with a diploma. But if we expose our students to greatness and excellence and if we develop in our young people a taste for these, they will continue to search for them. There is the chance that such a search may enable them to consider various ideals, from among which they can choose the best ones to organize their lives around. A good and fully developed man will not be a slave. He will find the energy and the means to protect his freedom and that of the people committed to his charge.

The second task of education is the preparation for a vocation. This should come only after a young student has acquired a basic acquaintance with the fundamental disciplines. These will set standards of critical exactitude and suggest ways of approaching new and old problems, as well as the methods required in the pursuit of free and independent inquiry.

Premature specialization or overspecialization will produce a lopsided mind and an unbalanced individual, who may not be able to draw intellectual, moral, or spiritual strength from other branches of human knowledge—strength he will need in order to get the full and most creative use out of his own special field.

The recent outcry for more scientists stems from despair and not from wisdom. Our difficulty today is not the shortage of scientists and engineers, as so many believe. We know that many scientists and engineers were looking in vain for jobs during the early seventies. What we need is a better type of scientist. We need more Einsteins, Fermis, Tellers, Bohrs, and Lawrences, as well as statesmen who will give them an opportunity to utilize their genius. Such men cannot be produced by more science education but they can be cultivated in part by an equally thorough education in the arts, literature, philosophy, and religion. Giants of science are artists, who derive creative and intuitive ideas for the work in their fields from other branches of human knowledge. Most of the men just mentioned were, or are, at home in some forms of music, literature, religion, and philosophy.

It was Albert Einstein who said, in *Ideas and Opinions:*

> I cannot conceive of a genuine scientist without profound faith. . . The most beautiful experience we can have is the mysterious. It is the fundamental emotion which stands at the cradle of true art and true science. Whoever does not know it and can no longer wonder, no longer marvel, is as good as dead, and his eyes are dimmed. It was the experience of mystery—even if mixed with fear—that engendered religion. A knowledge of the existence of something we cannot penetrate, our perceptions of the profoundest reason and the most radiant beauty, which only in their most primitive forms are accessible to our minds, it is this knowledge and this emotion that constitute true religiosity. [Then he added:] Science cannot give us a sense of the ultimate and fundamental ends; they come into being not through demonstration but through revelation. The highest principles for our aspirations and judgments are given to us in the Jewish-Christian religious tradition. [1]

Natural science can only ascertain what is, but not what should be. Value judgments that lie outside its domain remain necessary. Natural science has a useful and honorable place among branches of human knowledge, but its goals must be derived from and subordinated to the humanities. Again, to quote Einstein: "Science without religion is lame; religion without science is blind."[2]

The motivation and goals for human existence are not produced or satisfactorily explained by science. When Einstein was asked what the meaning of human life was, he answered as follows: "To know an answer to this question means to be religious. You ask: 'Does it make any sense then, to pose this question?' I answer: 'The man who regards his own life and that of his fellow creatures as meaningless is not merely unhappy but hardly fit for life.'"[3] We need wise, courageous men with vision, who can synthesize complex situations and utilize free men's capacities for the mutual benefit of all men.

We would do well to orient our education toward excellent students, by expanding to the limit the individual's capacity and desire for self-education for seeking and finding meaning, truth, and enjoyment. That means as thorough a training in the liberal arts as possible, after which can come specialization. As for the less gifted and the less industrious, they will gain more from a program that appears to exceed their capacity than from one that makes no demands upon them.

We must recognize that nature did not distribute blessings to each person uniformly. We can correct this only in part. The progress and survival of the majority depends upon the gifts and accomplishments of the minority. Since we do not know who the potentially great are, we must provide an equal opportunity to all. This does not mean leveling down to the lowest denominator but aiming at the highest attainable peaks. The less gifted will find a better place for themselves than they do under a program that fails to use even their limited resources.

The greatest problem in educating youth lies in the proper institutional arrangements for utilizing most effectively the best products of the whole educational system. This means enlightened political leadership, which leads us to the third requirement of education, namely, education for citizenship.

The free world needs not only better scientists but also better politicians. It needs statesmen who, through wise, farsighted leadership and the effective use of natural resources and the best available knowledge, can lead humanity toward a better future. The present crisis is due primarily to the failure of Western leadership.

The most important qualification for high office in the Western world appears to be the "know-how" of getting elected. In many cases, the "virtue" and charming personality of the candidate is nearly all he can offer. A politically undereducated public accepts platitudes for realistic policies, salesmanship for statesmanship. Whenever it becomes obvious that the elected candidate violated the voters' trust and endangered the country's safety, partisan loyalty and public apathy combine to protect him from the consequences of his ineptness.

It is an old saying that people get what they deserve. If a free people are politically educated, they will choose a wise man to lead and govern them. Our high schools, colleges, and universities must educate the young in the basic principles of democracy. This education can be given through a historical study of how various ideas come into being in a well-organized society, thereby showing our own ideals in their proper perspective. Every citizen, and especially every student, should be familiar, not only with those ideals and political institutions that make men free, but also with the theory and practice of old and new totalitarian systems that promise freedom, abundance, and justice but in actuality produce slavery, hunger, and concentration camps. We need a thorough knowledge of all types of political systems so that we can make intelligent choices and strengthen the will to protect and extend freedom. Ignorance of hostile doctrines and despotic systems is one of the most vulnerable points in a democracy such as ours.

Since, in Western democracies, every citizen determines political leadership from the local to the national level through the ballot, it is imperative that every chemist, engineer, pharmacist, lawyer, economist, and member of other professions and trades be well acquainted with politics, including international politics. The intricacies of politics cannot be left to politicians or students of politics alone. The survival of freedom depends upon the intelligent behavior of every person who profits by it and upon his knowledge of its fragility and the forces that strive to destroy it. Unquestioning loyalty is not enough. It is necessary that the largest number of idealistic, courageous, and able citizens become involved in this process, thus matching the fanaticism of the disciplined and effectively organized enemies of democracy, who are experienced in various forms of subversion and conquest.

Today, the battle for the minds of men is going on in the classroom. Young people will undoubtedly decide the eventual outcome of the struggle between freedom and tyranny. The Western democracies have never lacked patriots willing to give their lives on the battlefield. But we also need a different kind of courage, a sustained moral and intellectual courage, applied every day by every individual, as if the future of Western civilization depended upon individual action.

These are not merely lofty or nebulous ideals, but the price necessary for survival. It means hard work for students, less emphasis on sports, and fewer social distractions. It means a stiffer curriculum of study and entrance examinations that will make greater demands on the high schools.

It also means harder work for faculty members—more research and preparation for classes, more encouragement of competition among students, more recognition for good work. Perhaps every teacher should burn his lecture notes at least every two years. New preparation and a fresh approach would include the latest scholarly achievements in the field. Many teachers, repeating the same lectures year after year, become sterile and dull, and students are quick to sense this.

In recent years, it is obvious that many institutions of higher learning seem to have become the base for an attempt to realize instant Utopia. Instead of being sanctuaries of reason, the universities have become staging areas for an assault upon free society.

The basic ideological climate of opinion among faculty members and students has a direct bearing on the terrible crisis in our academic institutions. The Cornell Alumni Committee for Balanced Education stated:

> For the past three or four decades the majority of the professors in the social sciences have been of the liberal and collectivist persuasions. Thus we have had an entire generation of college graduates enter their careers, including teaching, with the views of our society and economy which their liberal professors have imparted to them. The students receive, directly or indirectly, a steady diet of the currently respectable liberal doctrines from professors who for the most part are proficient proponents of that persuasion. On the other hand the students receive only minimal instruction in the free-market—limited-government point of view, and much of that is from men who are basically opposed to that philosophy. Continuing existence of this self-perpetuating liberal orthodoxy in social science departments is preventing most students from receiving a fair and unbiased exposure to the economic, political, and philosophical doctrines upon which this country was created and which make possible a free society.[4]

Lawrence Fertig, an economist and writer on economic subjects, and for eighteen years a member of the board of trustees of New York University, expressed a similar observation:

> My point is that in many departments of American universities, such as economics, sociology, history and the other so-called social sciences, the ideological content taught to students is entirely one-sided. It is of the modern liberal persuasion, and often does not even make a bow to the old traditional liberalism or the modern conservative viewpoint. As an example, there are cases I personally know of, where capable students have received their Doctor of Philosophy degree in Economics from a major university although they had never even heard of, or been taught about such distinguished free-market economists as Ludwig von Mises, Friedrich Hayek, or Wilhelm Roepke—three world-famous economists. Imagine that for a Ph.D. in Economics! What kind of an education is it that refuses to expose students to other than the modern liberal point of view so that students may have all the ideas and information necessary to arrive at a sound conclusion for themselves? When a great university virtually hides opposing viewpoints, it is really guilty of spreading propaganda instead of learning. I believe that we should strive for a better balance in the teaching staffs and curricula of leading universities—a balance between the modern liberal and conservative viewpoints.[5]

The task of a teacher in a classroom is not only to present his subject but also to stimulate the interest of his students in the search for knowledge. He should galvanize his students' minds and wills with the significant relationship of the subject taught to the larger problems of humanity.

A dedicated, intelligent teacher can explain the basic problems of a given subject, stimulate interest in it, teach the methods of research and study, and show the way to an independent advance in learning. Obviously, the proper environment is needed for both student and teacher.

An educational institution that provides an atmosphere for learning and rewards scholarly achievements will have no cause to be ashamed of its product. It is the responsibility of society at large to utilize to the utmost its most precious possessions: the highly developed mind and spirit.

We shall lose our freedom and possibly perish unless we change our present pattern and give more encouragement and better opportunities to new Fermis and Tellers, as well as new Washingtons, Jeffersons, and Lincolns. We need philosophers and spiritual leaders who can guide us away from the perils of enslavement at this dark moment in human history. To develop intelligence is the task of educational institutions and of a society of free men.

NOTES

1. Albert Einstein, *Ideas and Opinions* (New York: Crown, 1954).
2. *Ibid*.
3. *Ibid*.
4. Letter to Members and Friends, Spring 1971.
5. Lawrence Fertig, Letter to the Cornell University Alumni Committee for Balanced Education, Spring 1971.

Academic Freedom and Authoritarianism

Henry R. Novotny
*California State College,
Bakersfield*

The ideal of a pluralistic society, a democratic polity of free and autonomous men endowed with dignity, self-respect, and individual responsibility for their actions and decisions has come again under direct attack. The notion of a "society of consent," whose members willingly
obey consensually validated laws (adopted to provide a civilized framework for both cooperation and competition) is again derided and proclaimed slow, if not unworkable, by those in a hurry. These people are
less impressed by the objective progress achieved today than by Utopian visions of tomorrow, for which today—and often those living
today—are to be sacrificed. Under attack by these would-be saviors of
mankind are the key concepts that make the ideal of a free, pluralistic,
and tolerant society tangible—namely, the *assumption* of man as a
creature capable of intelligent, willful, and purposeful behavior.

What is challenged is the proposition that empirical reason, experimental logic, and the predictive scientific strategies employed in a
tolerant, democratic environment of an informed society represent the
intellectual and social structure through which cultural and material
social progress, as well as individual happiness, can be best achieved.
The New Left calls for a "higher logic and a higher reason." Herbert
Marcuse attacks "technological rationality" as repressive and "one-
dimensional." He urges the adoption of "negative, dialectical
thought," whose "function is to break down the self-assurance and self-

contentment of common sense, to undermine the sinister confidence in the power and language of facts," and to usher in a "qualitive change: the explosion and catastrophe of the established state of affairs."[1] In *The Greening of America*, Charles Reich states: "Accepted patterns of thought must be broken; what is considered 'rational thought' must be opposed by 'nonrational thought'—drug-thought, mysticism, impulses."[2]

Attacking from yet another angle is B. F. Skinner, who wants to abolish the "autonomous man" and proposes a society whose members have progressed "beyond freedom and dignity." Skinner starts along familiar lines when he sees man as a deterministic mechanism without the faculty of "free will." However, he then confuses the issue—perhaps in an effort to justify his own intervention—by circular arguments that leave key concepts undefined. Consider, for instance, his treatment of the terms "responsibility" and "control."

> A scientific analysis shifts both the responsibility and the achievement to the environment. [3]
>
> Those who undertake to do something about human behavior—for any reason whatsoever—become part of the environment to which responsibility shifts. [4]
>
> The mistake . . . is to put the responsibility anywhere, to suppose that somewhere a causal sequence is initiated. [5]
>
> The simple fact is that man is able, and now as never before, to lift himself by his own bootstraps. In achieving control of the world of which he is a part, he may learn at last to control himself. [6]
>
> We all control, and we are all controlled. As human behavior is further analyzed, control will become more effective. [7]
>
> Man has "controlled his own destiny," if that expression means anything at all. The man that man has made is the product of the culture man has devised. [8]
>
> [Man] is indeed controlled by his environment, but we must remember that it is an environment largely of his own making. The evolution of a culture is a gigantic exercise in self-control . . . We have not yet seen what man can make of man. [9]
>
> It does not matter that the individual may take it upon himself to control the variables of which his own behavior is a function or, in a broader sense, to engage in the design of his own culture. He does this only because he is the product of a culture which generated self-control or cultural design as a mode of behavior. The environment determines the individual even when he alters the environment. [10]

I submit that Skinner's logic as exemplified by the preceding quotations makes one agree with one of his characters in *Walden Two*: " 'A curious case of eating your cake and having it too,' said Castle. 'You seem to be in and out at the same time. Pray, how do you manage to do it?'"[11]

One of the objectives of the present symposium, as I understand it, is to evaluate and possibly to criticize the performance and products of existing institutions of higher learning. Since the most recent—and probably the most prominent and widely publicized—contribution of the academy has been its involvement with and promotion of such alternatives to the present social order as those just mentioned, I first want to examine briefly certain implications of these intellectual undertakings and then focus on their creators and their colleagues. Two aspects of these proposed social alternatives concern me most.

First, none of these socio-philosophic systems challenging the scientific and democratic "society of consent" seems to rely on a mode of reasoning that can demonstrate predictive power. (Skinner's "descriptive" system is not predictive in the usual sense, since his variables, such as "reinforcement," cannot be defined independently from a particular case, that is, a particular experiment carried out with a particular organism under particular conditions. That reinforcement has occurred is *inferred* from an increase of the frequency of relevant behavior. In Verplanck's words, "Prediction . . . is represented by extrapolation, by analogy; its use for the generation of propositions that may be put to experimental test is avoided."[12] Skinner himself recommends that we forget prediction and analyze instead the behavior and the reinforcement history of the scientist.)

Ostensibly aiming at a "higher" knowledge, wisdom, and virtue, the challenging schemes make frequent use of scientifically obscure concepts and processes such as universals, intuition, instincts, and various postulated historical or other mysterious forces; in any case, they all offer formulations from which one cannot draw propositions that possess predictive power and can thus be experimentally tested and verified.

Second, all such proposed social alternatives rely on leadership by a small, elite group of individuals that, without suprise, includes the founder.

ACADEMICIANS AS AN ELITE

Several decades ago, Ortega y Gasset observed: "Properly speaking, there are no barbarian standards. Barbarism is the absence of standards to which appeal can be made."[13] Let me suggest a related proposition (perhaps obvious, but not widely recognized): despotism and oppressive authoritarianism represent the absence of *consensually validated, objectively defined, and publicly known* standards to which appeal can be made. The root difference between a tolerant, democratic, or pluralistic society of free and autonomous men and a coercive, tribal and ideologically purified dictatorship seems to me to be this: in the former case, social power is based on the authority of empirical evidence, experimentally verified facts, scientific prediction, and publicly demonstrable superior performance and competence; in the latter case, social power is based on the authority of a privileged (perhaps inherited) social status, ex cathedra proclamations, a presumed gift of oracular prophecy, and unverifiable claims of moral and intellectual superiority.

In fact it appears that all socio-philosophic systems that rely on nonscientific modes of reasoning and use terms and formulations that do not allow open scientific analysis and public inquiry are intrinsically authoritarian in their very structure. They all depend on the services of high priests and expert ideological interpreters to furnish official guidelines for social action and legal and ethical standards for individual behavior.

Once installed, a nonscientific and nondemocratic socio-philosophic system represents a vehicle through which the leading elite expects to achieve its private ends. Official edicts, as well as current social prescriptions, proscriptions, and moral imperatives, reflect the personal idiosyncrasies and preferences of the system's inventors and caretakers. For obvious reasons, nonscientific social schemes invariably praise and demand a concentration of social power, a *totalitarian* social power. They lead to totalitarian social systems, in which leaders with supposedly superior virtue and insight direct, by force if needed, the moral health and the daily labor of all the other, presumably less gifted and less enlightened, members of the community.

One consequence of such a totalitarian take-over is, of course, the destruction of academic freedom and the independence of the educational enterprise.

The events of the last few years have indicated quite clearly that academic threats to the democratic system are more than theoretical possibilities. Those who want to see more advanced stages of this phenomenon need only examine the condition of most South American universities and note the ensuing polarization between the academic communities and the governing structures.

With all these considerations in mind, then, are academicians an elite? My reply is that they should be and I hope that they are. But if so, it must be by virtue of their superior competence, a publicly verifiable competence, and not by membership in an exclusive, and mostly self-selected, organization.

The urgent task at hand is to find a formula with which to design the structure and select the social role of institutions of higher learning—a formula that would preserve both a free, rational, and democratic society and an educational enterprise that is viable and independent of external interference. In particular, the question to examine is how to deal with an academic community that claims the privileges of academic freedom but also strives for "social relevance."

UNIVERSITIES AS INSTRUMENTS OF SOCIAL CHANGE

As long as the academy adheres to a democratic and scientific philosophy, or at least as long as academicians remain satisfied with discussing ideas rather than trying to find means through which to implement them and to change the community at large, few difficulties arise. However, with an increasing frequency, parts of the academy seem to confront our basically imperfect, but improving, scientific and democratic egalitarian society with demands for a public accommodation of academically taught and trained shock troops trying to establish one or another of the nonscientific and nondemocratic social alternatives.

To find the needed perspective, it is necessary to fall back on fundamental principles; two are of relevance here. One, of course, is that of academic freedom. The other and, at least pragmatically, more basic one is the framework of our republic as specified by the Constitution. It should be observed that, while the average citizen may not be a member of the academic community, an academician remains a member of the larger community whether he likes it or not.

I concede that the academic community is special and unique and that its processes cannot be blindly judged by any simple measures. Certainly, the social merits of a free philosophic discussion may not be readily measured by any available formal, objectively definable criteria any more than the artistic merits of a masterpiece can—although the requisite qualifications for prospective philosophy and art teachers may and should be clearly stated. In some ways, nevertheless, centers of higher education cannot ignore the imperatives and implications associated with the concepts of scientific methodology, open and free critical discussion, and democratic tolerance, as well as individual rights.

My suggestion on how to preserve the democratic structure of the entire community and, at the same time, insure maximum academic freedom and independence is to adopt as a guide the proposition that follows (and if it were accepted by the academy, it should lead to a significant reduction in present-day turmoil):

Any applied science and any discipline taught at a center of higher education that claims to be socially relevant in a direct manner (that is, whose teaching is undertaken to propose, prescribe, justify, facilitate, or teach methods or skills of bringing about a social practice or change of any kind) should be so formulated and presented as to promote intelligent and democratic behavior.

By "intelligent behavior" I mean any conscious, functional, and purposive act, or a series of acts, designed to achieve some specific, desired objective. Intelligent behavior implies an understanding of what one is doing in terms of the predictable consequences. It is justified by its outcome, as well as the means and methods it employs. *One cannot behave intelligently without depending on a mode of reasoning that has predictive power.*

By "democratic behavior" I refer in this context more to the egalitarian connotations of that term than to political and voting processes and procedures through which the rule of a majority is established (which is necessarily accompanied by some degree of disenfranchisement of a minority). I refer to such attitudes of behavioral conduct as exhibiting tolerance to opposite viewpoints, permitting critical discussions, allowing independent and free research and intellectual inquiry, sharing scientific results and findings with as many interested individuals (of academic standing or otherwise) as possible, and relying on consensual processes as the appropriate method of selecting and establishing social goals. It is unnecessary and useless to defend the proposition that one should behave intelligently; to the intelligent that is obvious, and there is no way to employ intelligent persuasion to convince the fanatic, the irrational, or the unintelligent.

As for the possible objection that democratic requirements would interfere with academic freedom, let me say this. First, on a more abstract level, it seems obvious that the processes of free intellectual inquiry can take place only in a tolerant, democratic, and therefore most likely a pluralistic social environment. Anyone arguing for the former must of necessity accept the latter. Second, on a more practical and pragmatic level, it seems quite absurd to expect that the society would tolerate and finance, under the guise of academic freedom, supposedly educational institutions that would, in fact, be training grounds for hostile guerrillas and totalitarian fanatics. The most the academy can expect is to have their *ideas* tolerated. Academicians who desire social change can promote it, in their *academic* roles, only by disseminating ideas, not by training warriors.

To sum up then, I am proposing neither to interfere with the freedom and independence of intellectual inquiry, no matter how irrational the methods, nor to ban philosophic speculations, no matter how totalitarian the premises or conclusions. Nor am I attempting to force the fine arts into a logical or formalistic straitjacket, no matter how bizarre their products and ideas. I am concerned here exclusively with intellectual and educational undertakings that involve *social action*.

Since I believe that the condition of open-ended debate is essential to any institution of higher learning and also that, as Edward Teller pointed out, where action starts debate ends, I conclude that action-oriented instruction must be singled out for a special restriction. To preserve free education, we must preserve a democratic environment. However strongly the intellectual and the educator may feel about the need for social reforms, they must recognize an even stronger need for a firm commitment to democratic processes.

Having outlined constraints that reform-minded academics endeavoring to restructure the society might be reasonably expected to recognize, let me add a personal view regarding the present mass-production of intellectuals.

ONE MILLION, TWO MILLION, MANY INTELLECTUALS

Zbigniew Brzezinski of Columbia University has suggested that one should differentiate between "intellectuals" and "members of the intellectual class." Qualifications for the latter category, I assume, would derive from a professional status rather than from a performance of truly intellectual quality.

It seems to me useful to make such a distinction. It helps point out several consequences of the "vertical invasion" that has been taking place during the last few decades. For instance, it indicates (1) that some, perhaps most, of the class-intellectuals may, in fact, be only pseudointellectuals, as measured by performance, and (2) that, in many cases, intellectuals, perhaps even genuine intellectuals, cannot be accepted any longer as unbiased scholars but must be considered members of a pressure group with political and economic class prejudices.

The creation of a sizable intellectual class (which in the United States includes over half a million college and university professors) is in large measure a by-product of the technological progress that has made our society affluent enough to support a large number of people not directly involved in the production of life's necessities. With technological efficiency expected to increase still further in the future, one may anticipate that the number of intellectuals will grow as well. In fact, in the not-too-distant future life in a society where a majority of adults belong to the intellectual class is becoming a distinct and frightening possibility.

I wish I could believe that the sound of a million hammers, or even a million marching boots, replaced by the sound of shuffled papers and a million scribbling pens would signal a better future. Unfortunately, in the light of recent history, the million scribbling pens might easily be followed by the cries of a million innocent victims. Though mine may still be a minority view, I believe the blame for most of this century's massacres should be placed primarily on aberrant intellectuals, not on so-called military establishments.

With the creation of an intellectual class there emerges a very significant group of articulate voters and community leaders, frequently found in the forefront molding public opinion and influencing vital public decisions, such as those related to defense, "national priorities," and so forth. Yet, these are individuals who, as a rule, are destined to spend their lives without ever having experienced a meaningful "dialogue with reality," without ever having had the kind of corrective feedback that teaches man to respect facts and check his propensity for rationalization.

We live in an apparently orderly universe, imposing certain constraints with which man has to learn to live and work. Technology with scientific research, planning, and prediction are our tools by which the effect of these constraints may be moderated and made more bearable, but they can never be fully eliminated. In my opinion, these constraints represent the most authoritative and effective teacher of discipline there is, at least for those not shielded artificially from the effects of their influence.

The fact that a rapidly growing number of academicians and those in positions of leadership have never had the opportunity to learn the strict discipline of mind acquired through purposive transactions of a practical nature—and that is indispensable for the learning of true intellectual honesty—concerns me gravely. Regrettably, one can hardly learn this kind of discipline vicariously from books. Incidentally, while I agree that skills are not, as a rule, transferable from one field of endeavor to another, I believe that attitudes are; and attitudes, such as the respect for facts, are not irrelevant to the outcome of one's efforts.

The current explosion of the so-called "knowledge industry" seems to involve as much of an explosion in the production of potentially dangerous nonsense as that of validated knowledge; it is paralleled by an explosion in the number of mediocre individuals who seek art without discipline and discipline without sacrifice, and who seem invariably to achieve only pretenses without substance.

WHAT IS TO BE DONE?

The present discussion would be incomplete without at least a brief list of specific social and educational recommendations that one might hope would help restore tranquillity to both the campus and public life, sanity to academic discourse, civility to personal conduct of students and teachers, as well as democracy to educational and other social institutions. The following suggestions are offered without a claim to completeness.

The scientific, democratic, and humanitarian pretensions of the self-serving, prescientific mode of dialectical reasoning—as well as of any other oracular and authoritarian modes—should be vigorously challenged. Rhetoric should be rejected as an inappropriate substitute for factual evaluation, scientific analysis, and experimental findings. A special effort should be made to explain to nonscientists, such as liberal-arts students and their teachers, that, to achieve set objectives, it is wise to rely on the efficient and democratic epistemological strategies of scientific methodology, since they alone can provide reliable guidelines for intelligent, functional, and purposive behavior. Objectives that cannot be defined clearly should then be approached with utmost caution and tentativeness.

The traditional American approach of judging action and profession by the predictable consequences will have to be reasserted. The medieval practice of divining individuals' motives and mental health by oracular interpretations of ritualized, dogmatic ideologies will have to be diligently discouraged. Social scientists will have to classify individuals on the basis of observable behavior rather than by lumping them into artificial sociological, economic, and ideological groupings that frequently depend on outdated stereotypes and do little justice to many so labeled.

Social mechanisms and institutions that provide corrective feedback, especially on the local level—and which therefore promote dependence on purposive and intelligent behavior—will have to be developed; those that tend to shield individuals from the consequences of their actions—and hence may lead to random, reflexive, ritualistic, and superstitious behaviors—will have to be reformed.

The academic community, and intellectuals in general, will have to take a hard look at the results of their activity. The ongoing metamorphosis of yesterday's culturally leavening intellectual minority into tomorrow's culture-defining majority is a radically new social development, whose possible consequences must be investigated very carefully. It may turn out, for instance, that as more and more academics are shielded from reality, more and more delusions are generated and disseminated by them. In such a case, fundamental reforms will have to be instituted to reverse the trend. Otherwise, we could easily reach the point at which the dominant segment of the academic community would fail to develop adequate awareness of the facts of life and would present visionary social demands without any sense of history and historical possibilities and limitations. At this point most academicians would start acting less as impartial scholars and more as missionaries, preachers, and prophets.

Should the House of Scholarship ever cease to resemble a House of Intellect and take on the appearance of a House of Tarot Cards, the general public would be justified in ceasing to listen to the magicians inside it and in shaking the structure instead.

NOTES

1. Herbert Marcuse, "A Note on Dialectic," preface to the 1960 edition of *Reason and Revolution* (Boston: Beacon Press, 1960), p. ix.

2. Charles A. Reich, *The Greening of America* (New York: Bantam, 1971), p. 394.

3. B. F. Skinner, *Beyond Freedom and Dignity* (New York: Knopf, 1971), p. 25.

4. *Ibid.*, p. 76.

5. *Ibid.*

6. B. F. Skinner, *Cumulative Record,* rev. ed. (New York: Appleton-Century-Crofts, 1961), p. 4.

7. B. F. Skinner, *Science and Human Behavior* (New York: Macmillan, 1953), p. 438.

8. *Beyond Freedom and Dignity*, p. 208.

9. *Ibid.*, p. 215.

10. *Science and Human Behavior*, p. 448.

11. B. F. Skinner, *Walden Two* (New York: Macmillan, 1948), p. 35.

12. William S. Verplanck and Burrhus F. Skinner, *Modern Learning Theory* (New York: Appleton-Century-Crofts, 1954), p. 311.

13. José Ortega y Gasset, *The Revolt of the Masses*, 25th Anniversary ed. (New York: Norton, 1932), p. 72.

PART THREE

THE CRUCIAL PROBLEMS
OF THE MODERN UNIVERSITY

The Role of the Faculty

John R. Searle
University of California,
Berkeley

We now appear to be at the end of the period of intense student activism that began at Berkeley in 1964 and spread across the nation, culminating in the demonstrations against the Cambodian invasion in 1970. I say "appear to be" because it is impossible to predict what the next few years will be like, but one can at least say with confidence that we are now in a more peaceful atmosphere than we lived through during the late sixties. That being the case, it is a good time to reflect on the quality of our response to the disorders of the sixties. In my view, the American professoriat, as a class, responded feebly and inadequately to the challenges of the past decade, and I want now to discuss some aspects of the response.[1]

As I am about to continue painting the rather bleak and depressing picture of ourselves and our colleagues that was begun earlier in this symposium, let me at least begin on a more cheerful note. There are two achievements of the American university system—hence of American faculties—that seem to me to be quite remarkable, indeed, unprecedented. First, we have raised a higher percentage of the population in this country to a higher intellectual level than any other country past or present that I know of. In spite of the tremendous gaps in this achievement—the unevenness of educational opportunities, the low quality of much university instruction, the incoherent prose written by many university graduates—more people are exposed to and benefit from advanced instruction than anywhere else.

A second achievement is in research. Having worked and lectured at universities in several countries, I am inclined to say that the quality of the research done at the best American universities is as good as or better than that being done anywhere in the world. The prodigious international impact of the research in this country testifies to its quality. I was really quite puzzled by one professor, who said that he thought intellectual standards were declining. It seems to me the contrary is true in the fields I am most familiar with—philosophy and linguistics. The standards are higher now in these two fields than they were thirty years ago and even higher than they were a decade ago. More good books and articles are published now than formerly. True, most of what is published, now as before, is mediocre at best. But that does not alter the fact that the amount of high-quality research is now greater than at any time in my academic lifetime. In any appraisal of our professional weaknesses as a class, we should bear in mind these two achievements: the spread of mass higher education and the high quality of original research.

Having said that, let me now turn to the failures and inadequacies of our response to the events of the past decade. One could discuss any number of topics, but I shall concentrate on two: first, we have not responded adequately to the attacks made on academic freedom; secondly, we have not responded consistently or intelligently to the various proposals for educational reform. Both of these topics have a special interest because both reveal, in varying degrees, an intellectual failure.

As an illustration of the sort of failure I have in mind in the area of academic freedom, note that the same distinguished faculty that will defend a professor's academic freedom when it is attacked by right-wing agencies in the outside community (such as the state legislature or right-wing members of the California Board of Regents) will often look the other way when one of their fellow professor's classes is disrupted by left-wing students. I can testify from personal experience that many of the same faculty members who vigorously defended the rights of Professor Angela Davis, when the Regents attempted to fire her for her political views, showed no interest in the case (one of many, I might add) of Professor Robert Scalapino, whose class was disrupted by left-wing students. I knew many of the people active in the strike at San Francisco State College; many of them have a long history of defense of academic freedom. They were vigorous and eloquent fighters for the rights of dissident professors, but when there was a bomb attack on Professor Bunzel or physical attacks on the editors of the student newspaper, these same people had nothing to say. They simply looked the other way.

I have been frequently puzzled to find that when I was in a position to defend the rights of students against harassment by the administration—as for example, during the Free Speech Movement—I had one class of allies on the campus, but when the time came to defend the rights of other students and faculty against the depredations of left-wing students (many of them the students whose own free speech I had been defending), many of these allies were not interested. Not only were they unhelpful, but they regarded a consistent civil-libertarian position as a kind of betrayal. They found it impossible to conceive that one could defend the rights of both the radicals and their adversaries unless one had undergone a change of heart. "How could you, of all people, attack the movement? You must have changed your views." These phenomena reveal a very serious weakness both in the degree of commitment to academic freedom and in the intellectual grip upon what academic freedom really is—what it is to be consistently committed to the free marketplace of ideas. I shall have more analysis of this phenomenon later, but now I want to identify my second topic.

In recent years, we have had an enormous outpouring of rhetoric and action about educational reform. Black studies, field studies, interdisciplinary studies, and experimental courses have all been established. Some of these innovations have been of excellent quality, but an unfortunately large percentage of what passes nowadays for academic innovation or reform is not intellectually acceptable. More to the point of our present discussion, I am constantly amazed that my colleagues, normally so meticulous and careful when asked to approve a new appointment or a new course, are suddenly too timid to question the intellectual standards of these innovations. Take ethnic or Black studies. Are we really convinced that the intellectual level we routinely demand as a minimum in physics, history, or English is being maintained in the various Black-studies programs? Have we rigorously scrutinized these programs to make sure that the students who place such a touching hope in their success are not being intellectually shortchanged?

I cannot answer these questions with confidence in the absence of a thoroughgoing national study, but I can report my impression that faculty members in general are not anxious to pose these questions. They are not anxious to make a public show of placing rigorous academic constraints on these or other forms of educational innovation. I have not yet seen any clothes on the Emperor, but the point is that I am unable to arouse much interest in the question of whether he has any on. It is rather as if we have tacitly conceded that the purpose of these programs is not primarily academic but political, that they were designed to satisfy the essentially political demands of various insurgent minority groups and have little or nothing to do with serious intellectual efforts. If that is the case, I believe we should say so and abandon our present hypocritical stance.

Let me give an example from my personal experience of the kind of faculty attitudes I am discussing. (Incidentally, I use these autobiographical examples, not because my own experience has been especially rich in academic atrocities, but because I can speak with more confidence and authority about cases I have actually lived through.) The famous Eldridge Cleaver course at the University of California seemed to me to have rather low academic standards; however, it had been approved as an experimental course through regular procedures. The Board of Regents, in a clear violation of academic freedom, attempted to deprive the course of academic credit on political grounds; and, as I was chairman of the Academic Freedom Committee at the time, I was heavily involved in its defense. I was happy to defend the course because I am willing to defend the right of my colleagues to institute academic experiments even when I think they are imbecilic. My contempt for the intellectual level of the course did not diminish my enthusiasm for defending the right of the faculty and students to have it. Much larger issues were involved than the quality of this course. However, I did make a statement to the campus newspaper to the effect that, while it was obvious that we had to defend the course on grounds of academic freedom, it was a dumb course. Many of my colleagues were outraged that I would say in public that it was a dumb course. "Well, don't you agree that it is a dumb course?" I asked. "Of course, we agree that it is dumb, but you must not say in public that it is a dumb course."

Each of us, no doubt, has his own litany of atrocity stories, and I have no desire to heap anecdote upon anecdote. Rather, the question I want to pose is: How are we to explain these curious lapses from standards in the two areas closest to the academic bone—academic freedom and intellectual standards? What is it that has made us respond so feebly to the challenges of the past decade? If one were looking for mere "causes," there are certain obvious ones such as the Vietnam war, the racial crisis, and the various headline topics of the 1960s. Professors proved to be almost as vulnerable to the intellectually unsettling effects of social upheavals as students were. These moments of hysteria provoked recurring lapses from rationality.

It has been repeatedly argued that because the war and other problems are so frightful, somehow attacks on academic freedom and intellectual standards are justified or are at least excusable. A typical specimen of this form of argument occurred in a recent review of a book by

Professor and Mrs. Handlin. The reviewer argued that the Handlins were unjustified in their criticism of the more extreme forms of radical behavior because such criticism ignored the fact that there was a war in Vietnam and a racial crisis at home. The assumptions behind this line of reasoning are so grotesque one is never quite sure of how seriously it is intended. One assumption is that somehow it is all right to burn down university buildings and disrupt classes as long as one is doing it with the intent of ending the war in Vietnam or putting a stop to racial injustice. Either there is an enormous logical gap in this argument or else its advocates have a most extraordinary hypothesis about the nature of the political process. I believe the underlying structure of the argument is what I have elsewhere called the two-wrongs fallacy: because the war and racism are so dreadful, it is acceptable and indeed justifiable to engage in further irrational and malicious behavior, however remote this behavior may be from having any effect on either.

A second feature of the response to the events of the past decade has to do with the characteristics of the professoriat. During a crisis one discovers that many of our colleagues are rather timid souls. It is much easier in terms of one's own personal life to defend the rights of fashionable left-wing heroes such as Angela Davis than it is to defend the rights of one's colleagues to do research on behalf of the Defense Department or the CIA. I find the activities of both Miss Davis and the Department of Defense researchers more or less repellent, but that is not the point. The point is that there is far more social pressure in favor of the former than in favor of the latter. There is a certain irony here, in that if one defends fashionable left-wing views or even the right of people to be free to express these views, one generally is hailed as being remarkably courageous. But at present, unlike the situation during the McCarthy era, it takes no courage whatsoever, as is quite obvious to anyone familiar with the winds of opinion on university campuses. But when one takes a truly courageous position and defends the right of one's colleagues and students not to have their classes disrupted by left-wing activists, this is regarded as taking the easy way out, as selling out to the establishment, or worse.

Social pressures on professors from both students and faculty have been quite remarkable. I believe that what Merton calls the "locals" are more vulnerable to these pressures than the "cosmopolitans," because, professionally speaking, the students are the only clientele the locals have. This makes them reluctant to place themselves in an adversary relation to a large number of an important, opinion-making element among the students. But even as cosmopolitans, we are not such free spirits, and there is a large percentage of prudent men among us. There is hardly any question about what the course of prudence has been in the past few years: it has been to go along with the prevailing rhetorical climate.

These factors then—the social upheavals of the past decade and a cautious and timid reluctance to fight hard for one's values—are part of any explanation of the phenomena we are describing. But they are by no means the whole story. There has been a loss of nerve in our sense of mission, in our confidence in our official philosophy of higher education. The traditional theory of a liberal education in this country, a theory that culminated after the end of World War II, was that the undergraduate student acquired a general education in those areas of knowledge that were supposed to be a requirement for any educated person, together with a more specialized knowledge of his major subject. The core of the general education was usually a corpus of "Western culture," or "Western civilization," together with certain basic intellectual skills such as the ability to write English prose or speak and read a foreign language. From Stanford to Columbia, the better universities instituted required courses and even special programs (such as the Wisconsin Integrated Liberal Studies Program) built around this philosophy of undergraduate education.

Now, for a variety of reasons this theory has exhausted itself. Many requirements that universities used to impose routinely on undergraduates have now been abandoned, and the courses that were supposed to give people a broad general education are now taught in a perfunctory and uninspired manner by junior professors, because senior faculty members don't want to teach these "service" courses for "nonmajors." Man's great cultural achievements are more and more being conveyed by bored junior faculty to equally bored and even rebellious students.

The traditional philosophy of a liberal education has not been refuted; nor, indeed, has it been superseded by a more rigorous and penetrating conception of how undergraduates should be taught. It has simply lost much of its appeal. The interesting thing about our present situation is that, though we are now under more pressure for educational reform than at any previous time in my lifetime, most of us are without a coherent philosophy of higher education. This means that, in this period of great demand for educational reform and innovation, most of us have no articulated and coherent set of standards by which to judge proposals for new educational programs. All kinds of feeble educational projects are permitted to move into a vacuum, because there is no coherent educational ideology to oppose them.

As an experiment to test your colleagues' capacity to withstand assaults on higher education, I suggest you try the following: ask your fellow researchers to articulate their philosophy of undergraduate education. What intellectual objectives do they try to achieve in their own undergraduate courses and how do these objectives fit into the overall objectives of undergraduate education? I would predict that a sizable percentage will not be able to give very impressive answers to these obvious questions; they simply never give these matters a thought. They are much more concerned with pursuing their own research and working with their graduate students. It is, in part, this absence of any well-defined set of educational objectives that gives rise to the attitude one hears over and over again in discussions of educational change. "Look, the kids want it, and besides, we've got to be willing to experiment. After all, are we opposed to educational experimentation?"

Turning from educational reform to academic freedom, I think the events of the past decade have uncovered some interesting inadequacies in what, for want of less rebarbative jargon, I shall call the "liberal mode of sensibility." The single worst effect, internally, during the period of campus unrest was the creation of more or less permanent attitudes of hostility and mistrust among various factions in university faculties. I am constantly amazed to find attitudes of bitterness and resentment persisting to this day about battles that occurred many years ago. Partly, this occurred because the leaders on *both* sides in these battles tended to be drawn from the ranks of what used to be called liberals. From the faculty point of view, the battles were characteristically civil wars of academic liberalism, and they engendered the passionate hostilities characteristic of civil wars. The other side seemed not merely wrong, but traitors, betrayers of sacred principles.

In the mid-sixties, most senior liberal professors in our universities had certain paradigms of what constituted an issue of academic freedom and certain paradigms of what constituted a defense of academic freedom in the public or academic arena. We have in this country a long history of great fights for academic freedom, and they almost always have one thing in common. They are almost always defenses of the rights of left-wing or radical nonconformists against the attacks of a right-wing establishment outside the university or in authority within the university. The result of this is a kind of hardening of categories, as many liberal professors tend, more or less unconsciously, to define the struggle for academic freedom as an attempt to defend the rights of the dissenting Left against the establishment Right. For many of our colleagues, it has been quite unthinkable that attacks on academic freedom could come from left-wing sources and even from left-wing students inside the university. Such events simply could not get over the threshold of their perceptual apparatus. The dramatic categories possessed by many of those with the liberal mode of sensibility were not adequate to cope with the events. For many of the people who fought hard against McCarthyism and resisted loyalty oaths, it is too bitter a pill to swallow that their new enemies come from a quarter from whence they usually drew their allies. What broke the unity of academic liberalism—such unity as there ever was—was the fact that many other liberals do possess a consistent position on the subject of academic freedom. They are as ready to defend these values against attacks from the Left as they are from the Right. For them, academic freedom is a formal concept, which Jensen and Huntington have as much right to as do Angela Davis and Eldridge Cleaver. For this reason, the civil war of academic liberalism over the subjects of student disruption and academic freedom was, in large measure, a fight over the double standard.

Another feature that led to a certain feebleness in the defense of academic freedom, as well as the defense of intellectual standards, stems from the peculiar organization of authority and decision-making in American universities. I hardly need remind anyone that, in almost all American universities, final governmental authority rests in a lay board of trustees, which delegates administrative authority to an "administration" consisting of president, deans, department chairmen, and such. In theory, the administration is independent of the faculty, who have their own little corner of authority separate from the administration. This organizational structure is a gem for theorists of social institutions in that it manages to be both incoherent in theory and—in the 1960s at least—disastrous in practice. I have attacked it at length in *The Campus War* and will not repeat the criticisms here.

The most important consequence of this system (at least as far as our present discussion goes) is that it encourages the faculty member to believe that he is not responsible for defending the university's intellectual standards and protecting academic freedom from antiadministration sources. If some students are misbehaving or if some educational program is not maintaining decent intellectual standards, surely, reasons the faculty member, that is the responsibility of the administration and not his responsibility. The artificial separation of educational authority, which necessarily lies with the faculty member, from administrative responsibility, which constitutionally devolves upon the administration, encourages the faculty in a sense of isolation from the immediate crisis of university authority and in an attitude of indifference to the long-run welfare of the university.

For example, most faculty members do not regard the current HEW affirmative-action programs as their problem; it is an administration problem. This indifference to questions of the general welfare of the university would not be so bad if the administration actually had the power to maintain rigorous standards and protect academic freedom.

But it is quite obvious from the events of the past decade that, in a crisis of authority, the constitutional delegation of authority from the trustees to the administration is simply not sufficient to govern the university effectively; witness the careers of Clark Kerr, Grayson Kirk, and Nathan Pusey, for example.

Not only does the artificial separation of powers in the university encourage the faculty member to be indifferent to the welfare of the institution, it actually engenders an attitude of mistrust and hostility toward the administration. Most liberal faculty members believe they must defend their rights against the administration, and they are in a more or less permanent adversary stance against the administration. The traditional liberal paradigms of the battle for academic freedom— that it is essentially a struggle against established authority—combines with the artificially induced adversary relation between the administration and faculty to further weaken the liberal faculty's ability to defend intellectual standards and academic freedom from attacks by anti-administration sources.

One could continue this analysis of the faculty role more or less indefinitely. I have been concerned chiefly to point out those failures of sensibility, of philosophical clarity, of rationality and understanding that have led to the weaknesses of the faculty I mentioned at the beginning. There is one last feature that I want to mention. Most faculty members do not have an overall intellectual grasp of the events of the sixties. To some, it seems that their universities went through a more or less unrelated series of upheavals: here, it was the draft or ROTC; there, it was Dow Chemical or Black studies. Earlier, it was racial problems; later, it concerned the Cambodian invasion. It seemed, so to speak, "one damned thing" after another. I disagree.

I think that, insofar as these events involved assaults on the university—and most of them did—they sprang from a more or less coherent vision of what the attackers want the university to be. Often, the vision is only partly conscious and seldom is it clearly articulated. It is a vision of the university as a kind of youth city, a city-state of the young. The ideal of the youth city is that the university ought to be converted into a city-state, whose primary population consists of young people between the ages of about eighteen and thirty. Like all democratic states, it ought to be governed on the principle of one man, one vote; and like all city-states, it ought to have a foreign policy and a domestic policy. Its foreign policy will be to try to change the larger outside society to conform to the values of the citizenry of the youth city; its domestic policy will be to provide for the individual self-realization of its citizens, to get rid of their psychological hangups, to help them over identity crises, and so on. There is to be nothing essentially intellectual about the youth city. There may, of course, be some citizens who are "into" mathematics or history, just as others are "into" Zen or macrobiotic cooking. For some people the intellectual "bag" is their "bag," but others need have no commitment to intellectuality at all.

It is this concept of the university as a city-state of the young that gives rise to much of the demand for more student power: in the ideal youth city, one man, one vote, as in any democratic polity. Minority populations—faculty, janitors, secretaries, and so forth—have a right to vote but no special right to govern.

One of the most striking things about many American professors in the sixties was their hand-wringing timidity and inarticulateness in the face of the twin demands of the youth-city partisans for "student power" and "relevance." Lacking a coherent theory of the university or a philosophy of higher education, many of them were no match for the passionate advocates of the youth city. I believe that the notion of the university as a youth city should be met head on. The university is not a general institution like a city or a country; it is a specialized institution like a hospital or an airline. Its special purposes are the advancement and dissemination of knowledge. As a special-purpose institution dedicated to intellectual values, it is not a democracy but an aristocracy; more precisely, it is an aristocracy of the trained intellect. Since Americans tend to be panacea democrats anyway (even at this symposium I have heard a great deal about how democratic the university ought to be), it is important to hammer this point home: The university is not, by its very nature, a democratic institution; it has an inherent class structure. And though our existing universities no doubt fall far short of the ideal, the ideal we are aiming at is not that of the youth city, but the aristocracy of intellect.

NOTES

1. Limitations of space force me to deal here rather briefly with several complex topics. A more detailed discussion can be found in my book *The Campus War* (New York: World Publishing, 1971).

Collective Bargaining in Higher Education

John H. Bunzel
*California State University,
San Jose*

One of the most significant developments in the field of education during the past decade has been the growing interest among professional educators in collective bargaining as a method of influencing the disposition of issues affecting their professional lives. First to take root and flourish among elementary- and secondary-school teachers, the seeds of collective bargaining have, within recent years, been borne on the winds of faculty discontent onto college and university campuses, where they have found fertile soil. The emergence of university faculty organizations espousing collective-bargaining objectives has posed a challenge to existing decision-making arrangements and patterns of institutional governance. The halls of academe have echoed with responsive, often vigorous debate, while faculty clubs have simmered with more muted expressions of concern and with discussions of the import and impact of this new phenomenon.

THE STATE OF COLLECTIVE BARGAINING

One of the more noteworthy responses to the challenge of collective bargaining has been the American Association for Higher Education's study of faculty influence and governance in higher education. The 1967 report by its prestigious task force gave support to internal partici-

Note: I should like to express my gratitude to Professor George Halverson for his invaluable assistance on the original and later drafts of this paper.

patory arrangements based on a concept of "shared authority." Although the task force acknowledged that one such arrangement could be collective bargaining, it clearly gave preference to the consensual form, typified by a faculty senate.[1] Noneconomic issues, particularly those related to faculty participation in internal decision-making, were given more weight in the report as sources of faculty dissatisfaction than were strictly economic and personnel issues. Since 1967, however, economic and personnel issues appear to have become far more potent sources of dissatisfaction, while noneconomic issues have not decreased but, if anything, have increased in severity.[2] Concurrently, and no doubt partly as a result of these circumstances, the movement toward collective bargaining has grown in prominence and strength.

Scanning the collective-bargaining movement in higher education today, we find three principal geographical centers of activity: the states of New York and New Jersey, the state of Michigan, and the Chicago area. The movement is by no means limited to these areas, however, and the situation is anything but static.[3] Whether desirable or not, pressures to recast faculty-administration relationships in the collective-bargaining mold—or something akin to it—may be expected, if they have not already appeared, on almost every large college or university campus.

Of the roughly twenty-five hundred accredited institutions of higher learning in the United States, about one hundred and sixty were estimated in 1972 to have been covered by collective-bargaining contracts, although not all conform to the conventional model of such contracts in nonacademic organizations.[4] As an educated guess, some forty-five to fifty thousand members of college and university faculties are included in established and recognized collective-bargaining units—approximately 10 per cent of the total teaching faculty across the country.[5] The movement has made greatest headway in New York State.[6] Among the reasons for New York's preeminence (besides factors affecting faculties generally, which will be discussed later) are (1) a favorable climate for faculty unionism, created by the existence of a strong and influential industrial trade-union movement throughout the state, (2) the extensive and intensive union activity among teachers in the New York City public-school system, and (3) the existence of a state public-employee-relations law (the Taylor Act), which gives legal sanction to collective bargaining in public jurisdictions.[7]

The collective-bargaining movement has staked out a firmer beachhead and grown more rapidly in the publicly funded sector of higher education than in the privately funded sector. One reason is that the movement has claimed its earliest and most aggressive support from among faculties of two-year community colleges, which, in the main, derive their funds from tax sources.[8] But the movement honors no boundary between public and private institutions. Private institutions, however, are not subject to state laws governing public-employee representation, as are public institutions, but rather to the Federal National Labor Relations Act administered by the National Labor Relations Board.[9] Because the NLRB occupies a preeminent place in the legal structure governing collective bargaining in the United States, its decisions have tended to shape, in the industrial image, the evolution of legal concepts applied to educational institutions. These decisions do not appear to have fully recognized the unique characteristics of these institutions as compared with industrial enterprises. As a result, faculty-administration relationships are viewed legally more in the employee-employer context than in the "professional collegial" frame of reference.

HIGHER EDUCATION AND SOCIETY

To put the present-day, academic collective-bargaining movement in perspective requires a brief review of the change in character of higher education in American society over the last two centuries. A view of the university as a community of scholars, somewhat remote from everyday life and the ebb and flow of social forces and drawn together to pursue intellectual inquiry and teach students, who become part of the community as a center of learning, has its roots deep in the culture and civilization of Western Europe. it is, admittedly, a somewhat idealized and simplistic view of most American universities, past and present.

During the colonial period, colleges were carefully controlled by the dominant forces of a conservative colonial society. They were little more than secondary schools, and their faculties were composed more of teachers than scholars. During the middle half of the nineteenth century, a rash of new colleges erupted. Many were founded by individuals and groups, often religious in orientation, responding to a "call" to serve mankind. Trustees and presidents tended to dominate these institutions in order to shape them to the philosophy and goals of the founders. Their faculties were not marked by a high degree of professionalism, either in training or in goals and standards. Tenure was a rarity. "The vision of a college professor as an independent expert with a mission transcending the college where he happened to teach was almost unknown."[10]

With the rise of a society based on industrial technology in the later nineteenth and early twentieth centuries, American higher education underwent a metamorphosis. It took on a more established and enduring framework, undergirded by more adequate and diversified sources of funds. These changes were accompanied by a professionalization of the faculty, a shift from a solely teaching role to one of scholarship. The emergence of larger and more stable institutions and more professionally oriented faculties generated many pressures to curb the powers of administrators and the intrusions of trustees. Many such struggles took place, the cumulative effect of which was that the faculties at many institutions carved out a large sphere of influence over educational policies and professional personnel matters. Even today, however, this situation is not yet universal throughout American higher education. Great diversity reigns in the degree and scope of faculty influence and the extent of self-governance, ranging all the way from highly developed systems of "shared authority" at prestigious universities to virtually no faculty participation at some community colleges.

The evolution of a complex industrial socioeconomic system in the United States, with its egalitarian and utilitarian strains, has brought higher education into a closer and more integrated relationship with society. "Education," wrote Arnold Toynbee, "was bound to come to be thought of, no longer as a preserve for an elite dedicated to particular 'liberal' professions, but as a ladder up which everyone has a right to climb as far as he has the ability. . . . [University] education has come to be thought of as an education for everyman."[11]

Colleges and universities responded early to the rapid industrialization and rationalization of society by accepting the responsibility for supplying the educated and highly trained manpower upon which this development depended. Campuses have become the gateway for "opportunity for all," in what has evolved as an essentially middle-class society, and the streams of young people pouring through the campus gates have forced a great expansion of our system of higher education, financed to a great extent by massive injections of public funds. More and more, these institutions have been asked to serve the continuing educational needs of their respective communities through extension programs, institutes, conferences, and various special programs of professional and vocational development. Research being conducted at colleges and universities, both theoretical and applied, has become increasingly more oriented to the needs of society and less to the personal whims of the scholar in search of new knowledge. Professors in ever larger numbers have been called from the classroom to perform an endless array of public services. In sum, there has been created what may properly be called the "knowledge industry." [12]

CONDITIONS GIVING RISE TO COLLECTIVE BARGAINING

These characteristics of higher education in American society bear a relationship to the emerging collective-bargaining phenomenon in the academic world. First, there is the growth of individual institutions and of whole systems. The expansion has been particularly acute during the past two decades. Private institutions, freer to control their own destinies, have been affected the least. Publicly supported institutions, however, which are more directly influenced by public policies reflecting society's educational needs and objectives, have had to absorb the major part of the surge of youth into higher education.

One effect has been a huge growth in existing four-year institutions. This has led to a necessary formalization of administrative policies, practices, and relationships. Internal patterns of communication have become more complex and subject to pressures and breakdowns. As the gap between faculty and administration has widened, the preceptions of each side held by the other have grown more fixed and stereotyped. A college president today is seen by the bulk of the faculty, more likely than not, as a remote figure in an executive suite they rarely visit—a figure who is more a symbol of power than a human being. The problems of management of such institutions have increased in number, variety, and complexity. These conditions have forced a certain tightening of some administrative practices, which tend to be perceived by the faculty as cramping their professional style and limiting their accustomed freedom.

All too frequently, the machinery for faculty participation in institutional governance has functioned too slowly and too cumbersomely to enable institutions to deal most effectively with problems created by new conditions. This deficiency is seen by many faculty to be particularly true when matters "involving professional working conditions are in question." [13] As a result, some segments of the faculty have become disenchanted with faculty senates and other traditional participatory arrangements, which they think tinker superficially with, but do not actually solve, problems affecting their professional lives." [14]

Another consequence of the vast increase in demand for higher education has been the creation of large multi-institutional systems supported by public funds, such as the State University of New York and the California State University and Colleges systems. The conditions brought on by bigness in individual institutions assume macrocosmic scale in such systems. Superimposed on the administrative structure of each college in the system is an overarching administrative superstructure, which is responsible for molding a coterie of colleges into an integrated system bound together by legal structures, a unitary budget, and a common set of policies and administrative controls. It is easier for many faculty members in such an institutional environment to regard themselves as *employees* of a remote employer, rather than as *colleagues* in an educational enterprise. Another seat of power, farther removed from influence by local faculties, has been added to those on individual campuses. Pressured by state legislatures and governors to achieve efficiency through uniformity, the trustees and system administrators are prone to issue directives that are not always suited to local conditions. Local faculties (and, it should be added, campus administrators) react with dissatisfaction and feelings of impotence as system uniformity clashes with local diversity.

The tremendous influx of new faculty needed for the expansion of higher education has changed the tone of collegial relationships on individual campuses. Large-scale hiring has reduced the capacity of the institution to absorb new faculty into an existing professional culture. The newcomers are not so easily conditioned by the attitudes, traditions, and ways of behaving that make up a culture shaped by senior faculty with established careers. We find the clustering of faculty into a younger group and an older group, each reflecting differences in professional attitudes and, to some extent, values. Each group finds itself vying with the other for influence in shaping policy, as it relates to career aspirations and working conditions.[15]

Another result of the relationship between American higher education and society, which bears on the movement toward collective bargaining, is the shift from predominantly private to predominantly public funding. A small number of private colleges and universities are still in a position to retain an isolated independence behind a barrier of private endowments. But the vast majority of public institutions are subject to a form of accountability born of their dependence on public funds. This situation has led to what Claude T. Bissell has described as "the governmentalization of higher education."[16]

Administrative changes required in response to demands by state legislatures, government agencies, and private foundations for fiscal accounting and operational efficiency have increased the number of administrators needed in educational institutions and—or so the faculty think—the power they wield. These developments have a tendency to upset the traditional balance between academic affairs and administrative support activities, and the faculty find it more difficult to maintain their assumption that the main task of administrators is to support academic activities.[17] Some academic professionals think that they are coming out second best in a shift of power within the institution, and they fear, as a result, that their traditional freedom and flexibility will continue to be eroded.

Public funding of institutions of higher education has affected the perceived professional status of professors in those institutions. To the taxpayer, the legislator, and the government official, they are public servants and are expected to fit the usual image of the civil servant responsible to the public for his behavior and performance. While resisting this stereotype when it impinges adversely on their professional role, many faculty members are influenced by the rapid spread of unionization among public employees at all levels of government, especially when public authorities are yielding to pressures to adopt collective bargaining in one form or another. If they are to be cast in the mold of public employees, they ask, why then should they not join other public employees on the collective-bargaining bandwagon? The temptation becomes greater as the benefits achieved by organized employees, in private as well as in public employment, continue to grow.[18]

The close relationship between higher education and society has had yet another result. The modern college or university "is more and more a microcosm of our society."[19] Social unrest and social forces pressing for change permeate the campus, as they do society. One of the crucial issues in higher education today relates to the role of the university in a time of social turmoil. Some argue that it should become an instrument of social and political change. Fortunately for the preservation of the integrity of higher education, the proponents of this view represent only a small minority of the total faculty at any institution. However, many of their colleagues, while rejecting the idea of "politicizing the campus," are left with uneasy concerns regarding the neutrality of the university in the face of what they believe are basic moral questions on the Vietnam war, war-related research on their campuses, and the allocation of societal resources to defense and space exploration. They are disturbed also by the paucity of resources diverted to the alleviation of poverty and unemployment, to the solution of minority problems, and to the check on the continued despoliation of our natural environment.

There is an increasing tendency to apply to the college or university the same political and legal forms that are built into the fabric of our democratic society. This is evidenced by attempts on the part of faculty organizations to have academic personnel policies, including faculty grievance and disciplinary procedures, recast in a legalistic mold corresponding to the legal concepts and structure of society's other institutions. Such attempts overlook the differences between society as a pluralistic system of social and political relationships, on

163

the one hand, and an institution within that system with specific operational objectives, on the other.

The "pluralism of contemporary society," says William Boyd "is replicated on our campuses and reflected in a pluralism of goals."[20] The result has been the diffusion of what were once held to be common professional and academic goals and the dilution of a "shared sense of purpose." Authority has become suspect and accustomed professional relationships confused. Traditional attitudes and methods are no longer seen as legitimate or potent. Such a climate fosters a mood of uncertainty and a casting about for new ways out of uncomfortable dilemmas. Many academic professionals, nursing a variety of other dissatisfactions, view collective bargaining as an option that may provide qualities of firmness and certainty to the academic climate. One may question, however, how thoughtful their evaluation has been in weighing perceived gains against costs to the academic community.

The last few years have witnessed a marked deterioration in the external environment in which educational institutions function. This change has undoubtedly caused a number of faculty members to view collective bargaining with favor. The "taxpayers' revolt," severe inflationary pressures, and the recent decline in economic activity in the United States have adversely affected the economic condition of both public and private educational institutions. This combination of circumstances has led recently to a reduction in the rate of increase in faculty positions (and, in some cases, an actual reduction in positions); a lag in salary improvements; and pressures for larger classes, more time spent in the classroom, and the scheduling of classes over more hours of the day. Many institutions are suffering from reduced financial support for research from governmental and foundation sources. Pressures to reduce costs are adversely affecting educational programs and methods, posing a serious threat to the maintenance of the quality of education at desired levels. Faculties are beginning to experience cost-reduction layoffs even of tenured professors.[21] And they see ominous threats to their independence in the mounting criticism by the public and by some students of the time-honored institution of academic tenure.

These conditions have combined to undermine the economic security and professional status of the faculty, especially those most affected by the significant shift in the supply-demand pattern in the academic labor market during the last half of the 1960s. At the same time that institutional growth, with its generation of new academic jobs, tapered off, the Ph.D. population exploded. Those who have been able to obtain academic appointments find that they have less assurance of eventually receiving tenure—even of continuing to receive renewals during probationary periods at the same institutions. Those with tenure find promotion slow in coming. The result has been a sprouting of criticism of the traditional peer-evaluation process, which many younger faculty members see as a device employed by senior faculty members to maintain entrenched control at the departmental level.[22] In a more favorable academic labor market, many dissatisfied faculty members would probably react to these conditions by looking for jobs in other, and perhaps for them more compatible, institutions. In today's tight job market they find this option virtually closed to them, and some, wisely or not, look to collective bargaining as a way to improve their condition.

SOME IMPACTS

The cumulative effect of the many circumstances and conditions that fuel faculty interest in collective bargaining is to emphasize the "employee" role of the faculty over the "collegial" role. One of the likely impacts of collective bargaining in higher education derives from this shift of emphasis.

Industrial union-management relations exist in an institutional environment marked by a clear distinction between managerial personnel, who possess management responsibility and authority, and non-managerial employees, who normally do not share in either. In this sense, the former are collectively the "employers" and the latter are the "employees."[23] The difference between employer-employee relationships in such an organization and the traditional faculty-administration relationships in an academic institution is clear, although it must be admitted that this distinction is not always found in the pure form implied here. In most institutions of higher education, especially four-year colleges and the universities, there exists at least a fair degree of "shared authority," based upon a collegial relationship between faculty and administrators. In many institutions, of course, it exists in a highly developed form. In the main, the faculty determine how they shall carry on their professional work within the context of a set of minimal institutional requirements. Faculty members are partners with administrators in their influence on educational policy and on personnel decisions affecting the jobs and careers of their faculty colleagues. They participate, through various forms of governance, in shaping the goals and programs of the institution. Professor Clyde Summers, commenting on the uniqueness of the academic institution, described it as "a strange animal . . . where the employees determine the raw materials to come in, productive processes to be used and the procedures to change the raw material into the finished product."[24]

In its purest form, the relationship between the faculty and administration is one of colleagues sharing a common sense of purpose, working together to shape and implement policy, and jointly influencing the programs and goals of the institution. This collegial relationship depends upon open sharing of information, appeals to reason, and mutual acceptance of the ideal of community.

One result of collective bargaining is likely to be the injection of an adversary quality into this relationship. Neil W. Chamberlain, a respected authority on industrial relations, described the essential nature of collective bargaining in these words: "Collective bargaining is a power relationship. The resolution of differences between union and management rests on the balance of the relative bargaining powers of the two parties. This power aspect of industrial relations is fundamental and inescapable. An effort to conceive of the collective-bargaining process in other terms is sure to lead to error."[25]

In sparring for advantage, each party will undoubtedly tend to become more firmly defined in a role, at the expense of the pluralistic nature of the relationships in a less structured context. The administration may find it impossible to deal directly with individuals and faculty groups on matters of mutual concern relating to issues covered by collective-bargaining agreements. Such matters will have to be funneled through the official and legally established machinery of faculty representation. In order to preserve its options at the bargaining table, the administration may well be forced into a defensive posture on certain matters of joint concern, withholding information that previously was released freely to the faculty. In some cases, the administration may find it necessary, or at least strategically desirable, to retreat behind a barrier of "management rights," in order to draw a clear line between what is subject to bargaining and what is not. The result could be the closing of opportunities for the faculty to exert influence in making many decisions. Decisions involving the differential allocation of budgetary resources for various academic purposes not covered by a collective-bargaining contract might have to be reserved for unilateral administrative determination, because such decisions might relate to other matters with financial dimensions that must be dealt with at the bargaining table.[26] There is even the possibility that the professional freedom of faculty members to teach what they want to teach, and to do so in the manner in which they want to, may be restricted. In at least one case, course content has already been the subject of discussion in bargaining negotiations.[27]

The "power relationship" described earlier would seem to represent the antithesis of the collegial relationship traditionally found in colleges and universities with professionally oriented faculties. Not always, however, does either exist in pure form. In spite of the fundamental reality postulated by Chamberlain, industrial unions have been known to work with management in cooperative efforts to deal with matters where their mutual interests have taken precedence over their differences. And the interests of faculties and administrators are not always so identical and harmonious as to preclude conflict in which relative power is a factor, however subtly it may be employed.

On balance, it seems clear that collective bargaining will introduce qualities of formalism and rigidity into faculty-administration relationships, which will militate against the formulation of policy and the resolution of issues in the traditional collegial spirit. These developments may not occur, however, without some compensating advantages. The machinery of faculty institutional governance, for all its benefits and values in a professional situation, does tend to function with frustrating slowness. Although the committee device permits differences to be aired and harmonized and usually produces results that reflect a workable acceptance by most diverse faculty groups, it sometimes leaves problems and issues ambiguous in their definition and yields results too diluted by the need to "come up with something" to be realistically implemented. On essentially administrative matters, the input by committee members, who in most cases have been drawn from their primary academic concerns, sometimes reflects a lack of requisite knowledge of such matters, of expertise in dealing with their complexities, and of sufficient application of time and attention to produce high-quality solutions. The reverse, however, is more likely to be true when the faculty is involved in determining educational policies and methods; there, the entire justification for direct faculty participation rests on the possession of expertise

Under collective bargaining, on the other hand, there is the possibility that faculty representatives in negotiations, buttressed by paid expert assistance, will approach administrative (management) problems with degrees of interest, involvement, and sophistication beyond that of most participants in voluntary governance systems. By its nature, collective bargaining may make for clearer definition of issues and resolution of differences, however related they may be to tactical considerations. Fewer committee reports may be left forgotten in files and fewer recommendations left dangling in limbo. When matters are decided, they will be implemented at a certain time.

Faculties and administrations at institutions with developed systems of "shared authority" based on consensual traditions may lose some of the cherished benefits of those systems in a shift to collective bargaining; but at institutions where such systems are either immaturely developed or, for all practical purposes, nonexistent, little if anything may be lost, at least in the eyes of the faculty. In fact, the faculty may look upon collective bargaining as offering them a chance to obtain a degree of influence they had not previously enjoyed. This may be particularly true in the case of institutions where administrators have used their powers with insufficient sensitivity to real faculty concerns. Such a possibility should cause administrators to take heed. If they wish to avoid faculty participation through collective bargaining, they should take steps to establish, without delay, effective "shared authority" arrangements.

Under collective bargaining, decisions will be arrived at more in the spirit of trading than in a spirit of consensus based on the mutual exploration and evaluation of the merits of issues. The university will pay a heavy price for this change of emphasis in the decision-making process. In the words of one authority, decisions will be the product of a "process of proposal and counter-proposal, of action and reaction, of give and take—resulting finally in 'deal' or 'no deal,' in agreement or stalemate."[28] Collective bargaining will tend to elevate tactical maneuvering over rational analysis and to give predominance to factors external to the instrinsic elements of an issue over those dictated by the internal logic of the issue. At the bargaining table the ultimate objective of arriving at an overall "package settlement" works against the reasoned approach to each issue on its merits. This change in style will be hard for those faculty members imbued with ideals and habits of rational analysis, especially in an atmosphere of conflict, when the bargaining gets tough and the threat of strike is in the air.[29]

In the final analysis, collective bargaining is a process in which the relative balance of power between the parties is the primary factor determining the resolution of conflict. When bargaining is adopted at academic institutions, this portends the incursion of outside influences into the decision-making process. The ultimate pressure tactic is the strike or lockout. Although neither is likely to be used frequently, since professional people (especially in the university) do not easily take to such tactics, whenever either *is* used, the resulting situation immediately becomes a serious community concern. Parents and community leaders—and, in publicly supported institutions, state officials and legislators—will attempt to influence the parties in an effort to end the conflict. This will be especially true in states where a strike by public employees is illegal.

Other devices short of the strike are more likely to be employed. These could also have the effect of injecting outside influences into the resolution of academic issues. The faculty union could appeal to the public to bring pressure on the "employer." This could be done in a number of ways, including direct appeals for improved employment or other conditions on campus, mass failure of faculty to report to campus because of "illness" or other alleged reasons,[30] and joint student-faculty meetings and demonstrations designed to create an impression of "campus furor" to embarrass the administration. Another tactic that might be employed by the faculty union would be to seek the support of the local labor council for funds and some type of sympathetic action (for example, asking the Teamsters Union to refuse to make deliveries of food and other materials to the campus or a building-trades union to refuse to do repair or maintenance work). But such support is purchased at a price, for it means that the faculty union must be prepared to support strikes by other unions attempting to pressure the college administration or that unionized faculty engage in sympathy strikes in the outside community. In the view of one industrial-relations authority who lives in the academic world, that price would "almost certainly be considered by many in the academic fraternity as being too high."[31]

Outside influence could be brought to bear on internal decision-making in yet another way: the faculty union could appeal directly for outside political support. This would make most sense where public academic institutions are involved. Leaders of faculty unions are likely to be sensitive to the nature of the political process in a democracy. In one sense, collective bargaining itself is a kind of political system, and union leaders must be politically oriented and employ political tactics to achieve and function in their positions as representatives of their members. They understand that the effective mobilization of political power can be an important pressure device. Although they are inclined to oppose government intervention when it is perceived as detrimental to union objectives and faculty interests, faculty bargaining representatives will be strongly tempted to solicit political support to bring pressure on the administration when it can be used to advantage.

Another possibility of influencing internal decision-making by outside intervention is the use of fact-finding boards and arbitrators to resolve conflicts between the parties. Inquiry and reporting by a fact-finding board are less influential, because the findings and decisions are not binding on the parties, whereas under arbitration they are. Whether voluntarily constituted by the administration and the faculty union or imposed by outside authority, fact-finding boards exert pressure by hearing the arguments of both sides and then making public a report of their findings. The report may be accompanied by recommendations for the settlement of unresolved issues. While neither side is bound to accept the recommendations, the recalcitrant party usually feels a strong public or political pressure either to do so or to let the report influence further negotiations. Although binding arbitration is not often used to resolve basic contract issues (both sides want to avoid having terms dictated by a "third party"), it is customarily employed to achieve final resolution of differences on contract interpretation or employee grievances.

Both of these processes of conflict resolution run counter to ideals and traditions of collegial self-governance. They open educational and other professional issues to the weight of influence or ultimate decision-making by outside parties, who may be unfamiliar with the academic world and insensitive to important academic considerations. Certain safeguards may reduce this disadvantage: exempting some issues of educational policy or faculty status (perhaps academic freedom or tenure) from being decided in this manner, or laying down clear standards and guides to be followed by the arbitrator.[32] But the fact is, a measure of internal decision-making traditionally subject to collegial determination will come under the influence of persons outside the academic world. This could have serious repercussions on how the line is drawn on matters that seriously involve academic freedom and other important issues.[33]

Consider another problem posed by collective bargaining. Who exactly is the employer with whom faculty representatives will bargain? Who constitutes management, that is, who possesses effective authority to make decisions and commitments? The question is more easily answered for private colleges and universities than for those funded by public sources. In the case of the former, the president and trustees would normally constitute the contracting authority. In the case of public institutions, the problem can be much more complicated. Would the bargaining party be the chancellor, the president, the trustees, the governor of the state, or the legislature? The budget in state-supported institutions is greatly influenced by the governor, and the power to commit funds ultimately rests with the legislature. How can realistic bargaining take place without both being involved in some stage of the process? This problem, or a comparable one at local and national levels of government, confronts all collective bargaining involving public employees.

This problem will undoubtedly be worked out in one way or another. In community colleges controlled by locally elected trustees or by local government authorities, the solution may consist in having representatives of whichever is appropriate sit as "employer representatives" at the bargaining table. Even here, implementation of agreements will inevitably depend upon the voting of funds by legislative bodies and taxpayers. In state-supported institutions the governor's office would need to be involved in some fashion, either formally or informally, before final contract terms could be formulated with some expectation of their being implemented. Again, however, the final result would depend upon the appropriation of funds by the state legislature.

Another area of impact of collective bargaining concerns professional standards and faculty personnel matters. The egalitarianism that seems inevitably associated with decision-making under collective bargaining is likely to have a leveling effect upon the application of professional standards to faculty performance. The practice of rewarding excellence and quality in individual performance may give way to, or at least be circumscribed by, demands for spreading benefits more equally among all members of the faculty. Meritorious performance and scholarly achievement may become less significant in individual tenure and promotion decisions than seniority and other generalized, but less discriminating, standards of competence. Conflict may be engendered between the "haves" and the "have-nots" in a faculty covered by a common collective agreement, resulting—if experience in industry is a parallel—in the narrowing of differentials in salary and other benefits that are based on differences in performance and career achievements.[34]

It cannot be denied that the flexibility in personnel decisions that has prevailed in academic institutions has been attended by occasional abuses of discretion, even outright discrimination and favoritism, especially in institutions marked by a low level of peer influence. Infrequently as they may occur, such abuses are found in all human systems. Collective-bargaining agreements, by reducing that flexibility, may operate to curb these practices. It will do so, however, at the price of reducing the flexibility appropriate to academic professionalism in favor of the rigidity and uniformity more characteristic of the civil service. It is also likely to do so at the expense of participation in personnel decisions, which faculties in institutions operated largely on the collegial model have become accustomed to. This will be the result where collective-bargaining agreements spell out mechanical or quantitative criteria and other restrictive guides designed to encourage uniformity in appointment, reappointment, tenure, promotion, and other personnel decisions. When agreements establish grievance machinery that terminate in arbitration by outside persons, the tendency will be to substitute legalistic interpretations for academic peer judgments.

CONCLUSION

Collective bargaining has become a much more likely possibility in higher education than was foreseen only a few years ago. It may be, as many have alleged, that it represents an "idea whose time has come."

Whether or not this prophesy comes true in any given situation will certainly depend, at least in part, on how administrators, trustees, and nonacademic authorities (government officials and legislators in the case of public institutions) react to expressed faculty dissatisfactions and aspirations.

It is probably true to say that until recent years most faculty members accepted the collegial policy-making process based on "shared authority," which had evolved on college and university campuses as higher education consolidated its position in American society in the twentieth century. It was accepted, not because it was a finely tuned and efficient instrument for making decisions, but because its characteristics were suited to the values that have traditionally permeated the academic community: the full and free flow of information, the open examination of diverse points of view, the use of reason and persuasion rather than organized pressure, and the accommodation of conflicting opinions and judgments, rather than the exercise of superior power in the form of caucuses, interest groups, or bloc-voting. Informality in the academic community, as well as the pluralistic network of relationships between faculty and administrators, has made it possible to enlist a wide range of skills and competences for the special tasks at hand. The strength of the committee system has been the way it has permitted participation to be an outgrowth of suiting the person to the task.

The university has depended upon a concept of collegial trust, which has been a powerful force in maintaining the fragile understandings among members of a professional community. The atmosphere it produced has allowed, at least until recently, the existing consensual processes to serve its needs. By and large the potential for conflict has been successfully managed and reduced through open discussion between faculty members and administrators, thus avoiding the harsher forms of influence and power.

For a variety of reasons there has been an erosion of collegial trust. Consensus as a way of academic life is being pressed to yield to adversary relationships and other forms of conflict. Informal processes of accommodation and decision-making are being replaced by more conspicuous and formal procedures. The tradition of "shared authority" appears to be held in disrepute by some elements of the faculty, with efforts being made to recast it in a design that locates power and authority in explicit terms. "Professionalism" is giving way to "institutional citizenship" as a model serving to condition faculty attitudes and behavior. In this context, collective bargaining challenges administrators and faculty to improve existing representational forms and practices so that important issues affecting the well-being of the faculty are dealt with effectively, while the essence of academic professionalism may be preserved.

Thus a critical question is raised. Will the university be able to preserve its way of life as a community of self-governing professionals, who share responsibility and authority for achieving mutually held goals? Or will it be reshaped in the image of "industrial democracy," under growing pressure from faculty unions seeking to contest their power against the power of administrators, trustees, and other public authorities cast in the role of employer? The present trend is away from a system that has subsisted on persuasion, discussion, and reason toward one that incorporates a concept of conflict resolution through the use of organization, pressure, and power.

American colleges and universities are in a crucial phase of their development. The stakes are a measure of the importance of the choice they must make.

NOTES

1. *Faculty Participation in Academic Governance,* Report of the AAHE Task Force on Faculty Representation and Academic Negotiations (Washington, D.C.: American Association for Higher Education, 1967). Composed of industrial relations specialists under the chairmanship of Arnold Weber, then professor of industrial relations at the University of Chicago, the Task Force studied 34 colleges and universities where there was evidence of faculty discontent.

2. Joseph W. Garbarino, "Precarious Professors: New Patterns of Representation," *Industrial Relations,* Feb. 1971, p. 1.

3. Considerable faculty support for collective bargaining has emerged in Massachusetts, Pennsylvania, Hawaii, and Wisconsin. In addition, scattered activity has been noted in several other states, among them Nebraska, California, New Mexico, South Dakota, Arizona, and Colorado.

4. Unpublished and undated document by Richard C. Peairs, associate secretary and director, Western Regional Office, American Association of University Professors. Garbarino estimates that the number of collective bargaining agents designated at institutions of higher education reached 130 by the summer of 1971. See Joseph W. Garbarino, "Creeping Unionism and the Faculty Labor Market," preliminary draft of a monograph prepared for the Carnegie Commission on Higher Education, p. 3.

5. Garbarino, "Creeping Unionism," p. 19.

6. Approximately one-third of the bargaining units composed of professionals in higher education are to be found in institutions in that state. They include two of the largest collective bargaining systems presently established: (1) the City University of New York system (CUNY) encompassing thirteen institutions, and (2) the State University of New York system comprising 15,000 professionals in a unit spanning 26 campuses. William F. McHugh, "Collective Bargaining With Professionals in Higher Education: Problems in Unit Determination," *Wisconsin Law Review,* 1971, No. 1, pp. 55-56. Together the units in

these two systems contain over one-half of the professionals in higher education covered by collective bargaining contracts in the United States. Garbarino, "Creeping Unionism," p. 19. As viewed by a well-known industrial trade union leader: "For teachers, signing up these big ones (CUNY and SUNY) is like the Auto Workers [Union] signing GM and Ford." Gus Tyler, "The Faculty Joins the Proletariat," *Change*, Winter 1971-72, p. 41. The author is the assistant president of the International Ladies Garment Workers Union.

7. The existence of omnibus statutes covering collective representation of college and university faculties in other states where significant activity in collective bargaining in higher education is evident (for example, in New Jersey, Michigan, Massachusetts, Hawaii, Pennsylvania, and South Dakota) has led some informed observers to conclude that such statutes do indeed give impetus to this activity. See, for example, Donald H. Wollett, "The Status and Trends of Collective Negotiations for Faculty in Higher Education," *Wisconsin Law Review*, 1971, No. 1, pp. 4-6, and Garbarino, "Precarious Professors," p. 6.

8. Since 1966, over one-half of the community colleges in Michigan have adopted collective bargaining. By 1969, 16 contracts had already been negotiated among 30 such colleges in New York State outside of New York City. The junior college system in Chicago is presently covered by a system-wide collective agreement. (McHugh, p. 55). One reason why faculties of community colleges seem to demonstrate such interest in collective bargaining may have to do with their status in relation to college administrations. Faculty influence in the shaping of educational policy through patterns of shared authority with administrators is not so well developed in community colleges compared with the traditional four-year colleges and universities. Community colleges are more likely to be governed by administrators given to directive, non-consultative styles of management, reflecting to some extent no doubt the kind of pedagogical relationships between administrators and teachers that have tended to persist in lower public schools. As a result, some community college faculties, seeking the academic status and rights of participation associated with academic professionals in the more traditional and established four-year institutions, may be tempted to see in collective bargaining a route to the achievement of such goals.

9. This situation has prevailed only since 1970. Previously private colleges and universities had floundered in a kind of legal "no man's land" as a result of a decision by the NLRB, in a case involving Columbia University in 1951, that Congress did not intend the National Labor Relations Act to apply to employees of educational institutions. In a 1970 case involving Cornell and Syracuse Universities, however, the Board, in a startling reversal of its earlier decision, asserted its jurisdiction over private colleges and universities with a gross annual revenue of $1,000,000 or more. For further details, see McHugh, p. 57, and Dexter L. Hanley, "Issues and Models for Collective Bargaining in Higher Education," *Journal of Liberal Education*, March 1971, p. 5 ff.

10. Christopher Jencks and David Riesman, *The Academic Revolution* (Garden City, N.Y.: Doubleday, 1968), p. 13. My brief review of the early development of higher education is based primarily on this work.

11. Arnold J. Toynbee, *Higher Education in a Time of Accelerating Change*, Academy for Educational Development, Paper No. 3, 1968, p. 6.

12. Clark Kerr has described the current transformation of the American university in these words: "The university is being called upon to educate previously unimagined numbers of students; to respond to the expanding claims of national service; to merge its activities with industry as never before; to adapt to and rechannel new intellectual currents . . . [The] university has become a prime instrument of national purpose. This is new. This is the essence of the transformation now engulfing our universities . . . Basic to this transformation is the growth of the 'knowledge industry,' which is coming to permeate government and business and to draw into it more and more people raised to higher and higher levels of skill. . . . Knowledge has certainly never in history been so central to the conduct of an entire society. What the railroads did for the second half of the last century and the automobile for the first half of this century may be done for the second half of this century by the knowledge industry: that is, to serve as the focal point for national growth. And the university is at the center of the knowledge process." Clark Kerr, *The Uses of the University* (Cambridge, Mass.: Harvard University Press, 1964), pp. 86-88. Other sources found to be helpful for this discussion of the relationship of institutions of higher education to society are: Irwin T. Sanders, "The University and the Community," in Charles Frankel, ed., *Issues in University Education* (New York: Harper and Row, 1959); Claude T. Bissell, *The Strength of the University* (Toronto: University of Toronto Press, 1968), pp. 231-242; Edward Gross and Paul V. Grambsch, *University Goals and Academic Power* (Washington, D.C.: American Council on Education, 1968), pp. 2, 46-50, 66; Ernest A. Jacobsen, *Obligations of Higher Education to the Social Order*, Fourteenth Annual Faculty Research Lecture (Logan, Utah: The Faculty Association, Utah State Agricultural College, 1955), pp. 28-29.

13. Garbarino, "Precarious Professors," p. 11.

14. It should be noted that these observations do not have the same relevance for those private universities which occupy the most prestigious position in the higher educational structure, and which have attracted professional academicians strongly attached to aspirations and standards of scholarship. While these institutions are not necessarily free of faculty discontent, their more moderate growth rates and their strong collegial traditions in faculty-administration relations appear to have spared them the degree of strain and institutional stress found elsewhere.

15. One writer has described this competitive struggle in these words: "In some sense . . . the certification of a bargaining agent can reflect an attempt by a group outside the existing power structure to oust the oligarchy and supplant it. On the other hand, it can reflect a protectionist measure by the oligarchs to retain their power in the face of changed circumstances." Mathew F. Finkin, "Collective Bargaining and University Government," *Wisconsin Law Review*, 1971, No. 1, p. 131. For a discussion of the functioning of the "oligarchy in the faculty," see Burton R. Clark, "Faculty Authority," AAUP Bulletin, Dec. 1961, p. 298.

16. Bissell, p. 232.

17. Gross and Grambsch, pp. 1-2.

18. Benjamin Aaron, "Faculty Participation in Decision-making: Some Painful Realities," text of a keynote address delivered at the First Annual Confer-

ence of the California Higher Education Association, Dec. 9, 1971, Los Angeles, Calif., p. 6. Relevant comments regarding the relationship of public employee unionization to the collective bargaining movement on campuses may be found in McHugh, p. 56, and C. Dallas Sands, "The Role of Collective Bargaining in Higher Education," *Wisconsin Law Review,* 1971, No. 1, pp. 151-153.

19. Bissell, p. 240.

20. William B. Boyd, "Collective Bargaining in Academe: Causes and Consequences," *Liberal Education,* Oct. 1971, p. 311.

21. This trend is reported by Larry A. VanDyne in "Some Budget-Cutting Colleges Firing Tenured Professors," *The Chronicle of Higher Education,* Nov. 15, 1971, p. 6. The author cites a recent study of the Association of American Colleges, which reveals that seven out of 54 responding colleges had terminated one or more tenured faculty members as a way of reducing costs. An additional number of other institutions surveyed anticipated the need to take similar action. An AAUP committee has reported that ". . . the greatest single cause of requests by faculty members for assistance by this Association during the last year (1970) has been dismissal or nonrenewal on grounds of financial exigency." Quoted by Carl N. Stevens in "The Professors and Collective Action: Which Kind?" a paper presented at the twenty-fifth anniversary of the founding of the Minnesota Industrial Relations Center, May 18, 1971.

22. Wollett, pp. 8-9.

23. This conceptualization ignores nice distinctions between levels of management which make managers at one level the "employees" of managers at a higher level, and it avoids the confusion of calling all persons working in an organization "employees" in a collective sense , only the stockholders (owners) being technically the "employers."

24. Quoted in the brief (p. 28) filed by Fordham University "In the Matter of Fordham University (Employer) and American Association of University Professors (Petitioner) and Law School Bargaining Committee (Petitioner)" before the National Labor Relations Board (1971).

25. Neil W. Chamberlain, *Labor* (New York: McGraw-Hill, 1958), p. 97.

26. On this point, see Hanley, p. 9. In this author's view, "The University would be foolish to permit the union, through the faculty, to sit on both sides of the bargaining table. Thus the faculty can properly be excluded from areas of management decision in which they now play an important part as colleagues."

27. Boyd, p. 315.

28. Wollett, p. 2.

29. The *quid pro quo* nature of the bargaining process might conceivably be turned to advantage in certain circumstances, irrespective of the incompatibility of a trading approach with one characterized by reasoned inquiry and analysis. It is an often voiced criticism of higher education that curricula, teaching methods, and other elements of the educational process have lagged in their responsiveness to changed conditions both in society and on campus. Although this situation is defended by the proposition that "change comes slowly in the academy" by the very nature of the collegial process of consensus, college and university administrations are confronted with pressures from external sources (society) and internal sources (students) to modernize the educational process and to achieve more effective utilization of scarce resources. Existing faculty

governance machinery has not distinguished itself so far (with some exceptions) in dealing with these problems to the extent of producing truly significant results. It is not beyond the realm of possibility that something akin to the "productivity agreement" which has emerged lately in the industrial union-management sector may eventuate from academic collective bargaining. The essence of this type of agreement is the trading of a major concession by management (in the form of substantial improvements in worker economic benefits) for a major concession by organized workers (in the form of the abolition or modification of traditional work rules and practices having the current effect of restricting a company's ability to adapt to changed market conditions). Where such agreements have been negotiated, it is because both parties have gained something. Their respective self-interests have been served by recognizing a basic mutual interest to improve the viability of the enterprise to function under changed conditions. Conceivably, a similar result might accrue in the university from framing the issues a certain way for negotiating purposes. A more dramatic break with traditional educational practices that have outgrown their time might be achieved through collective bargaining than through the systems of faculty participation to which we have been accustomed. For further details on the application of the "productivity agreement" concept to collective bargaining in higher education, see Garbarino, "Precarious Professors," pp. 18-20.

30. For a discussion of "illness" and similar tactics as used by public school teachers, see Michael H. Moskow, *Teachers and Unions* (Philadelphia: Industrial Research Unit, Wharton School of Finance and Commerce, University of Pennsylvania, 1966), p. 197 ff.

31. Benjamin Aaron, member of the faculty of the University of California, Los Angeles. Professor Aaron commented more fully on this point as follows: "Apart from ideological arguments that groups of wage and salary earners somewhat arbitrarily labeled 'workers' and 'intellectuals' should join forces to create a new and better world, which do not appeal to me for a variety of reasons, there are two practical advantages to be gained by an alliance between professors and other unionized workers both within and outside the college or university. The first is money . . . (and the second is) . . . sympathetic action by other unions. . . . As the economists say, however, there is no such thing as a free lunch; the price that would have to be paid to secure these advantages would almost certainly be considered by many in the academic fraternity as being too high." Benjamin Aaron, pp. 10-11.

32. As has been attempted in at least two bargaining contracts recently negotiated, one at St. John's University in New York and the other covering the CUNY system. See *Agreement Between the Administration of St. John's University, New York, and the St. John's Chapter of the American Association of University Professors-Faculty Association at St. John's University,* July 1, 1970, Article X (10.2.2) (a), and *City University of New York: Agreement Between the Board of Higher Education of the City of New York and The Legislative Conference,* Sept. 15, 1969, Article VI (6.4: *Nota Bene*).

33. See Sands, p. 172.

34. In the words of one authority who has written on the effects of academic collective bargaining: "With tight budgets and loose labor markets, the con-

vergence of compensation packages is likely to take the form of holding down the rate of increase, or even of actual reductions in benefits and working conditions enjoyed by the upper end of the distribution, while improving the position of the occupational groups that have been at the lower end." Garbarino, "Creeping Unionism," p. 15.

The Affirmative-Action Program of HEW

Paul Seabury
University of California,
Berkeley

In the early months of the organization of the University Centers for Rational Alternatives I regarded it as something of a club which we would convene periodically to tell our horror stories—the most terrible things that had happened to us. Since then, the stories have become so familiar that I am persuaded to be brief on stories and to turn rather to questions about what might be done. This is especially true with respect to the so-called affirmative-action program, or governmental intervention in the affairs of universities. I have written an article on this; Professor Hook has, I guess, fired the first gun. But that great organization known as "Wealth, Education, and Healthfare" remains unscathed and seemingly unmoved. The movement against us continues, and we are, I believe, in somewhat unfortunate straits.

First, I am convinced that the attempts by the federal government to enforce a ban on discriminatory hiring on university campuses is probably unconstitutional and certainly contradicts the doctrines embodied in the Civil Rights Act of 1964. Secondly, I am more disturbed about the prospects of affirmative action at some of those universities that effectively and zealously adopted their own policies of affirmative action even before HEW arrived on the scene. Known as preemptive discrimination, this is being practiced very widely.

We do know that when the guns of HEW were turned upon the academy, they were turned first on the great universities: Columbia, Harvard, the University of Michigan, and later on Berkeley. The public struggle that has been fought in these conspicuous places is now in very dubious battle, as John Steinbeck once wrote. The outcome of this battle in these great and distinguished universities—namely, whether universities will establish specific quotas of an ethnic and sex character—is going to be critical with respect to those other institutions watching carefully to see how we behave. When the administration of the University of California at Berkeley decided to permit officials of HEW to have reasonably full access to confidential personnel files, this decision was rightly marked by administrators in other universities and state colleges in California. There is a ripple effect when these things occur, and, I think, any responsible administrator in any major institution should bear in mind that what he does is being very carefully watched. Meeting a friend from Columbia, I egged him on, saying, "Well, Columbia's got to stand up and fight," and so forth. He turned to me and said, "You sound exactly like Neville Chamberlain advising the Poles to resist the Nazis in the spring of 1939." I found the comparison somewhat alarming. But the problem still remains.

Several months ago when I was doing some "gum chewing" (as I call my research) on this national problem of affirmative action, I was struck wherever I went by one singular political phenomenon: campus by campus the faculties were silent. No one was speaking to this issue. On the contrary, university administrators seem to have a high incentive to keep the thing contained in as small a circle as possible, that is to say, to confine the issue, as far as possible, to a quiet zone of the administrative apparatus. I found it interesting that university administrators do not encourage wider discussion among their faculties. I suppose one reason for this has been that the faculties are a cipher. Nobody knows what we think because we don't say anything at all. On this issue there has been an extraordinary silence. I find this silence bizarre because the whole question seems to me to be absolutely critical to the selection and advancement of our colleagues in the future. The silence has been ubiquitous, and I hope it does not continue. But in view of that, I suppose, the canny administrator chooses to hope for the best in dealing with his counterparts in the federal government, to hope that some satisfactory settlement can be made that will not basically damage the autonomy of the university.

I thought for several months about the question of how the government's affirmative-action program might be resisted in a more effective way than it has been. One might argue that the responsible administration of a university might dig in its toes, might balk at some critical juncture in negotiations, might say, "Here I stand, I cannot do other," and then just wait and see what happens. We do know that the more distinguished a university is, the more there is at stake financially. One of the bizarre features of this peculiar procedure of the Department of Health, Education, and Welfare is what I call the thermonuclear capability. It's a kind of Curtis LeMay educationism, in which the weapon brandished by the federal government is the weapon of contract termination, of contract nonrenewal, or, in fact, the declaration that a university is ineligible for further funding. This extraordinary weapon means that, in case after case, the administrator has to inquire into the kinds of damage that might be caused by resisting on behalf of principles. Somewhere in the United States that first resistance may occur. Somewhere a university may say, "We will not do this; let us see what you are going to do to us." If that were to happen, needless to say, what has heretofore been a somewhat obscure issue—not widely publicized in the press—could become an issue of monumental importance in our national life overnight. But this has not happened yet. I predict that it will eventually happen somewhere. And I would hope that when it does happen, it will happen in a distinguished university, one in which the issues could be most clearly drawn. I am not here in the role of a Neville Chamberlain; I am here simply in the role of a prophet, prophesying what will have to happen at some point.

After my article on this matter was published, I received a letter from a colleague in the State University of New York system. It was a very long letter in which he told me about what was happening on his own campus, and he made the following point: He had thought and thought and thought about what kind of an organization might come to the help of a campus such as his, where numerical quotas are already set up, and one by one he had to cancel them all out. One could consider the American Association of University Professors; one could think of the American Civil Liberties Union; as one went down the list striking off organizations, the list dwindled to virtually nothing. I am told, strangely enough, that one organization with lawyers is beginning to pay some attention to this; it is the Anti-Defamation League. At some point, the legality, the constitutionality of these devices is going to be tested in individual cases. And here we get, I think, into one of the most savage and uncomfortable features of this whole matter.

I don't want to bore you with the details of the evolution of affirmative action in federal executive orders. I do want to point out, though, that the executive orders in use by the Department of Health, Education, and Welfare in cases involving universities are derived from Labor Department models of executive orders, a tradition that dates back to 1941. President Franklin D. Roosevelt issued orders for the elimination of certain kinds of pernicious practices among employers with federal defense contracts, especially where the discrimination was on the grounds of race. It is from these executive orders, rather than from the Civil Rights Act of 1964, that the law enters the picture. This law applying to labor unions, business firms, and the universities was tested in Philadelphia. It was tested in the case of the so-called Philadelphia Plan, a plan requiring certain unions to establish preferential hiring patterns because they had been negligent or blatantly discriminatory in the past. This case was tested—again I will spare you the details—and in a federal court action the executive order was sustained. On appeal to the Supreme Court, it was refused review. I mention this because some have attempted to distinguish our situation from that which exists in the wider field of labor-management relations, in the hiring practices of industrial firms, and so forth.

I recall an article in *Minerva* by Professor Edward Shils, which I suppose was the first shot fired against HEW. Professor Shils attempted to make the following point: that preferential hiring was all right in certain categories; it was all right with respect to labor unions and hiring practices in industry. Further, he said, it might well be all right even in some of the undistinguished centers of higher education that were not really engaged in the kinds of things that we are engaged in. I find that particular form of snobbery singularly alarming. The Achilles heel of our case is the attempt to say we are better than they. Don't do it to us, but it is all right to do it to them; we are in favor of the Philadelphia Plan, but please don't bring the Philadelphia Plan to Berkeley.

This somewhat illogical position is not particularly attractive in public. But the very fact that this problem exists raises the most serious question for us, namely, are we prepared to take on the entire bag or not? Is there some intermediate position in which universities can distinguish themselves from areas in which preferential hiring is legitimate? I raised this question rather than addressing myself to an answer to it because I think it goes to the very heart of the situation in which we find ourselves. I personally am inclined to the view—the very uncomfortable view—that we have to be consistent, that the issue of preferential hiring goes to the very guts of the cultural norms of our society, and that, in fact, such backgrounds lead down a very long path away from the heights attained by the enactment of the Civil Rights Act of 1964.

Again, the question is what can the faculty do. I suppose, looking at the problem that John Bunzel raised from the perspective of the faculty, I have been struck by the singular silence of the University of California faculty on this matter. There, we seem to be philosophically resigned to the inevitable booming of guns in the distance, saying, "Well, when will the artillery arrive here?" I don't know why this is so. It may be, of course, that having gone through as much as we have in the last few years, we so appreciate the peace we now enjoy that the prospect of another major conflict is very discouraging indeed. Nevertheless, it seems to me that, on the issue of preferential hiring, we must inquire deeply into our own hearts about what we are going to do. I do not think that the matter is going to be satisfactorily resolved if we remain silent, if we entrust the resolution of these issues to harassed administrators facing those guns alone and wondering what we think and where we stand.

Excellence and Irrelevance:
Democracy and Higher Education

Paul Kurtz
State University of New York at Buffalo

PRELUDE

Imagine a society of the future that decides that symphonic music is the highest value and that everyone should learn to appreciate good music. This society then decides to encourage or compel everyone to enroll in a symphonic orchestra of his choice. There will be one hundred thousand orchestras and everyone will be admitted. There are no entrance requirements, and not even a person who is tone-deaf or hates music will be excluded. Once admitted, anyone can play any instrument he or she wishes. There will be no test of excellence or quality. There will be no music teachers and no conductors. No distinctions will be made between first and second violins, and no individual will be recognized as a concertmaster. Who is to say who is a virtuoso or not? To do so is to apply elitist standards. There is no basis for criticism of good or bad music, for to so argue is to impose archaic rules of music theory and harmony. There will be no discrimination based upon sex, race, or ethnic origins. Every orchestra must have 51 per cent women, 4 per cent Poles, 1.6 per cent Episcopalians, and so on, proportional to their percentages in the population. (It is undemocratic, for example, that Italians should dominate opera!)

The orchestras need not practice unless they want to. The members need not even play together if they do not want to. Any effort to impose rules of discipline and practice in order to develop musical skills is repressive. Beethoven and Bartok may be irrelevant and certainly are not necessarily better than Woody Allen, Frank Sinatra, or "The Internationale." Why consider some people to be creative geniuses and not others? That distinction masks an aristocratic prejudice against the ordinary man. Besides, how can we enjoy classical music while millions go hungry in the world every night? Hereafter, only the tunes that the people like, those that speak to their needs, will be played. Let the orchestra be what it wants. If it chooses, as its main social function, to become a day-care center instead of playing music, why should others object as the orchestra marches off to babysit? From the mouths of babes come musical truths, which corrupt, elitist professional musicians and composers, restricted by their class positions, usually ignore!

What cacophony, what bedlam, what vulgarization would result! But surely, the analogy does not hold. Of course it does not. Yet, if you could imagine a symphony based upon the egalitarian model, an egalitarianism with no distinctions based upon musical ability and no standards of excellence, then perhaps you can imagine a possible university of the future that some well-meaning egalitarians might create.

I

Is the idea of democracy incompatible with higher learning? The classical university as it evolved was committed to exacting standards of intellectual and aesthetic excellence and competence, and the university attracted scholars and students who pursued inquiries that were often "irrelevant" to immediate social interests. Is this idea now dead, a relic of things past, because it is basically contradictory to the values of democracy? Many of the current reforms in higher education are being done in the name of democracy; yet some of these efforts at reform, however commendable on moral grounds, may undermine the very idea of the university itself.

Let me state right away that I am in broad agreement with a Deweyan approach to education and that I consider my basic ethical, social, and political philosophy to be that of humanistic democracy. Let me also state that, like so many other students of John Dewey, I consider that many faddist reforms in higher education, often done in the name of Dewey, have the effect of undermining one of the essential premises upon which the university is based. In particular, a new strain of egalitarianism is running strong, and this is often detrimental to efforts to maintain high standards of excellence.

There are many synonyms for "excellence," including exceptional merit and matchless or peerless achievement or worth, but, fundamentally, by "excellence" I mean the development of rigorous standards of attainment in intellectual inquiry or a high quality of aesthetic value, as these emerge in different fields of human endeavor. The university, ideally at least, sought to nourish creative genius in the discovery of beauty and truth. And it also sought to encourage the work of dissenting individuals, who may not have had any interest in the reigning social or political orthodoxies or fashions and whose lonely work may not have been directly relevant to them.

Can both excellence and social irrelevance be defended in the university? Can they survive the current assaults upon them? Should they survive them?

II

One's answer to these questions depends in a sense upon one's definition of the appropriate role of the university. Although there are many common characteristics between a university and a college, I wish to focus upon higher learning in the university.

What is the university? What should be its function? Any definition that is offered is bound to be normative, for "the university" is not an ideal essence in some Platonic universe. It is an historical institution that is developing and constantly changing. Different kinds of organizations have been labeled "the university." In some contexts, the university has been used to inculcate belief in God, support the establishment or the state, train people for industry and the professions, develop a base for social change or revolution, indoctrinate in ideology, serve as a mother for the arts and sciences, or provide a home for the fraternities or for experiments in sexual hedonism. To ask "What is the university?" is to ask what it *ought* to be

Human institutions are, in a sense, whatever we choose to make them—within the constraints imposed by historic drift, tradition, and cultural lag. The multiversity surely has had a host of tasks given to it. Many of these are appropriate; some, in my view, are inappropriate. What I want to establish is that the university ought to be the institution of society preeminently concerned with the cultivation of learning and inquiry. It ought to be the repository of the best insights of past civilizations, and it ought to push the frontiers of knowledge in the future. It ought to be a place where a community of scholars and students together or singly can pursue their visions of truth and beauty as they see fit and without interference.

The university has as its function, of course, the teaching of the young and not so young. But the university does not, in my judgment, exist solely to educate students—central as this function is. (I assume the teaching of students to be the primary purpose of a college.) The university has at least a double function: teaching and learning, on the one hand, and research and inquiry, on the other. Thus the university should make possible the pursuit of free and independent learning and research, whether in the physical, behavioral, and social sciences, philosophy, history, classics, or the arts. This ongoing inquiry should not be compromised to the exigencies of the marketplace. It should not be sacrificed to the tyranny of the fads and fashions of the day or to the immediate demands for relevance. In furtherance of this aim, it should seek to develop in its students an appreciation of the virtues of excellence.

The task of a great university is to provide optimum conditions for the best creative minds—no matter what their point of view—to work on problems of intellectual challenge and artistic creativity. And it should provide the setting wherein divergent ideas can compete and be evaluated in the investigative process.

The test of the standards of excellence is largely internal to the subject matter at hand and to whether or not the process and the product of inquiry fulfill the criteria and methods of evidence and significance, as these vary from field to field and as they are determined by the community of qualified inquirers in each field, however fallible their judgments may prove to be. The major test of excellence is thus performance.

According to some people, ideas should be tested only by their consequences to society, but to insist upon this would unduly narrow man's intellectual horizons. Independent of social relevance, there is a kind of intellectual relevance that is often overlooked. That is, ideas, including merely abstract or esoteric ideas, can be tested by how well they help us to overcome puzzles encountered in inquiry. Ideas may be irrelevant to immediate social problems, but they may be relevant to the deeper intellectual interests of man.

The justification for the irrelevant is instrumental and utilitarian. Free and untrammeled inquiry may have the highest long-run good, both to society and the individual. Here I am talking about knowledge derived from both theoretical and practical science as well as the arts of civilization. The so-called irrelevant may have a deeper kind of relevance to the long-range interests of mankind, and this is often overlooked by the disciples of immediate practice. Thus, knowledge ought to be pursued for its own sake.

In this normative definition of the university, I am not saying that learning and research should be its sole function; society may wish to entrust other roles to it, many of which are appropriate. But a university is not a university unless this essential end, at least, is realized.

There are always threats to this task; most often they come from narrow establishmentarians, whether of church, state, party, or class, who are opposed to free inquiry, which they consider to be dangerous and subversive. There has been a long, hard struggle to defend and justify the right of a community of scholars to exist. The practical men of commerce do not see an immediate economic value in scholarship; the church is fearful of heresy; political leaders, of sedition; the party, of counterrevolution. And some students are impatient because scholarship and science do not satisfy their immediate existential interests and yearnings. Demands for immediate relevance at times may be as destructive to the process of free inquiry as outright suppression by the establishment. What is essential, if excellence is to develop, is that academic values prevail so that the brightest minds can pursue their inquiries, even if these are irrelevant to immediate social needs or psychological yearnings.

Paradoxically, one of the major threats to scholarship today comes from those who, in the name of egalitarian democracy, would smother the independence of the university because it is thought to be irrelevant to democratic ends. John Stuart Mill, in *On Liberty,* maintained that, though representative democracy had achieved a victory against authoritarian government, a new problem that emerged within democratic society was the defense of the individual against the tyranny of the majority. May we perhaps say that, at the same moment that the struggle for autonomy is being won in the universities of the United States, they are in danger of being sacrificed to excessive application of the democratic faith.

I think that I should make it clear that this ideal of the university as a community of scholars devoted to learning and research has not always been fully realized. Tenure was introduced to protect professors from intimidation and sanction by governing powers, but it has sometimes become a mask for the privilege of an entrenched professoriat. This means the end of genuine inquiry. Creative research often is done best outside the academy, not within it. Men like Karl Marx, John Stuart Mill, and Charles Peirce illustrate this fact; they did not pursue full-time academic careers yet were among the most seminal minds of their day. Moreover, institutions of higher learning often have been run, not by a community of scholars, but by absentee boards of trustees, who attempt to bind the university to the establishment and the status quo.

Only recently has the greater society itself come to recognize the need for freedom and autonomy for scholarship. And only since the nineteenth century have universities been able to begin freeing themselves from direct control by the church, state, or corporate interests, which, for over one thousand years, dominated and financed them. Religious commitment, loyalty-test oaths, and subscriptions were once the rule throughout the universities of the Western world.

Spinoza turned down a teaching post because he thought it would limit his philosophical freedom. The judgment of the University of Paris was that Joan of Arc was a witch, and the University of Toulouse condemned the Albigensian heresy. The University of Paris also later passed a resolution declaring Descartes' theories unsound. In 1798, Johann Fichte was forced to resign his professorship at Jena because of his atheism and his pro-French-Revolution sentiments. In 1916, Bertrand Russell was removed from his post at Trinity College, Cambridge, for his pacifism, and he was not permitted to teach at City College in New York in 1940 because of his moral views. Communists were hounded off some faculties in the United States during the McCarthy period.

Of course, none of this can compare with the completely repressive control that totalitarian societies maintain in their universities. The Nazis demanded of their faculties absolute loyalty to Hitler and the Third Reich, and universities in communist countries must not deviate from Marxism as interpreted by the party.

At the present moment in the United States and some Western countries, there are new kinds of pressures that threaten intellectual autonomy and excellence; sad to say, these do not come from reactionary forces, but from well-meaning and zealous defenders of democratic egalitarianism. Are democracy and excellence incompatible?

III

Democracy, I submit, is primarily a moral philosophy that is based upon two key principles. First, the *libertarian* ideal: a belief in freedom of belief and action and a wish to provide the widest degree of freedom of choice for individuals, so that they can satisfy their own needs and interests and pursue their moral values as they see fit. The end is the creative growth and realization of individual personality. Second, the *equalitarian* ideal: a commitment to the principle of equality. Here there is a wish to provide (1) equality of opportunity so that individuals can fulfill their unique interests and needs, and (2) equality of consideration, which expresses a concern for each individual as an individual. The principle of equality means further that (3) each individual is to be judged impartially before the law, and (4) if the individual is unable to satisfy his basic biological and cultural needs, it is the task of society to provide the minimal wherewithal for him to do so. All discriminations based on race, creed, sex, class, or national origin are to be overcome. The principle of equality is not to be equated with egalitarianism. Individuals are not the same, nor are they to be treated exactly alike. They are to be given positive assistance by society in order to allow them to express and fulfill their own unique talents and interests.

How does democracy apply to the university? In my view, democracy cannot function effectively unless it allows for the emergence of leadership based upon talent and demonstrated achievement. Unless a democratic society is able to recognize and reward merit and excellence in performance, it will undermine its own vitality.

Democracy and elitism are incompatible where elites are based upon class, race, ethnic origin, or sex. But democracy and elitism *are* compatible where leadership is chosen on the basis of merit, where membership is open, and elites are responsive or can be replaced. Egalitarians' uncritical application of democracy to the university threatens its viability as a free institution dedicated to learning and inquiry. I wish to discuss five recent abuses in this area: (1) the open-admissions policy, (2) the no-exit policy and the breakdown of standards of educational content and requirements for graduation, (3) student participation in faculty roles, (4) relevance, and (5) the quota system.

IV

The first abuse is the belief that the democratic ideal implies universal higher education. Clearly, the effort to extend free and universal education, particularly on the primary and secondary level, to all strata of society is progressive and democratic. No man can fulfill his potentialities unless he is afforded the opportunity for cultural enrichment. This is particularly true in contemporary technological society, where higher education enhances further development.

The open-admissions policy is an effort to fulfill this ideal of universal education. I support the open-admissions policy, but only in one sense. Those denied admission because of race, class, ethnic origin, sex, or economic deprivation should be given the opportunity to enter. (I might add that, in my view, universities ought to continue to seek out high-potential, disadvantaged youth and provide them with special programs of tutorial instruction so that they can succeed in higher education.) Indeed, in an ideally democratic system of higher education, the state or society ought to provide adequate scholarship aid for all those who cannot afford it. It is undemocratic to allow the white-shoe boy to get into the best schools because of family wealth or prestige, while the poor boy is excluded. The principles of equality of opportunity and equality of consideration should operate without equivocation. Indeed, the schools, in emphasizing mobility, can contribute to the breakdown of class and ethnic lines and give everyone, no matter what his background, an equal chance.

But, we should ask, should everyone go to an institution of higher education? Should everyone be admitted to a university or college of his choice? Would it be undemocratic to exclude some? It is a remarkable achievement today in America that virtually 50 per cent of the population attends colleges and universities, whereas most societies send only 2, 5, or 10 per cent of their young people to institutions of higher learning. If current projections are realized, this percentage may very well continue to increase in the United States to perhaps 80 or 90 per cent. There are those, apparently, who think that this extension of higher education to *all* members of society is necessary to achieve the democratic dream.

In my view, many young people now in universities ought not to be there; they have neither the talent nor the motivation. But social pressures compel them to go; only with a degree, it is thought, can they get a good job or marry well; otherwise, they would be a failure in life. But to attend a university is not necessarily the only way to achieve the good life or significant experience; indeed, for many students, it may deaden some of their creative life spirit. And it may not be the only road to increased income or success later in life, as Christopher Jencks and others have shown in the book *Inequality*.[1] Universities and colleges have become sacred institutions, thought to be necessary way stations of life. Too many employers require a B.A., thus forcing students into unproductive higher education.

I sharply dissent. Perhaps we need some deschooling. Why confine young people at the prime of life to four more years of extended education? Why not give them the opportunity to get out and live and to come back later in their careers if they so wish? It is a pity that so many jobs in society are closely geared to college education. I would prefer to see the development of more technical-training institutions in industry.

However, the notion that everyone should attend institutions of higher learning is questionable on other grounds. Ability and talent are unevenly distributed among individuals, and universities and colleges should only admit those who have the capability to achieve or show some promise that they can. Some egalitarians have misconstrued democracy. They believe the idea that "all men are created equal" means that intelligence and capacity are determined solely by environmental causes, and they dismiss distinctions based upon merit or talent as undemocratic or elitist. Democracy is committed, however, to the principle of equality, not to an oversimplified egalitarianism.

John Dewey is often appealed to as the philosopher who defends the role of the university in a democracy. Yet he made the same distinction I have made.

> Belief in equality is an element of the democratic credo. It is not, however, belief in equality of natural endowments. Those who proclaimed the idea of equality did not suppose they were enunciating a psychological doctrine, but a legal and political one. . . . Each one is equally an individual and entitled to equal opportunity of development of his own capacities, be they large or small in range. Moreover, each has needs of his own, as significant to him as those of others are to them. The very fact of natural and psychological inequality is all the more reason for establishment by law of equality of opportunity, since otherwise the former becomes a means of oppression of the less gifted . . . what we call intelligence [is] distributed in unequal amounts. . . . The democratic faith in equality is the faith that each individual shall have the chance and opportunity to contribute whatever he is capable of contributing and that the value of his contribution be decided by its place and function in the organized total of similar contributions, not on the basis of prior status of any kind whatever.[2]

We can parody the confusion here by asking: Should everyone be admitted to the M.A. or Ph.D. program of his choice, even if he lacks the requisite capability or motivation? Where do we draw the line? Admitting everyone to an institution of higher learning has become the national craze for parents, students, educators, and legislators alike. Our society is now committed to supporting this new style of life for a whole generation. We are the first society in the history of mankind that has created a new quasi-leisure class of those aged eighteen to twenty-five. If we were to admit 100 per cent of the general population, then we would need remedial training programs for the retarded as part of higher education, and universities would mean all things to all men. Why can't we make quality distinctions among institutions—junior and community colleges on one end of the scale, and research universities on the other—without being called undemocratic? Why can't we insist that *some* institutions retain exacting standards of excellence? We are warned by egalitarians that the so-called elite institutions are next on the list for an assault.[3]

Is not part of the great crisis of the university today caused by demands that it become a supermarket? It was only to be expected that a high percentage of students would find that much of what was being offered to them by academicians would not be to their liking. Is it the fault of "reactionary" universities and "archaic" faculties, or is it due to the fact that many of those now being admitted to universities have different interests and inclinations? Perhaps the failure of the university, if it has failed, is not due to the scholars so much as it is to the extension of the university to accommodate such a large part of the general population.

V

Perhaps we can argue for the open-door policy; perhaps the university should be, as John Holt has suggested, like a library or movie theater, and everyone should be allowed to enter, without prior qualification. But if so, shall there be a revolving-door policy as well? If students who are admitted do not make the grade, may we flunk them out? Or does democracy mean that everyone who is admitted has a right to graduate and receive a degree? This is the no-exit policy. Does it mean that students should be allowed to determine the entire content of the curriculum? Shall the nature of the educational process be determined by rigorous standards of intellectual excellence or chiefly by the consumer students themselves? Those who argue the latter are laboring under a second misconception about democracy. One can possibly argue that we ought to admit everyone who wishes to attend an undergraduate college, even a medical or law school. But still, should we not graduate only those who *succeed* in college, and should we not try to turn out competent surgeons and lawyers?

There are those who would go further and debunk all credentials. All standards and credentials, they say, are false, and all claims to objectivity, nonsense. These, they say, are imposed by entrenched professional elites, who are not infallible and often are resistant to new ideas. Therefore, they conclude, the student himself can better judge what he wishes to learn and what will qualify or certify him. Thus, they insist that not only does everyone have a right to be admitted to an institution of higher learning, but each has an inalienable right to determine what and how he learns. "He who wears the shoe best knows where it pinches" is the faith of the democrat in politics, and it should apply, it is said, to students in universities as well. Faith in the common man and the common student is unbounded.

There is some truth to the criticism of the professoriat—it *is* often resistant to change. Further, given the growth of the multiversity, which is pressured by the public to admit large numbers of students, many students feel dehumanized and find their course of study deadening. John Dewey was surely correct when he suggested that we should not teach dead subject matter but living human beings.

But how far do we go? Because some standards were mistaken and others were based on outdated criteria, does this mean that there are no standards of excellence or merit and that faculties are no more competent to judge than students? Here, an uncritical interpretation of democracy comes into conflict with the principle of competence. We need to reach a balanced view.

Some humanists in education today emphasize the need for a curriculum based upon affectivity and feeling. They seem to think that any discipline, rule, or regulation imposed on the students is foreign to them. The student should be encouraged to do his own thing. To require any course of study, even the weakest distribution requirement, is said to be oppressive. Students are held to be slaves or serfs forced to do the bidding of their lords and masters, the professors; they need to be liberated.

At many universities, for example, all course or distribution requirements for graduation have been eliminated. There are no English language, science, or literature requirements; if students are not interested, there often is no exposure to history or to the social sciences. Many experimental colleges now consider grades to be repressive and the students grade themselves. We are told that this stimulates learning and motivation. Students often write their own course projects. The main thing is involvement and commitment.

Under this kind of program no one flunks. Everyone graduates. We are told it is immoral, and makes invidious distinctions, to recognize or reward some and not others. The recognition of intellectual distinctions and achievements is even now considered by some people to be "undemocratic."

I do not wish to deny the need for innovative and creative methods. We need to experiment with curricula. We need to trust students as adults and to arouse within them an interest in learning. We should not insist upon grades or exams or attendance rules per se.

But nowhere in the literature of protest is there an emphasis on what I consider to be essential to higher education—the authority or discipline of *intelligence*. Dewey, often invoked to support creativity (which is an essential component of education), also emphasized the need to develop *critical intelligence*, a knowledge of and facility with the standards and methods of inquiry in particular fields. This focus on intelligence requires exacting work and diligent effort. Motivation and effort must come from the student, but faculties surely have a role in criticizing and guiding inquiry and in applying evaluative judgments of performance and achievement.

There are some who believe that the chief aim of education is experience—as long as the student experiences anything, he is learning. But experience and learning are not necessarily the same thing. Not every experience is a learning experience, unless some degree of cognition occurs; nor is every kind of learning good. I can learn how to play bridge or grow poppy seeds, to make love or drink gin—all are forms of experience and no doubt have a place in the complete life. But learning should also include the development and appreciation of the skills of the intellect.

I reject the notion that the student consumer is invariably the best judge of what is good for him or what he ought to learn. The cancer patient knows he is in pain, but he does not know how to treat his cancer. A person may enjoy good food but may not know the principles of good nutrition or health. There are objective standards and criteria in different fields that require disciplined intellectual effort.

Making the student a king in all cases and catering solely to his pleasure may lead to the vulgarization of learning. Many faculty members know that there is a good deal of nonsense prated by the new "quackademics." Yet for some, the way to attract attention is to say something new, to "innovate" and demand "change," even if it is for the worse, instead of the better! The rarest commodities in universities of late have been wisdom (there is plenty of intelligence) and courage, the ability to say "no." But, of course everyone wants to be liked. There is no fool like an old fool who curries favor with the young. He has neither wisdom nor courage.

VI

A third fallacy committed by the reigning democratic orthodoxy is the view that the university is exactly like the state or government. Hence, the notion of participatory democracy has been applied. Those who so interpret institutions of higher learning believe that the central component is power. For them the real issue is the division of power between trustees, administrators, faculty, and students. And they say each is to count for one. "People ought to have control over their lives," is a familiar slogan. The rage only a few years ago was for large town meetings, in which everyone decided in unison what should be done.

Let me grant that students ought to be involved in many or most decisions concerning themselves. They ought to be consulted about a wide range of problems affecting them and their institutions, especially concerning their moral behavior, in which they should be free to decide what to do, and they should insist upon good teaching. The institutions ought to be responsive to their needs, interests, and opinions. The best way to learn the ethics of democracy is by practicing it.

Yet, how far do we go? Should everyone connected with the university decide what to do? At my university there are twenty-three thousand students and fifteen hundred professors. There are also four thousand janitors, maids, guards, secretaries, and others in support services, and many of them have dedicated their lives to the university community. Should everyone's vote be equal in all matters? They should surely be consulted in matters that concern them—but in all matters? No, say the students. Why? Because they are not competent to judge matters of curriculum or education. In other words, specialization and the division of labor come into conflict at this point with democratic decision-making. Should the entire college or university vote on the type of heating plant to install, the best sewerage-disposal system, the professors to be chosen, who should get tenure and be promoted, who should be admitted or graduated, and which books or journals to purchase for the library? Obviously not. There should be wide consultation, but only those who have some competence and expertise should decide. Do experience and training mean nothing? Does the world of an educator who has devoted his life to education equal that of an incoming freshman who hates math and would rather experiment with drugs?

In my view, the faculty should be largely responsible for running the university or college, sharing some responsibility with students and administrators, and the president and board of trustees should be elected.

Should the democratic model apply to universities and colleges? If so, it might destroy them. In New York and California many citizens in the community at large seek to intervene in the running of their state universities. Many of their elected legislators have at the top of their agendas the "firing of radical and liberal professors" and the "expelling of recalcitrant students." Does "power to the people" mean that the people in the state at large should run the universities? Since they are often unable to appreciate what the idea of the university is, we argue no. Do we believe in the independence and autonomy of the university? Yes. In academic freedom? Yes. And in allowing those who are best qualified to judge make the decisions? Yes.

VII

A fourth major attack upon the independence and autonomy of the university is the demand for relevance, the view that the university exists within society and that the university must therefore serve the needs of society and contribute to the solution of its problems.

I accept this role to an extent. The university cannot exist in splendid isolation in a complete ivory tower of irrelevance. First, society will not support the university financially if it ignore its needs, and, second, the university, as an institution of critical inquiry, has some obligation to turn its attention to the pressing normative problems of society.

But I would not accept this role if it meant the extinction of standards of excellence and so-called irrelevant research.

Indeed, the problem that we have faced is that the multiversity has become the handmaiden of society; it has trained people for the professions—law, the ministry, medicine—for executive positions in business and industry, for careers in the army, and it has done research for the military-industrial complex. This slowly erodes the independence and autonomy of the university. Relevance can be a synonym for the most vulgar, or for immediate gain. In its name, Babbitt can reign.

That is not what those who argue for relevance mean, and those are not the kinds of problems that they would have the university meet. They want the university to deal with radical social change, urban blight, peace, international cooperation, racism, and the solution of ecological problems. Granted, the university should engage in analysis of social problems, and it should be concerned with some of the urgent social and normative issues of the day. But it should not pursue these at the expense of other kinds of pure research or quiet scholarship, of poetry and philosophy, biology and history—studies for which there seem to be no immediate social uses.

I am opposed to devoting the entire resources and efforts of the university to one end—political, moral, economic, religious—however commendable that one end may be. Those within the university who wish to deal with specific social problems should be *encouraged* to do so, singly or cooperatively. But we must not turn the *entire* university into an instrument for social change and amelioration; we must allow some freedom and diversity for nonconforming individuals. Thus, it is one thing to argue that those *within* the university, as individuals or in groups, should be socially or politically concerned. It is quite another to insist that *everyone* should be compelled to be involved, or that the university, as a corporate body, should take "official" positions. In my view, the university *itself* should still maintain some neutrality, save in the most extreme cases where it is vitally threatened. The university should not be for God or atheism, for or against South Vietnam, for the Arab or the Israeli cause, for or against women's lib or gay lib, virtue or sin. It should keep the door open to critical inquiry. It should be a place where everyone can feel at home—the Marxist and reactionary Republican, the liberal and the anarchist.

I grant that by existing in a society and by accepting support from it, the university, in some sense, is already part of the social structure. To that extent, it is "politicized." Its existence in a society unavoidably relates it in some way to the social system. But, in spite of this, the university should be the home of a variety of points of view, including dissenting and nonconforming views that may diverge from the dominant political or social interests of the establishment.

VIII

There is one final illustration of the current egalitarian assault on the university that is especially pressing. In my judgment, this new program of reform can, if carried out, alter the nature of the university drastically. I refer to the recent policies of affirmative action in the hiring of women and minority faculty and to the use of the quota system to achieve it. This has been initiated by the Department of Health, Education, and Welfare (HEW) and other governmental agencies and implemented by universities and colleges across the land. So much has recently been written about this that I shall confine my discussion to a few brief remarks.

Many well-meaning democrats, who are against inequalities and discrimination, are now apparently using quotas in reverse. But reverse discrimination is still discrimination, even if it is called something else. Because there is discrimination against women or minority members, does this entitle one to discriminate against the highly qualified individual who happens to be a male Wasp or a "Weej" (White Eastern European Jew)? Should we deny him a position in the university because some of those classified like him may be overly represented on faculties? Do not the rights of such persons also need to be protected?

Those of us who are genuinely committed to the democratic principles of equality and the open society believe that all discriminatory barriers should be broken down, that we ought to treat human beings as individuals and judge them solely on their merits. All invidious distinctions based upon sex, religion, race, or national origin should be abandoned. The only method of choice should be based upon equal opportunity and the only test, demonstrated competence.

Unfortunately, affirmative-action plans have often been construed to say that you *will* judge persons by their sex or group and not by their individual abilities. What this can mean, if implemented, is that some highly talented individual, if he is not a member of the compensated group, can be passed over for someone else. What about the rights of such an individual? Never mind about him, some seem to be saying; he must be sacrificed to repay the centuries of discrimination. In a period of tight budgets, some universities have been warned: Hire women or members of disadvantaged groups first, and exclude others, or your funds will be cut off.

What is at stake here is the ability of faculties to make professionally qualified judgments about applicants, without extraneous matters intervening. Granted, we need to get rid of all forms of inequality and discrimination. We should allow merit and talent to be the chief criteria. We should treat individuals as *individuals*, not as members of groups—either to discriminate or to reverse it. Even though the HEW affirmative-action plan was ill-conceived, we need to come up with new plans to ensure that everyone be treated fairly, that women and minority members be encouraged to compete on equal terms for positions in universities and other institutions of society.

IX

Is it impossible to defend the view that the chief end of the university is *learning and the quest for knowledge, teaching, and scholarship?* The point is, those who wish to use the university for other purposes, however commendable these may be, may end up by undermining and destroying the university as a free and independent institution.

I do not wish to defend the status quo in the university, nor to argue that universities are infallible. But neither are colleges and universities—often the most liberal segment of the society—composed of irrelevant and oppressive oligarchs, entrenched racists or sexists, as their critics charge. Is the university as I have outlined it elitist? I reiterate, my answer is yes. The university is an elitist institution; if it were anything else, it could not function. But it is elitist only in the sense that it seeks to bring to it the best minds and talents to work on the most difficult intellectual problems of mankind. It opens its doors to students and faculty who can participate in the difficult quests of inquiry; those who succeed earn the right to qualify for further inquiry. It is an elite of demonstrated competence, skill, and achievement.

But does this mean then that the university is alien to democracy or a democratic society? No. For a democratic society is open to anyone, regardless of origins. Democracy ought not to bar anyone who can contribute. It ought to encourage everyone who wishes to become involved and has the capacity to do so. But it should not compromise its principles, its standards, or its mission in the process. The appeals to universal higher education, to open admissions, to the students' unlimited right to choose curriculum; notions of the right to graduate and of participatory democracy; demands for relevance and the use of quotas—each has its place. But if these ideas are applied uncritically, there may be a deleterious effect upon the university. Other countries in other times have saddled their universities with religious, political, or ideological constraints. Hopefully, our society will not, in its excessive egalitarian zeal, impose a heavy burden upon the university from which it will be difficult to escape.

NOTES

1. Christopher Jencks *et al.*, *Inequality* (New York: Basic Books, 1972).
2. John Dewey, "Democracy and Education," *Problems of Men* (New York: Philosophical Library, 1946), p. 60.
3. See the article by Jerome Karabel, "Open Admissions: Toward Meritocracy or Equality?" *Change*, May 1972, pp. 38-43.

The Ethnic Revolution and Public Policy

Richard Gambino
*City University of New York,
Queens*

Many things determine the behavior of large groups of people and the shape of their society. Among the most significant determinants are the myths held and acted upon. A rich myth is rooted in reality but transcends it in reaching toward an idea or ideal. The energies people expend in this outreach define the values they esteem. To the consternation of "social engineers" pressing for more effective social management, myths are born, grow, die, and replace each other in a complex process that is highly nonrational, and hence not amenable to prediction or control. In short, it is very difficult to deliberately invent a myth and get people to believe in it. And it is equally hard to stamp out a myth that enjoys credence among large numbers of people.

The culture of the United States is as complicated as it is vast. Many myths are held by the American people. Among the most alive and prevalent ones are two classics of the American saga: first, the persistent myth of social and economic mobility based on individual merit and, second, a powerful mythical ethic of "fairness."

On the other hand, one of the myths dying in America is that of the ethnic melting pot. In fact, one may question whether this myth ever commanded belief among most Americans. Probably, it was believed only by a handful of people, found among all ethnic groups, who wished to erase certain ethnic characteristics in favor of the alternative myth of a uniform culture, purely American in nature. Attempts to impose this latter myth on the American people failed.

It is now clear that Americans in large numbers adhere to myths of ethnicity, which are contrary to the ideal of the melting pot. Whether ethnic myths have remained vital but submerged throughout the onslaught of the melting-pot ideal, or whether they lapsed and have now become revitalized is a moot question. Whether we are witnessing the birth of new myths of ethnicity or are merely becoming once again conscious of old, ever-present ones is comparatively unimportant. What is more significant is that ethnicity is a powerful force on the American scene and is likely to become more powerful in the future.

Any attempt to make sense of American society must probe the probabilities and possibilities in these three complex constellations of myths. Not only should we investigate the future of each constellation of myths, but also we must examine their interrelations. As the myths of ethnicity, fairness, and meritocracy become enmeshed, many problems and possibilities for the future take shape.

Accustomed in the 1950s, and even before, to thinking of our society as culturally homogeneous, or at least as moving toward cultural homogeneity, we were startled at the intensity with which ethnicity began to be asserted in the middle sixties. And in the 1970s, we are taking note of assertions of ethnicity in societies that we had hitherto thought of as monolithic. On July 31, 1972, the *New York Times* reported new affirmations of ethnic identity among the one hundred ethnic groups in the Soviet Union. More significantly, a major shift of official policy was reported. The Soviet government has for the last fifty years vigorously pressed a campaign to achieve a "melted pot" of Soviet culture, a cultural homogeneity rooted in "international" socialist ideology. In short, it tried to obliterate popular ethnic myths and to impose an exclusive myth in their place, using all of the formidable means of a totalitarian state in the effort.

Now, in evident recognition of the fact that the effort failed, the official policy of the Soviet government is to try to compromise with the forces of ethnicity rather than eradicate them. Speaking of the new policy, it was reported: "Within the limits of its republic, region or other autonomous area, each ethnic group was given the right to foster an education and culture in its own language, but under the over-all umbrella of a Communist ideology. In terms of a widespread slogan, ethnic cultural development became 'national in form and socialist in content.' "[1]

On the same day, another article in the *Times* reported a similar effort by the government of China regarding the fifty-four major ethnic groups that constitute most of that nation's seven hundred and fifty million people. The Central Institute for Nationalities in Peking is attempting to cultivate, among carefully selected young leaders, both Maoist ideology and different ethnic identities.[2] The present behavior of the Soviet and Chinese governments will provide perspective when our attention turns to ideas of what should be the policies of the American government.

We, too, need to balance divisive ethnic forces with the cohesive strength of a common culture. Whatever the reasons, the myth of the melting pot is no longer a viable basis of our common culture. In fact, it was never a genuine cultural foundation but only a psychological superstructure. On the other hand, the myths of fairness and meritocracy *are* fundamental to our culture. Their destruction would signal an acute social pathology. The very roots of the authority around which the majority of the American people center their lives, plans, and hopes would disintegrate. Without this strong center, centrifugal forces of ethnicity would cause American society to shatter into fragments. Restoration of a common culture of any sort would be very difficult. In the chaos, polarization between anarchy and totalitarianism would ensue.

For as long as the life of humanity has been recorded, people have identified themselves by their membership in groups. Among the most frequent criteria for group definition have been a common language, common culture, common history, and common racial distinctions, or, in a phrase, ethnic characteristics.

Today, gigantic forces of social life create mass feelings of rootlessness, anonymity, impotence, and hence meaninglessness among people. Among the many paths available to people to resolve their crises of identity and meaning—for example, religion, political ideology, personal achievement—ethnicity is outstanding in several ways. First, it is immediately available. One is already a member of an ethnic group by birth and upbringing. (Personal achievement, on the other hand, is an uncertain and long-term affair.) Second, recent events have demonstrated the effectiveness of ethnicity in providing identity at a time when other criteria, such as religion and political ideology, have proven to be of dubious reliability. Given the overwhelming need for identity today, ethnicity has a powerful psychological appeal, perhaps unmatched by any other criterion for defining identity and a meaningful life.

"Ethnicity," however, is a vague term. Each of its different meanings carries with it different possibilities for American society. For clearer understanding, let us distinguish between two classes of ethnicity, calling them by the loaded terms "tribalistic ethnicity" and "creative ethnicity."[3]

Tribalism involves the tendency to distinguish between us and them.

Grounds for distinguishing between members of the tribe and outsiders have been innumerable. They have included virtually every real or fictional criterion one could imagine, including religion, age, sex, class, interests, and even the cut of one's clothes or hair. Of course, ethnicity has been historically one of the characteristics most often used to define tribalism.

From the initial division of humanity according to the criterion of ethnicity, all other meanings follow in the mind of the ethnic tribalist. The very framework for all his thoughts, feelings, and actions follows. We may say of him what George Orwell said of a type we might call the "nationalistic tribalist," merely reading "ethnic group" where Orwell used "nation or other unit." "I mean first of all the habit of assuming that human beings can be classified like insects and that whole blocks of millions or tens of millions of people can be confidently labelled 'good' or 'bad.' But secondly—and this is much more important—I mean the habit of identifying oneself with a single nation or other unit, placing it beyond good and evil and recognizing no other duty than that of advancing its interests." [4]

Ethnic tribalism provides a strong sense of identity and security. Moreover, it provides answers—or at least directions for the solutions of problems. And it provides a clear guide for all relations with those outside the tribe.

But ethnic tribalism is a sham identity, a false security, and a potentially disastrous guide for human relations. For it stifles the very psychological characteristics needed for genuine identity, well-grounded security, and constructive relations. These include a free and active intelligence, sensitivity to the tragic dimension of life (all is not "black and white"), and positive appreciation and utilization of differences between people and groups. Instead, the ethnic tribalist is clannish, conformist, obstreperous, uncritical of himself or his group, overwrought, pugnacious, prejudicially critical of those outside the group, paranoid, and enormously energetic and determined; in short, he is potentially very destructive.

The creative ethnicist, on the other hand, uses his ethnic background as a point of departure for growth rather than as the proof of his worth. By inquiry and reflection, he shapes his identity by building upon inherited ethnic characteristics he judges to be valuable. In so doing, he gains insight into how the identities of other people are formed, and in the process learns how to appreciate their different inheritances.

Thus, ethnic awareness provides a substantial part of the identity, energy, and direction of the creative ethnicist. And it cultivates his respect for others, with possibilities of genuine communication and interchange of what may become valuable to all from each ethnic group. Thus, it is creative, for one learns to live beyond one's roots, helping to shape the emerging synthesis of contributions coming from various ethnic groups.

What our future will be depends on whether Americans turn toward tribalistic ethnicity or creative ethnicity. And as a corollary, the direction of the turn will be influenced by the policies and actions of the government. However, we do not begin with a blank slate. The influences of the past are already operating in setting the direction to be taken. Unfortunately, some recent events have moved us in the less desirable direction. As the "revolution of rising expectations" of the early sixties became one of rising nonnegotiable demands among tribalistic groups at the close of the decade, America entered a severe social crisis.

One of the key causes of the rise of ethnicity was the civil-rights movement. At first, impelled by the 1954 school-desegregation decision of the Supreme Court, the movement was a demand for equal rights for individuals, and hence it sought to tear down the walls of racial segregation that impeded the enjoyment of equal rights. At this stage the movement raised the ethnic consciousness of Blacks and raised both corresponding and responding awareness of their own ethnicities among many Whites. In the middle sixties, however, a concurrence of forces moved ethnic awareness toward tribalistic ethnicities. Although it did not cause the shift in direction, the slogan "Black Power" stands as the clearest symbol of the turn from ethnic awareness to ethnocentric tribalism.

The switch from concern with individual rights to alleged rights of ethnic groups has now become more pronounced. Large segments of various ethnic groups now think exclusively in terms of identity with their own ethnic groups—in Orwell's phrase, "placing it beyond good and evil and recognizing no other duty than that of advancing its interests." When challenged on the socially divisive results of their ethnic exclusiveness, tribalists of various ethnic groups answer with one or more of the following responses.

1. They maintain that America was always divided; it has always been each group for itself. This argument ignores the fact that the common-culture myths of fairness and merit have had considerable vitality until now. Although less than complete and although fairness and merit were denied to some groups of Americans, the myths have been operative. When the "have-nots" respond to the limitations of the myths by wanting to scrap them altogether, this is understandable, yet ill considered. It is more logical to try to *increase* the effectiveness of the myths and to extend them to cover all Americans.

2. Ethnic tribalists often cite the constructive aspects of ethnicity. Either those who do this are themselves confused about the differences between tribalistic and creative ethnicity, or they are consciously manipulating and exploiting this confusion in the minds of others.

3. They assert that tribalistic ethnicity is a necessary, temporary step toward creative ethnicity. The dynamics of how one would lead to the other are explained, if at all, in terms of a dangerously inadequate understanding of the self-perpetuating nature of tribalistic minds and tribalistic groups.

These apologies are used to legitimize violations of the moral myth of fairness so strong in the American mind. Double standards abound: great sympathetic attention is given to the objective conditions determining social ills among favored ethnic groups, but social ills among other groups are dismissed without sympathy or understanding. Segregation practiced by nonfavored groups is assailed, while segregation by the favored group is accepted. Legal sanctions against behavior abusive of basic individual rights are demanded only against the "others," but are never regarded as legitimate against the favored group. These philosophically crude positions are now finding sophisticated, if not sophistical, arguments to support them. Attempts are being made to impose other myths upon the American people that will replace the myth of fairness.

Two of the least subtle attempts are found in Michael Novak's *The Rise of the Unmeltable Ethnics; Politics and Culture in the Seventies*[5] and Peter Schrag's *The Decline of the Wasp.*[6] Novak makes an impassioned attack upon the melting-pot myth. He argues forcefully for the acceptance of cultural patterns of Southern and Eastern European ethnics. He pleads that their cultures and the neighborhoods and institutions nurturing them need and deserve respect from the forces that move and change society. In his argument, he shifts back and forth between stances of tribalistic and creative ethnicity.

Sometimes his tribalism is obviously silly, as when he suggests preserving old-world craftmanship by granting tax benefits to artisans. (One is reminded of Gandhi in his most unworldly moments arguing that India should reject all modern technology in favor of revitalizing traditional village crafts like home weaving.) But Novak's main thrust is dangerously tribalistic. He would have all non-Wasp ethnic groups unite in a political coalition to capture power from the Wasp establishment. He has greatly underemphasized the cultural and social differences among all these groups, including both Blacks and Whites, but this may be innocent. It belies, however, his exposition of the stubborn vitality of diverse ethnic characteristics. In his effort to create a non-Wasp coalition, Novak "melts" his unmeltables after his own fashion.

Then, in anything but an innocent manner, he resorts to a favorite tactic of tribalists. He invents a common enemy—the Wasps—and sets his "colorful" ethnics against this "drab" group. In the process, he slanders Wasps in ways that would create outrage—and rightfully so—if they were directed against any other ethnic group.

Novak does touch upon the dynamics and worth of creative ethnicity and in so doing makes a contribution deserving of attention. But his call for a non-Wasp political coalition is so divorced from today's social realities that it is hardly likely to have a real effect. Blacks and non-Wasp Whites are not joining hands to form a new American majority within the Democratic Party, as Novak thinks they should. Their views of their interests evidently are quite different from Novak's views of their interests. While Novak's indulgence in political fantasy is harmless, in his unconscionable attacks on Wasps he manipulates what one reviewer called the "social uses of hatred." Sadly, this third theme of his book, the call to ethnic tribalism—or to thinking "with one's blood," to borrow a phrase of Bertrand Russell—is virulent. It cannot help but accelerate an already widespread malignancy.

Peter Schrag's book is even more venomous. Ignoring the fact that the melting pot was touted by people from all ethnic groups (and that the phrase was probably first used by a Jewish writer), Schrag portrays it as the product of an evil conspiracy by Wasps to rob other Americans of their souls. Whereas Novak's stereotyping of Wasps as unfeeling robots is used in a deliberate effort to build a political force, Schrag's even worse slurs seem to be the product of an intelligence totally distorted by malicious rage. In the end, his book turns out to be another diatribe calling for the destruction of the utterly evil "establishment." This is familiar rhetoric from those who believe that America is synonymous with an evil that is doomed to the "trash heap of history." But Schrag's efforts culminate in an attempt to make the familiar polemics of the New Left and counterculture synonymous with the ethnic sensibilities of non-Wasps and the evils of "bourgeois, capitalist America" synonymous with another set of ethnic characteristics—those of the Wasps. Political cant is disguised as ethnic tribalism. The total distortion represents the "big lie" technique of propaganda that would boggle even superior analysts like Orwell.

A typical example of Schrag's "reasoning" is his explanation of why Judge Julius Hoffman punished Abbie Hoffman at the trial of the Chicago Seven.

> [Judge] Hoffman's insecure establishmentarianism skirted overt anti-Semitism. He appeared deliberately to be trying to deny not only identification with kids but his own Jewishness. They seemed, at times, to represent similar (or even identical) crimes. The link was hardly precise, yet it had symbolic validity in a society that had always made it difficult to be totally American and totally Jewish at the same time. Abbie Hoffman understood. "Your idea of justice is the only obscenity in this room," he shouted at the judge. "You *schtunk. Vo den. Shanda fur de goyim.*" For insulting the judge in Yiddish (accusing him of shameful behavior on behalf—and in the eyes—of WASP's), six days.[7]

Using this tortured logic, one can hang any rap on Wasps or on any other group. But American sensibilities no longer tolerate such obvious ethnic hatred in print, except when directed against the new scapegoat, the Wasp. Not only is it open season on him, but if the commercial success of Schrag's book is an indication, there is a bounty on his head. Where Novak would tribalize and politicize ethnic groups, Schrag would have them at each other's throats.

More subtle, abstract attempts to destroy the common-culture myths have been made by social philosophers. Two professors of philosophy, Marshall Cohen and Stuart Hampshire, favorably reviewed[8] *A Theory of Justice* by John Rawls.[9] Rawls' theory of justice, which presumably is to replace the operating American myths of fairness and meritocracy, is composed of two essential elements. One is that justice is to be pursued by institutions on behalf of *groups*, as well as of individuals. Second, and more important, justice demands that institutions cultivate inequalities of wealth, authority, and power, when such inequalities work in favor of some group that is socially or otherwise disadvantaged. In short, institutional unfairness to individuals or groups is justified if it benefits a favored group.

Thus, Rawls' thesis is already being used to complement the position explained by Harold Cruse in *The Crisis of the Negro Intellectual*:[10] meritocracy, which has been the operating framework for other ethnic groups, will not work for Blacks. From this, the next step was to favor quotas or "positive discrimination" to permit Blacks to break through racism and move upward more quickly than would be possible under meritocracy and fairness, which demand that Blacks learn the skills that enable them to compete with Whites. It is a reversal of the traditional American system, as explained, for example, in Richard M. Huber's *The American Idea of Success*.[11] Until now, all ethnic groups have operated under the myth that status is gained by "achievement rather than ascription," whereas now ascription rather than achievement is being pressed. Of course, the basis of ascription is not the old European class system Huber writes about but rather membership in a favored ethnic group.

The pluralistic society that results from multiple ethnic tribalisms after the ethic of fairness has been abandoned is a "mosaic society." This is an apt expression, for it connotes the static quality of such a society: each piece of the social mosaic is unmoving and isolated from the others. The mosaic aspect of our society has become increasingly evident. For example, on college campuses, Blacks and Whites separate from one another in dormitories and cafeterias, at extracurricular events, and on college newspapers. Even the seating patterns of Blacks and Whites in classes is a mosaic, for there is little mixing among members of the two races. The *New York Times* reported that "Dianne Howell, a graduate student of psychology at the University of California at Berkeley, likened her white classmates to 'the wallpaper.' 'They're there. They are just there,' she said."[12]

At an elementary school I know, P.S. 108 in Manhattan, where the majority of the children are Puerto Rican and the minority are Black, the pupils responded in a singular fashion to the televised showing of the movie *West Side Story*. Their behavior, as reported in a newspaper, was conspicuously more tribalistic, agitated, and violent in the days following the film. The children identified with both ethnic gangs in the film (Italian and Puerto Rican), were highly excited by the inter-gang violence, and imitated it both in play and in serious "acting out." According to the staff of the school, there was no evidence that the children either understood or were moved by the clear "moral" of the movie: a plea for intergroup tolerance and the renunciation of violence in intergroup behavior.

In my opinion, this is "where we are at." We are a society heavily "into" a static mosaic of isolated, even mutually hostile, ethnic and ideological units. It remains to inquire what, in light of this, should be the role of institutions, including governmental agencies, in the next decade.

The mosaic aspect of our society overlays all of the institutions that constitute what Peter Drucker in *The Age of Discontinuity* terms the "new pluralism" of our society.[13] This is a pluralism of types of large institutions, each type specialized in its basic functions and ultimate goals, yet exercising considerable influence on the whole society.

Accepting this part of Drucker's analysis as essentially correct, I offer two responses. First, the very nature of the society described by him and the nature of its component institutions add to the severity of people's feelings of social alienation and their yearning for personal wholeness and meaningful identity. Therefore, insofar as Drucker's picture of American society is accurate, its character will make the psychological appeals of ethnicity even more attractive to large numbers of people in the future.

Secondly, I must take issue with some of Drucker's crucial conclusions about the role of governmental agencies and other institutions, public and private. His conclusions need to be scrutinized, for there is evidence that some powerful individuals have been influenced by them since the publication of Drucker's book in 1968. More importantly, the behavior of governmental agencies reflects Drucker's opinions at key points.

Government, Drucker argues, should coordinate the operations of society's other institutions. It, and it alone, should make the key decisions about society as a whole and move society's institutions in directions it has charted. Drucker is vague about how these basic decisions are to be made. In response to his suggestion that government should be a special institution among institutions, or as he puts it, the "conductor" of society's "orchestra" of institutions, one may ask, "Who writes the music?" On this point Drucker is both vague and ambiguous. At times he sounds like a latter-day Rousseau, raising anew the notoriously vague notion of the "general will." "We need government as the central institution in the society of organizations. We need an organ that expresses the common will and the common vision and enables each organization to make its best contribution to society and citizen and yet to express common belief and common values."[14]

In other places, Drucker seems to suggest a theory of decisions by "consensus." "The purpose of government is to make fundamental decisions, and to make them effectively. The purpose of government is to focus the political energies of society. It is to dramatize issues. It is to present fundamental choices. The purpose of government, in other words, is to govern."[15]

What is clear in Drucker's view is, first, that the government should make all key decisions and, second, that the other institutions of society should merely be what he calls "doer" institutions, that is, they should carry out the roles and policies set for them by the government.

Drucker's views raise serious questions of political ethics and democratic theory that can be only cited here. (1) "General will" and consensus theories lead to de facto rule according to the whims of whoever controls the instruments of power. (2) Government's exclusive prerogative to make decisions and "orchestrate" society is totalitarian. The obvious danger is that of a corporate society ruled by an all-powerful state. Until now, the term applied to such a society has been "fascism."

In addition to these fundamental questions, other questions more operational in nature come to mind. There is no pluralism of decision-making in Drucker's scheme. This is a society in which each institution is specialized; thus, the people who know an institution best would be excluded from making decisions concerning its basic aims and functions. For example, is the university, a "doer" institution, one that must obey the commands of government agencies, even if academicians perceive those commands as destructive of the university's unique mission—the pursuit and dissemination of knowledge and ideas? In other words, the effective specialized functions of the doer institutions are ill served by Drucker's design.

One may also ask whether Drucker has too sanguine a view of social engineering. Indeed, in the two-page concluding chapter of his book, he admits that his thesis is flawed in that he has ignored all but the "social dimension of man." One may go further and charge that even within this dimension Drucker has ignored too much. He does not deal with many determinants of social life—for example, popular myths. In short, his model of society is both too mechanistic and too simplistic in its view of the dynamics of the social "machine."

What, then, should be the role of governmental agencies regarding ethnic groups? What policies of these agencies and of other social institutions will foster creative ethnicity, individual rights, a fluid pluralism of interrelations among groups, democratic decision-making, and social and economic justice? And what policies move society toward ethnic tribalism, violation of individual rights, a static mosaic society of insulated groups, and internecine fighting? Human psychology being what it is, any actions that are not clearly and unequivocally perceived as moving toward the first scenario ipso facto help to create the second.

The issue is nowhere more critical than in the affirmative-action policies of the Department of Health, Education, and Welfare and other institutions. The widespread public confusion surrounding these policies is fraught with dangers. In the operative, popular American myths of fairness and individual merit, our institutions, and especially governmental institutions, are viewed as "referees," who see to it that the ethics of the two myths are not violated. When a governmental institution is itself perceived as violating those ethics, the effect on society is extremely disruptive and destructive.

Several characteristics of affirmative action, as they are perceived by millions of Americans, are damaging for precisely this reason. They are:

1. the assertion of "group rights," specifically rights of certain ethnic groups, over individual rights and the "rights" of other groups;

2. the assertion of ethnic group membership over individual merit as

a criterion of reward;

3. the assertion of "compensatory justice" on behalf of members of some groups over the right and merits of individuals not belonging to those groups;

4. the partisanship of institutions, including HEW, that violates the fairness myth;

5. the capture of the powers of institutions by groups using them for partisan purposes;

6. the stimulation of a determination to "strike back," to assert oneself and one's group against other groups and the institutions favoring them.

It has long been realized that America is composed of a pluralism of ethnic groups. Walt Whitman called the United States a "teeming nation of nations." In this scheme, basic to the American mentality for a long time, government is viewed as the guarantor of the legal rights of individuals and as neutral regarding the relations between ethnic groups and the various expressions of ethnicity. The twentieth century has seen the rise of collectives, including ethnic groups. As collectives compete and clash with each other, the "nation of nations" has come increasingly to resemble the rivalry of nations in international society, a society composed of sovereign units, where the lack of effective, fair international laws is sorely felt. The woes of fragmentation have beset the United States for some time. That these are felt today by millions of Americans is reflected in "A Synoptic View of American Public Opinion."[16] Of five "hopes" and eight "fears" surveyed among Americans over a twelve-year period, the sharpest increase occurred in the fear of national disunity, which jumped 18 percentage points between 1964 and 1971 and 23 percentage points between 1959 and 1971.

As the nation is increasingly perceived as a collection of collectives competing with each other, it would seem essential that the traditional role of government be reaffirmed. For individual rights urgently need protection in a field of collective movements, and the myth of fairness dictates that government and other institutions remain nonpartisan in the competition between ethnic groups. The great emphasis on civil rights since 1954 attests to the interest in protecting individual rights. Ironically, however, some of the more ill-considered of these thrusts have weakened public confidence in the nonpartisan nature of their government at the very time when the more tribalistic assertions of ethnic groups are being multiplied and intensified.

The problem can be put simply. As the government is viewed, accurately or not, as using its power to implement ideas of "collective justice" on behalf of some *groups* as distinct from individuals, it is further seen as being unjust to those individuals who do not belong to favored groups. And government is also viewed as a partisan group itself. Belief in the notion of the fairness of American society is undermined. The cynicism that results is fertile ground for the growth of a new myth of a disjointed nation of tribalistic groups, each following a dog-eat-dog ethic.

The confusion surrounding the affirmative-action programs of HEW and other institutions has also fueled the drive toward ethnic tribalism. Since many people are convinced that membership in a favored ethnic group is given preference over individual merit, the natural response is to spend one's energies, not in improving one's qualifications and performance, but in strengthening the power of one's tribe so that it (and hence you) can survive and flourish in the war of tribes. In addition to creating disunity, this trend has another socially destructive effect.

Although it is now unfashionable to say, social and economic progress in the United States has been realized in large measure because of the efforts of its middle class, which greatly outnumbers both poor and rich. This is because the energies of the poor are wasted since they are not channelled into socially productive areas. Indeed, this is one of the outrages against the poor. And although much of the money of the rich is used in ways that contribute to socioeconomic growth, their energies have been largely deflected into pleasure-seeking and other individual pursuits that produce little or no social gain. The large middle class' desire for upward mobility is the yeast of America's social and economic growth, without which the resources, or "dough," of society would not be productive. This drive for upward mobility depends upon faith in the myths of reward for individual merit and fairness exercised by social institutions, especially public ones. Actions by government that subvert belief in these myths by rewarding ethnic membership vitiate the socially productive energies of those not in the favored groups and of those who are only condescendingly favored.

It is widely believed by members of all ethnic groups from all strata of our society that the term "equal-opportunity employer" is a code phrase meaning that members of favored minority groups and women will be given preference over other qualified individuals. It is also widely accepted that this is largely the result of pressure from government agencies like HEW, which have given in to pressure by aggressive tribalistic groups. Hence, HEW and other institutions are seen as unjust partisans that threaten the rights of individuals and the effectiveness of pressured organizations.

In the academic world, for example, where the job market is now very tight and competition for positions intense, it is widely believed that the affirmative-action policies of HEW place qualified members of

215

nonfavored groups at a disadvantage and thus lead to the hiring and promotion of the less qualified, subverting the quality of education and research in the university. The actual extent to which "reverse discrimination" is operative is a moot issue since the *belief* that it prevails has the same corrosive effect as the fact. Only a few recruitment letters from university departments expressing partial or absolute preference for women and members of specific ethnic groups are sufficiently destructive—and more than a few such letters have surfaced, some directly attributing the preference to pressure from HEW.

A recruitment letter from a department at Claremont Men's College in California states: "We desire to appoint a Black or Chicano, preferably female." (Incidentally, the device of hiring female members of minority groups satisfies pressures from two directions. One person now "represents" both categories of people. The ultimate result of this trend demeans people; individuals are quite plainly reduced to tokens.) From Northwestern University in Illinois: "We are looking for female economists and members of minority groups." From Sacramento State College in California: "Sacramento State College is currently engaged in an Affirmative Action Program, the goal of which is to recruit, lure and promote ethnic and women candidates until they comprise the same proportion of our faculty as they do of the general population." From Indiana University: "Preference will be given to women and minority group candidates in filling this position if candidates of equal quality are identified." From Connecticut College to a male applicant: "It is quite true that we have an opening here and that I have examined your dossier. It is very impressive indeed, and I wish I could invite you to come for an interview. At present, however, the department is interested in the appointment of a woman so we are concentrating on interviews of this kind."

A letter from New Mexico State University explains: "Your prompt response to my letter with four candidates all of whom seem qualified for our vacancy, is greatly appreciated. Since this is no indication that any of them belongs to one of the minority groups listed, I will be unable to contact them at present." From Washington State University: "women or members of minority groups." From Stanford University in California: "The Provost of Stanford has asked our Department to make a special effort to assemble a roster of Chicanos . . ." From the University of California at Berkeley: "outstanding candidates of minority background (Chicanos, Blacks, Women [sic])."

In trade unions, affirmative action is felt as an unjust threat by members of those ethnic groups next to the lowest rung of the socioeconomic ladder. It is they who must compete with the favored minorities and who suffer reverse discrimination. We should remember that many trade unions became ethnically homogeneous for good reasons. One was due to the attempt of foreign-language-speaking immigrant workmen to survive at a time when labor unions were underdogs in a hard and often vicious struggle.

Workingmen needed unions, and ethnicity served as one of the most useful criteria of organization. Unions became populated by the ethnic groups making up the labor force at the time of unionization. Thus, in New York City, Italian sanitation workers organized an Italian union, Jewish teachers organized the teacher's union, and the police association was Irish. In private employment, Italians populated construction unions, the Irish were synonymous with transportation workers, and the garment industry was unionized by Jewish and Italian workers. Similar ethnic identities marked the organization of the labor movement in the rest of the United States. For example, the steelworker's unions of the Midwest were organized by Poles, Slovaks, Croats, and Magyars.

Since their origins, the "ethnic" unions have frequently sought to exclude members of other ethnic groups, for three reasons. First, there is a natural desire to work and associate with those of similar background and culture. As has been emphasized, ethnicity has always been in the warp and woof of all peoples' identity. Second, ethnic tribalism has sometimes operated and outsiders were excluded, not only because they were different, but also because they were regarded as inferior. Third, outsiders were excluded as a result of an antiunion tactic once widely used by employers: dividing and conquering the workers on the basis of ethnic differences. Employers set ethnic group against ethnic group, telling Poles they could not trust Italians and vice versa. Great fears and hatreds between ethnic groups were cynically inflamed.

In *Toil and Trouble*, a history of the labor movement, Thomas R. Brooks notes the effectiveness of this divisive tactic against the fledgling labor movement. It turned ethnicity toward a panicky, threatened ethnic tribalism.

> Needless to say, each group protected its own as it organized its trade. The process—and results—were markedly different in industry where employers followed a deliberate policy of pitting one immigrant group against another as a means of forestalling unionization. In a report made by John R. Commons following a visit to a large Chicago packing company in 1904, he notes that he "saw seated around the benches of the company's employment office a sturdy group of Nordics. I asked the employment agent, 'how comes it you are employing only Swedes?' He answered, 'Well you see, it is only for this week. Last week we employed Slovaks. We change about the dif-

ferent nationalities and languages. It prevents them from getting together. We have the thing systematized. We have a luncheon each week of the employment managers of the large firms of the Chicago district. There we discuss our problems and exchange information. We have a number of men in the field who keep us informed . . . If agitators are coming or expected and there is considerable unrest among the labor population, we raise the wages all around . . . It is wonderful to watch the effect. The unrest stops and the agitators leave. Then when things quiet down we reduce the wages to where they were.'" This deliberate policy is one reason that unions failed to secure an early foothold in industrial plants. Among the skilled trades, ethnic lines reinforced craft solidarity. But among the unskilled in factories, worker solidarity was defeated by the babel of tongues. [17]

Thus the paradox that ethnic homogeneity was reinforced in the labor movement because it was successful as a tactic both to unify skilled labor and to "bust" the unionizing efforts among unskilled labor. In short, ethnicity and the early labor movement were inseparable.

Recently, the historic ethnic parochialism of trade unions has increased as members of White ethnic minorities (Irish, Italian, Poles) fear that they are, or may be, discriminated against by favoritism toward nonwhites. Violation of notions of fairness and merit is perceived by White ethnic workers as a continuity, running from the old practices of employers to the new affirmative-action programs.

A parallel exists in the academic world. Jews, and now even Wasps, fear ethnic and sex discrimination exercised by universities under pressure from HEW. Unfortunately, neither HEW nor other affirmative-action proponents have demonstrated appreciation for the complexities and nuances of intergroup relations. Like the media, they have been sensitive only to one facet of the complicated history of ethnic relationships—racism. Their single-mindedness has convinced many White ethnics that their legitimate needs, problems, and rights are not understood or respected. As a matter of fact, little hard data about these groups has even been collected. In government studies, they are simply lumped together as "Whites" or "others"—and ignored. The attempts of members of these groups to protect, or even explain, their rights and needs are usually immediately countered with loud, glib cries of racism or sexism. Instead of producing confusion and guilt among White ethnics, the dominant pattern until recently, these simplistic charges are now meeting a counterresponse of White-ethnic assertiveness and even tribalism.

The miasma surrounding affirmative action is dense. Within the limits of this brief essay, major points can only be illuminated.

1. There is widespread confusion over whether "affirmative action" implies the imposition of quotas. Quotas, by any name—for example, "goals" or "timetables"—are unjust and destructive.

2. The selection of favored groups, called "protected classes" by HEW, raises a number of complicated questions. Who decides which groups are to be favored and by what criteria? Choices will inevitably involve injustices. For example, is the son of a rich and influential Black family to be favored? Are Black men to be favored over Italian-American men in admissions to graduate schools in light of the finding by Glazer and Moynihan that in the New York City area the percentage of Black male professionals is higher than the percentage of Italian-American male professionals?[18] In short, any selection of favored ethnic groups is bound to violate the principles of fairness and merit.

In addition, the policy of favoring one group is an open invitation to another group to struggle to capture the levers of power and declare itself or its allies "favored." In this struggle, the most energetic, tribalistic, and politically "savvy" groups are best equipped to win the efforts of the government and other institutions to their side. These groups are not necessarily those suffering discrimination, nor are those who "lose out" in the struggle necessarily free from oppression.

3. The use of statistical data alone does not prove or disprove discrimination. Present affirmative-action policies rely too heavily on simplistic use of such data.

4. Compensatory justice is valid only as applied to individuals, not to groups. If a qualified individual has been discriminated against in the past, and thereby refused a job, he or she is entitled to compensation, entitled to be hired first by the offending employer. Compensatory justice applied to groups, however, leads to the absurdities of infinite regression. As the selection from Brooks' history of the labor movement indicates, it would be hard to find anyone who is not a member of a group that has been discriminated against at some time in the United States. Second, compensatory justice for favored groups is unfair to individuals who have suffered discrimination but are not members of a favored group.

5. The establishment of favored ethnic groups distorts the process by which society chooses which cultural contributions by which groups are to be accepted by the whole, making it less likely that the genuinely valuable or useful will prevail.

6. The argument that discriminatory affirmative action is a necessary but temporary cure is spurious. In addition to establishing undesirable precedents and entrenching discriminatory practices, it encourages ethnic tribalism and destroys social unity.

7. The application of the sanction of "preaward compliance review"

of financial aid and contracts against institutions is, in effect, a demand to prove innocence. This demand is not only morally unjust but also logically absurd.

Powerful governmental agencies like HEW should take the lead in reversing the drift of American society since the mid-sixties toward the undesirable scenario described in this paper and move it in the direction of a desirable scenario. This can be done by a clear and unequivocal announcement that "affirmative action" means programs designed to equip disadvantaged individuals to compete on the basis of competence in a social arena where fairness will be guaranteed by government protection of individual rights. Energies and resources should be shifted toward the creation of imaginative and effective programs of this type, coupled with a clear renunciation of all discriminatory affirmative-action practices.

Recommendations can be listed under three headings: first, those relating to general social policy; second, those that will meet the special circumstances of the academic world; and third, recommendations covering the particular conditions of trade unionism. General recommendations would include the following:

1. Special programs to recruit and qualify members of all ethnic groups, with the goal of widened job opportunity for individuals who are qualified, and special training and educational efforts to increase the pool of those who are not yet qualified. There should be a switch in affirmative action from ethnic categories to opportunity for all individuals who are in need. No ethnic group has a monopoly on poverty, need, or ambition. Widened opportunity to compete on the basis of merit is the goal where job or professional qualifications are relevant. When there is a surplus of qualified candidates for a job, selection should be by lot, that is, by the neutral laws of chance. This would be preferable to the proposed guidelines of the Office of Civil Rights of HEW covering colleges and universities, which states that women and minority applicants "must be recruited, hired, and promoted over all competitors where their qualifications are the same."

2. Vigorous enforcement of the 1964 Civil Rights Act and all prior and subsequent legislation against racial, ethnic, religious, and sex discrimination. Specific cases of discrimination should be pursued. Vigorous enforcement would not only punish offenders but also deter others from discriminatory action.

3. Careful use of statistical data according to rules governing meaningful interpretation. One of these rules is that statistics alone are not conclusive proof of discrimination and, at best, can give only a prima facie picture. Conclusive proof of discrimination requires other

evidence, independent of statistical data.

The other rules governing the use of statistics are complicated, but easily available through the many statisticians employed by government agencies and other large institutions. Among them are the stipulations that all the significant characteristics of a sample be included in the study and assigned appropriate statistical weight; that the statistical samples used be large enough to have mathematical significance; and that there be homogeneity among the statistical examples in terms of significant characteristics. Each of these important rules has been repeatedly ignored in compiling data that purportedly establishes discriminatory practices. The logical and moral burdens of proof are on those making an accusation, and not on the accused, as the Proposed Guidelines would have it in saying that "the premise of the affirmative action concept of the Executive Order is that systematic and institutional forms of exclusion, inattention and purposeful discrimination in employment have existed." Such a premise says nothing about any *specific* employer. To use it as a blanket a priori condemnation requiring proof of innocence from an employer is a logical non sequitur and a moral injustice.

4. Cessation of classification of favored groups by institutional fiat. Questions of discrimination should be objectively determined according to the rules listed under headings two and three.

5. Complete, unequivocal renunciation of all attempts to impose ethnic or sex quotas, however euphemistically labeled.

6. Government neutrality regarding the efforts of organized ethnic groups. These should be purely private and voluntary associations and government should not use its power on their behalf. This involves a clear and unambiguous commitment from government institutions to enforce, not group rights, but only the legal rights of individuals of all groups. Indeed, preferential hiring is quite clearly illegal under Section 703 of Title VII of the Civil Rights Act of 1964, which states:

> Nothing contained in this title shall be entitled to require any employer . . . to grant preferential treatment to any individual or to any group because of the race, color, sex or national origin of such individual or group on account of an imbalance which may exist with respect to the total number or percentage of persons of any race, color, religion, sex or national origin employed by any employer . . . in comparison with the total number or percentage of persons of such race, color, religion, sex or national origin in any community, State, section, or other area or in the available work force of any community, State, section or other area.

In addition to these recommendations, others should also be followed by colleges and universities.

1. Colleges should give maximum publicity to job openings, tenure and promotion opportunities, and should be required to make full disclosure of all information involved in decisions regarding these questions, including the qualifications of those accepted. Any aggrieved individuals would thus have the information necessary to initiate corrective action. Neither the principle of confidentiality nor the privileges of departmental personnel committees or of deans and presidents should be permitted to hide cases of discrimination or reverse discrimination. Colleges should be compelled to honor the merit system by vigorously scrutinizing their practices and punishment of any lapses. The long-established "old boy" discriminatory system and the newly established "preferential treatment" discrimination should both be combatted on behalf of the merit system.

2. It must be recognized that colleges recruit from a nationwide pool and statistical data must be carefully interpreted. For example, the great majority of college personnel decisions are made by individual departments. Most of these are too small (less than fifty) to permit conclusive statistical results without statistically independent evidence. In enforcement of antidiscrimination policies, therefore, stress should be upon good-faith efforts by the employing departments to hire the best-qualified person without ethnic or sex discrimination.

3. Programs for recruiting college and graduate students should be enlarged. Their special needs (educational, social, financial) should be met so that they have a fair opportunity to become qualified for college teaching or for other professions and occupations.

I wish to make four recommendations regarding labor unions.

1. Apprenticeship programs should be opened. For many years, craft unions have required that admission be based on successful completion of an apprenticeship training program, which may run from a few months to as long as six years. These programs are designed to meet two needs: to assure a supply of fully trained labor, and to control the numbers of trained workers entering a particular field. The second purpose is grounded in bitter memories of past unemployment, which wrecked many unions, with disastrous results for all workers in the trade.

Affirmative-action efforts were at first aimed at winning admission to apprenticeship programs for selected minorities. Openings for these programs should be widely publicized. Then applicants should be selected by lot in a supervised process. Each person desiring entry would then have a mathematically equal chance to that of every other applicant, which would guarantee fairness for each individual, avoiding both discrimination and reverse discrimination. Recent attempts to bypass apprenticeship programs, exercised on behalf of favored groups, should cease. In addition to the objections already raised in this essay, undertrained workers create hazardous working conditions.

2. Unions which are de facto closed should be opened. Some craft unions favor the admission only of relatives of members. Obviously, this tends to preserve the ethnic status quo within these unions. This is illegal under the Taft-Hartley Act, but like the illegal closed shop it persists in practice because of sub rosa agreements between unions and employers. Closed unions should be opened by close government observation of practices in the field and swift prosecutions of Taft-Hartley violations.

3. Union leadership should be opened. Union leaders tend to perpetuate themselves in office, even when the ethnic composition of the union has changed dramatically. For example, in New York City, the garment-workers union has shifted from a Jewish and Italian membership toward a largely Black and Puerto Rican composition, but the leadership does not reflect this change. Similarly, the fire, police, and transportation departments, once solidly Irish, now have large numbers of Italians and a growing number of Blacks and Puerto Ricans. The union leadership, however, remains Irish. The remedy calls for close government scrutiny of union elections under existing laws, a remedy local governments have been loath to employ for fear of labor troubles.

4. The seniority system must be modified. Seniority is the most troublesome issue in labor unions. Seniority systems require laying off the latest arrivals first; they also require all rehiring on the basis of length of service. Thus, newcomers are last hired, first fired. In addition, in industries where seniority affects promotions, those who lack seniority because they were hired late, as a result of past discrimination, are not promoted. This perpetuates the original discrimination against these individuals.

The situation could be remedied by bypassing seniority requirements for 50 per cent of all firings, hirings, and promotions. Thus, those who have seniority (and who are individually innocent of past discrimination) continue to have some protection. And those who are newcomers have a chance to get where they should have been. Because none of the newcomers are guilty of any past discrimination, the 50 per cent rule would apply to all of them. Those to benefit from it should be chosen by lot, as should those whose accumulation of seniority is to be waived. Such a compromise is necessary because questions of individual rights regarding seniority are mixed, as they are not regarding other issues.

Governmental policies, and those of large private institutions, tend to concentrate on short-term results at the expense of long-term considerations. This is so not only because these institutions are highly vulnerable to political pressure, but also because most of the social scientists they employ are trained to work only with quantitative models of analysis and are blind to different value priorities of data. Such values can only be assigned by informed, sensitive social thinkers. It is time to restore to public policy-making a longer vision and a more sophisticated perspective.

NOTES

1. Theodore Shabad, "Soviet Is Pressing the Blending of Its 100 Nationalities," *New York Times*, July 31, 1972, p. 2.

2. John Burns, "China Strives to Integrate Her Minorities," *New York Times*, July 31, 1972, p. 2.

3. For a fuller exposition of my thoughts on tribalism and creativity, see "The Militant Mentality," *Freedom At Issue*, July-Aug. 1972, p. 8.

4. *The Collected Essays, Journalism and Letters of George Orwell*, Vol. 3 (New York: Harcourt, Brace and World, 1968), p. 362.

5. Michael Novak, *The Rise of the Unmeltable Ethnics* (New York: Macmillan, 1972).

6. Peter Schrag, *The Decline of the Wasp* (New York: Simon and Schuster, 1972).

7. *Ibid.*, p. 104.

8. Marshall Cohen in the *New York Times Book Review*, July 16, 1972, p. 1. Stuart Hampshire in a special supplement to the *New York Review of Books*, Feb. 24, 1972.

9. John Rawls, *A Theory of Justice* (Cambridge, Mass: Harvard University Press, 1971).

10. Harold Cruse, *The Crisis of the Negro Intellectual* (New York: Morrow, 1967).

11. Richard M. Huber, *The American Idea of Success* (New York: McGraw, 1971).

12. Thomas A. Johnson, "Campus Racial Tensions Rise as Black Enrollment Increases," *New York Times*, April 4, 1972, p. 57.

13. Peter F. Drucker, *The Age of Discontinuity* (New York: Harper and Row, 1968).

14. *Ibid.*, p. 225.

15. *Ibid.*, p. 233.

16. Reprinted in *H.E.W. and the Future*, a paper of the Department of Health, Education and Welfare, Nov. 26, 1971, p. 30.

17. Thomas R. Brooks, *Toil and Trouble* (New York: Dell, 1964), pp. 76-77.

18. Nathan Glazer and Daniel Moynihan, *Beyond the Melting Pot* (Cambridge, Mass.: M.I.T. Press, 1970), p. lvi.

The Decline of Professional Morale

Glenn R. Morrow
University of Pennsylvania

One of the more ominous conclusions to be drawn from the campus disturbances of the past few years is that there has been a serious decline in the quality of our faculties. By this, I do not mean a decline in scholarly and scientific competence; in this respect, our professors today may well be—and I suspect they are—definitely superior to their predecessors. What I mean is a decline in their commitment to the idea of a university as a "setting for scientific and scholarly imagination," to use Professor Nisbet's fine phrase. A professor who holds such a commitment regards himself as especially privileged, as set apart in a real sense for some important purpose, and he regards his special privileges as validated only by his devotion to this high purpose and to the institutions that make it possible for him to pursue it. His profession is for him something akin to a sacred calling. Without this commitment, a professor becomes merely another individual seeking personal profit or advancement in a competitive order. This idea of the university and of the professor's calling is so obvious to most of us who have spent our lives in the academic world that I will not pause to defend it, especially since those to whom it is not obvious would scarcely profit by my defense. It is this idea of a university that has made it the most desirable of all places for scholars and scientists, indeed for all those who cherish the intellectual life; and this idea is responsible for the immense prestige that universities have traditionally enjoyed and for the numerous benefits their existence has brought society.

The most striking evidence of a decline in faculty quality is that many members of university and college faculties (my observation is that they are usually the younger members) have openly sympathized with the extreme activists during the disturbances, and have directly or indirectly encouraged the forceful occupation of administrative offices, the closing of laboratories, and the prevention of visiting speakers from speaking and of teachers from meeting their classes. Faculties who have tried to discipline offenders have often been unable to act resolutely because of the strident voices of dissidents within their own ranks; sometimes, when a faculty has a tradition of obtaining consensus before action, it has been unable to act at all.

Such behavior is a scandal to the profession. I think, however, that we can partly explain the reasons for it. During the recent period of rapid expansion, many persons have been appointed to positions in our colleges and universities who have been hastily trained and even more hastily screened before appointment. Universities had to have teachers; graduate departments felt that they had to place their graduates, whether or not they had completed their formal preparation; and a host of colleges and so-called universities, improperly equipped for the purpose, have initiated programs for advanced degrees, often moved by a lofty but misguided intention of helping satisfy a public need. It is inevitable that many persons appointed under such conditions should have had no clear commitment to the life of the university. Or, if they once had such a commitment, they have become alienated because of failure to attain immediately what they fancy they deserve and have thus ranked themselves among the underprivileged. Their dissatisfaction has had its danger to others; for even senior professors, finding themselves unable to attain distinction or preferment as teachers, scientists, or scholars, are sometimes tempted to obtain notoriety, at least, by courting the campus rabble.

Another factor also has been at work to lower the quality of appointments. Professors are no longer poor. There has been such a marked rise in faculty salaries during the past two decades that the academic career now offers prospects of financial reward sufficient to attract persons who otherwise would have no interest in it. The relative poverty in which professors traditionally had to live, as compared with lawyers, doctors, and businessmen, served a useful purpose in deterring applicants whose minds are directed toward matters other than the intellectual life. When a professor has to resign himself to going without some things enjoyed by his fellow citizens, we can be fairly sure of his commitment to his profession. We cannot take this for granted in the case of persons who have joined the ranks in the more recent affluent days. Seen from this point of view, the new era of professorial prosperity has been anything but an unmixed blessing. We look back with some nostalgia to the days when a professor was happy to live only in return for the satisfaction of advancing his field of study and training students in its background and techniques. I shall never forget a remark made by Professor H. J. Davenport to an economics class of which I was privileged to be a member early in my career. He said that if Cornell University were not paying him five thousand dollars a year, he would be willing, if he had the money, to pay that amount to Cornell for the privilege of teaching. I need not add that he was an excellent teacher and an eminent scholar.

I am told that financial rewards have been compounded for many members of our faculties by the proliferation of government-subsidized research in the universities. I have no firsthand knowledge of such operations, but I have witnessed their effects. They have distracted professors from teaching; indeed, they have greatly helped give currency to the view that a man's eminence is judged not by how much salary he receives but by how little he teaches. They have diluted the loyalty of professors to their universities. They have diverted professors' attention from problems to which their scientific imaginations might have led them to those for which they can obtain supporting grants. Project-hunting has become a rather vulgar enterprise, to judge from the behavior of some of my colleagues and from the elaborate organizations set up in major universities to facilitate the search for government and foundation grants. As universities have become more and more dependent on such outside funds, their policy choices have become limited in ominous ways, sometimes even threatening their fundamental commitment to the nurturing of excellence in science and scholarship.

Finally, I find enlightening the experience of the American Association of University Professors, in which I have been an active member for practically all of my professional life. I have usually found the AAUP's pronouncements on professional matters to be the most thoroughly considered and statesmanlike ones available. The officers and committees of AAUP have had to pronounce on a variety of issues, and these very issues provide invaluable insight into the temper and concerns of our members, particularly since our membership is broad and the officers are acutely responsive to their demands. For these reasons I have come to look upon the AAUP as something like a barometer of the profession. I note with sorrow that the barometer has been steadily falling in recent years.

To begin with, the Association is no longer the elite organization that was envisaged at its founding. When I was admitted to

227

membership more than forty years ago, our constitution made membership dependent upon three years of previous service as teacher or researcher in an approved college or university, and required nomination by three members and approval by a two-thirds vote of the council. The requirements have become much less exacting over the years. Membership is now acquired by mere application, and application is open not only to faculty members in four-year colleges and universities but also to those of junior colleges. Paralleling this progressively more liberal policy of admission, and probably in consequence of it, our announced purpose has been significantly changed. Originally it was to promote the "standards and ideals of the profession." The latest version of the constitution, amended in 1957, states it as being "to advance the standards, ideals, and welfare of the profession." (The original proposal for amendment in 1957 read "economic welfare," but the more responsible members outvoted the proponents and deleted "economic" from the amendment as adopted.) Nonetheless, the Association's attention within recent years has had to be focused increasingly on the economic status of the profession, and there has been persistent agitation by some of our members for the adoption of collective bargaining and for the use of the strike as a weapon. The defense of academic tenure as a necessary guarantee of academic freedom, to be attained only after a prolonged period of probation, has come to be regarded by more and more of our members as a program for assuring security of tenure at all ranks. Thus the main aim of academic freedom in a university context has been increasingly overlooked, and the significance of tenure and the requisites for attaining it have been, I think, seriously downgraded. The Association has seldom yielded to the more extreme demands, but their very presence is disheartening evidence of decline.

Is it too late to correct the trend toward deterioration in our standards of professorial competence? Must we continue to drift with the prevailing currents, or are there measures we can take to stem the tide? A resolute insistence upon merit as a condition of appointment and promotion is the obvious first step, but it should be supported by a renewed commitment to the idea of the university as a haven of the intellect, as a training-place in science and scholarship for the elite and for all students who show themselves able and willing to participate in this higher training. But whether that reversal of attitude will occur remains to be seen in the future.

Equality and Quality in Education

Marvin Zimmerman
*State University of New York
at Buffalo*

Does democracy presuppose the principle of equality, that all human beings are equal? If so, does democracy imply the equal right of all to learn and teach in institutions of higher education, to be admitted as students and faculty? Does belief in equality contradict commitment to knowledge and excellence? Are equality and quality in education compatible?

If democracy can be justified only on the principle of equality and if the principle of equality is untenable, so much the worse for democracy! Though belief in equality may imply or require belief in democracy, fortunately the converse is not the case. One can defend democracy on utilitarian grounds and on grounds of self-interest, as well as by other means. Whatever the relationship between equality and democracy, the principle of equality needs to be judged on its own merits.

One can conceive of a society in which all were made to conform identically in education, experience, and wealth. All would receive the same education, and be forced to spend and save the same amount of money and have identical experiences. This sounds like a nightmare, hardly what advocates of equality could really have in mind. Even this nightmare would face problems of achieving and sustaining complete equality, identity, and sameness, if only because of innate differences among people.

The belief in equality is not to be taken literally, for there are few things in which all humans are the same, such as having the same number of eyes, legs, and arms. Even here, there are obvious exceptions; some individuals have only one eye, leg, or arm. In general, it would be closer to the truth to proclaim the principle of inequality. The claim of equality is a moral or ethical one at most, and it raises fundamental questions of justification. The claim of inequality is also a moral one. In a time of widespread ritualistic egalitarianism, it may be appropriate to urge the support of the moral principle of "inegalitarianism," the right of all humans to be treated unequally. The myth of equality needs debunking and deflating.

Is the term "equality" any more deserving of approval than the term "inequality," since there are more sound reasons for treating people differently than similarly? Egalitarians concede that reasonable differences in treatment are compatible with equality, though unreasonable ones are not. If so, an inegalitarian can also maintain, without contradiction, that reasonable similarities in treatment are permissible, though unreasonable ones are not. If an egalitarian may treat an individual with an IQ of 60 differently from one with an IQ of 160, an inegalitarian may treat two individuals, each with IQs of 100 equally. Even in the latter case, equal treatment would apply to only one of an indefinite number of different traits that call for different treatment.

Differences may arise concerning the presence or absence of a valid reason for equal or unequal treatment. Thus, an employer may hire the first qualified applicant to arrive though there may be other equally qualified ones who show up after the first one. One might argue that there was no valid reason to hire the first one before interviewing the others. On the other hand, the employer may have specified that he would hire on a "first come" basis, that he needed someone immediately, that time spent interviewing was too costly, and so on. But, in the absence of valid reasons, one could plausibly maintain that either there was an invalid reason for treating them unequally or there was a valid reason for treating them equally.

Some kind of utilitarian appeal is being made in looking for valid reasons for treating people equally or unequally. Thus, reference is made to harmful consequences from prejudice and beneficial consequences from treating individuals on the basis of ability, knowledge, and experience in performing a job or in acquiring an education.

The problem of what constitutes a valid reason for equal or unequal treatment raises certain difficulties. Though ability, in the sense of knowledge, experience, and intelligence, is generally acknowledged as a valid ground, questions of personality, sociality, personal attractiveness, and other psychological factors possess degrees of validity that cannot be ignored. Personality and attractiveness may be relevant to effective functioning in certain jobs. Emotional and psychological stability may be relevant to success in certain educational pursuits. Unfortunately, factors like race, color, sex, and creed are so frequently intermingled with personality and ability factors, unconsciously as well as consciously, that it is not always clear what the motivating considerations are in human relations.

There is a twofold danger here. One may treat individuals unequally on what appear to be grounds of personality or ability and thus are reasonable, though in fact the grounds involve prejudice and are thus unreasonable. On the other hand, one may be accused, or fear being accused, of prejudice where there are legitimate grounds for unequal treatment. Both dangers, particularly reflected in recent Black-White relations in the United States, have contributed to unreasonable treatment of individuals, whether equally or unequally. It has also caused both White and Black racism, both discrimination and reverse discrimination, to appear as valid, on the basis that the "others" are guilty of discrimination.

In the call for open admissions to higher education, one must distinguish between encouraging further education commensurate with one's abilities and achievements, on the one hand, and the equal or even preferential right to be admitted to a higher education for which one is unqualified, on the other. The former could provide for preferential financial treatment for disadvantaged groups without violating the principle of educational merit. The latter, however, could have the effect of destroying certain educational functions and diverting them into quite different ones. Research and scholarship may give way to remedial work.

There is nothing wrong with individuals, students and others, taking courses and teachers of their own choosing where degrees or other forms of certification are not involved. In principle, this is like going to a library and taking out any book one desires. This constitutes informal learning, where no representation or claim is being made to the authorities or public that an individual is qualified in some profession, discipline, skill, or area of knowledge, where feasible, formal courses may be used to satisfy this informal kind of pursuit. But degrees, certificates, licenses, and other forms of credentials must retain the kind of meaning, validity, and integrity upon which the public can rely and trust.

Of course, one may radically transform the function of a university to that of a political, social, or remedial institution. This would not do away with the original academic needs of learning, teaching, and research. It would merely require society to find other means of fulfilling these needs to the extent that universities failed to fulfill them. It would also reduce the burden of other institutions that formerly dealt with social and remedial needs. Society would still allocate resources to satisfy these diverse needs as it saw fit, no matter which institutions or agencies happened to be carrying them out. In one sense then, one wonders what is the point of it all, in rearranging different institutions to carry out the same kinds of functions and needs.

In the push by government authorities for minority quotas, it is not clear what the overall consequences may be where minority or other groups are given preferential treatment in situations in which they are equally qualified. Bitterness has arisen on the part of Whites and others who object to reverse discrimination. This may promote more racial polarization and racism than that from which the original call for preferential treatment stemmed. Thus preferential treatment may be more than self-defeating. The Reconstruction era after the American Civil War lends some historical support to this notion.

However, it is one thing to give disadvantaged groups preferential treatment where they are at least equally qualified. It is quite a different thing where they are less qualified. Racism resulting from reverse discrimination will be (and already has been) supplemented by racism from less qualified and unqualified performance on jobs and at school. The costs of poor performance and deterioration of standards, not merely economic costs, have to be considered also.

Those who ask for alternatives to quotas in dealing with discrimination in education can invoke the models used in fighting discrimination in housing and employment. Let those who believe they are being discriminated against take legal action and utilize the judicial processes for redress. No process guarantees complete certainty against discrimination nor, for that matter, against false or erroneous accusations of discrimination. But individual claims, judicially processed, are far more conducive to avoiding abuses than quota systems imposed by government authorities.

Reflections on the Agonies of the University

Abba Lerner
*City University of New York,
Queens*

The troubles of academe that led to the formation of University Centers for Rational Alternatives in the first place, arose from a technological breakthrough in the art of disruption. In Berkeley in 1964, Mario Savio discovered, to his own and everybody else's surprise, how easy it was to demoralize the faculty. When the university was attacked by allegedly progressive forces instead of by reactionary forces and by students or alleged students instead of by government or by business, the professors were so shocked at the unexpected direction from which the attack came that they capitulated. The newly discovered vulnerability of universities was soon tested at Columbia, in Paris, and elsewhere, and was found to be applicable wherever the disrupters could find active support by even a small minority of the faculty.

The resulting disruption of university education and erosion in academic standards led to the alienation of important sections of the public from the universities. The alienated public, even while blaming the universities for giving in to, or encouraging, the disrupters, themselves took over some of the questionable charges leveled by the disrupters against the universities: namely, that professors did not teach enough and that their teaching was not "relevant" enough. As a result of this alienation, the universities found themselves in increasing financial difficulties and this made some of the disrupters' charges self-fulfilling.

The capitulation of university faculties and administrations to the violence and threats of violence seemed to be due to the cowardice discovered in the Berkeley "technological breakthrough," rather than to the numerous genuine and imaginary faults of the academic establishment—and indeed of our whole social system—that were in turn honored as "causes" of the trouble. But behind the apparent cowardice was a compounding of guilt and confusion.

The disrupters originally got their main support from the masses of young people who were at the universities for irrelevant reasons and who therefore failed to see much relevance in their studies. These were the young men who came to the universities to avoid the draft, to satisfy the pride of relatives, or to obtain degrees as tickets of entry to jobs. To this last group, their studies seemed only sadistically inspired obstacles, and to all of them the disruptions were welcome escapes from boredom and frustration. When these students began to be bored with the demonstrations and disruptions, the organizers turned to the genuine grievances of Blacks and other minorities. This greatly enhanced the guilt and confusion of the professors—guilt over past injustices, primarily to Negro slaves and their descendents, and confusion between past injustices and some of the continuing results, such as poverty, inferior preparation for university study, and lack of family help and encouragement to study.

From this confusion between past injustices and the resulting present handicaps grew another confusion: one between removing the old injustices (by eliminating racial and other such unjust discriminations) and balancing them with new and opposite injustices (by engaging in unjust discrimination *in favor of* groups that had suffered from discrimination). These were to be in the areas of admission and grading of Black and other disadvantaged students and of appointment and promotion of Black and other teachers in response to violence and threats of violence by students. Later, this philosophy found its way into the affirmative-action policy of the Department of Health, Education, and Welfare, which brought pressure for quotas (euphemistically labeled "targets") for faculties in the appointment and promotion of women and members of minority groups, with inevitable damage to the rational and legitimate principle of discrimination only in favor of greater competence.

The alienation of a great part of the public from the universities, which seriously damaged many universities financially, together with a decline in the number of new students, for demographic as well as other reasons, led to a worsening of the employment opportunities for university teachers and in the rate of increase of their pay. In some cases, pay was frozen in the face of a continuing increase in the cost of living. The natural dissatisfaction of teachers with this development gave impetus to the movement for the unionization of university teachers.

Here we find a strange symbiosis of two quite different notions of the nature of the university, able to coexist perhaps because both have claims to be "liberal" in the widest and most meaningless sense of that word. One is the view that the university is a democracy in which students, professors, administrators, and janitors should have equal voice in all university matters—one man (or woman), one vote is the hypnotic liberal slogan. We have seen great universities turned temporarily into chaotic communes. The other is the view that the administration, as employer, and the teachers, as employees, are natural enemies, the former trying to get as much work as possible from the latter for as little pay as possible in the industry of processing freshman materials into graduated products. The teachers must, therefore, protect themselves by organizing a union, and a union, in the liberal theology, is a "good thing."

I am not persuaded by either of these ritualistic liberalisms. I see the university as an institution in which teachers, students, and administration are engaged in a common educational enterprise, but in which they have clearly different roles that they are continually trying to integrate into the common purpose. Their positions are neither purely identical nor basically antagonistic.

So, I have been disturbed by the mail I get every day at Queens College from rival unions trying to organize me. I am bothered because I do not share the liberal view that trade unions are always a good thing, that they always protect the weak against the strong. I know that trade unions are not able to increase the real wages of workers in general. They can increase *money* wages in general, but they can do nothing to prevent prices from being raised to cover the increased costs caused by increased wages; thus *real* wages—purchasing power—remain the same. The only general result is inflation, with its manifest unfairness to pensioners and the like.

But trade unions *can* increase the real wages of some groups of workers relative to others. These others are hurt in the process, since what they earn does not keep up with the prices of what they buy: items made by the groups whose wages have risen more. There is, therefore, a pressure on these others to try to make their own group one of those that is ahead in the game, even if they understand that it is not possible for all to win.

I am therefore tempted to give in to my selfish interest in getting my pay raised and hence to support the union. But, I would do this with some regret and a little guilt, since I feel that unionization tends to foster a more antagonistic relationship between teacher and administration, rather than a cooperative interest in the educational enterprise. And, since I feel that I am not unique in my desire for higher pay and better fringe benefits, I am inclined to agree with those speakers who prophesy success for the unionization drive.

The question then is what can we do and how can we hope to protect and improve the university as an educational institution. What can we do to maintain the standards that are the concern of all those at this symposium?

It seems to me that our best hope, if I am right in expecting a great increase in trade-union power in the university, lies in getting the unions to work for *codetermination*. The more responsibility the union has in running the university, the less likely it is to consider itself solely engaged in trying to get more for its members out of the exploiting bosses. Among the fringe benefits it will try to get for its members will be the pride they feel in doing a good job.

I am reminded of the three stonemasons who were asked what they were doing. One said he was working for a living. Another said he was cutting a stone. The third said he was building a cathedral. All the discussion I have heard at this symposium came from people engaged in building a cathedral. With codetermination the trade union can become interested in building the cathedral—in running a better university in which its members would be helped to resist the forces that tend to corrupt and degrade it. After all, trade unions can be used for good purposes, just as senates or congresses or other faculty organizations can be.

I would like to return to another point in connection with HEW. I thought at first that I was going to disagree with Professor Seabury, but I was relieved to hear him say that we cannot claim to be treated differently from other people who are suspected of engaging in racial or other unjust discrimination. I do not think it good politics for us to say that we will not cooperate with HEW when they ask for information as to how many of our staff or our students are women, how many are Negroes, and information like that. We should not be afraid of providing any kind of information. Fear of information is a thing we are fighting on many fronts. We must recognize that statistics have helped to establish the existence of discrimination against Blacks, against other minorities, and against women.

It is true that this has been effective only in industries where there was some implausibility in the argument, for example, that the small number of Negro bricklayers was because they lacked the native ability or the long training required for competence. But university teaching does have such requirements. For us to resist giving out information lends plausibility to the charge that we are, in fact, discriminating unjustly and have something to hide.

Even if we believe, and with cause, that the statistics are going to be misused in attempts to show that we are discriminating against minorities—when we are, in fact, discriminating only in favor of competence—and in attempts to force us into unjust and harmful reverse discrimination, we must still say: information, yes—discrimination (other than for competence), no. We are neither against nor in favor of members of any race, color, creed, "language of name," or gender. We must insist that only discrimination for competence is justified and that every unjust discrimination in favor of anyone is inevitably unjust discrimination against others. But we must never hold back information. No misuse of the information can be as harmful to our just cause as the false charge that we are withholding information in order to hide unjust discrimination.

A Case Study—May 1970

Cyril Zebot
Georgetown University

Three presentations on three different themes at the symposium revealed that these topics are closely related. It seems to me that the troubles we have had all have one basic common cause. There have been four major intrusions onto our campuses. First, we experienced several years of student violence. Parallel to that were the pressures for dilution of our academic standards and programs; these pressures have continued. Next, there are inroads due to experiments in faculty unionization. Finally, we have heard of specific instances of dangerous government interference in university structures and governance.

What is common to these troubles, to these difficulties, to these dangers? It seems to me that the common cause lies in the basic confusion about the relationship between democracy in the society at large and the governance of a university. This is the central problem we should seriously address ourselves to when we go back to our respective universities. Resolving this confusion, solving this problem, it seems to me, is the great task and mission of University Centers for Rational Alternatives, which Professor Hook established in New York.

The reason that we at Georgetown feel rather strongly about this and have, perhaps, more explicitly realized the common cause of our difficulties is that in a few days in May of 1970 we experienced what can suddenly happen to a university if the academic faculty does not have a proper place in the university governance. For, by any meaningful definition of an institution of higher learning, the academic faculty is the key input in its production function—to use economists' terms.

As on many other campuses, a minority of Georgetown's vocal student activists, without consulting the student body, proclaimed a "boycott of classes" in support of a "bill of particulars," which listed seven issues and demands. As an afterthought, the issue of the invasion of Cambodia was added *after* the strike had been called. The boycott was to last three days, from May 6 through May 8, but it fizzled from the start. Not even 20 per cent of the students heeded the call. Virtually all classes were held, and there was no physical interference with professors or students or classrooms.

To rescue a political cause they could not assert by themselves through voluntary student participation, a group of students staged a sit-in around the president's office to force the administration to close the university, suspend classes, and end the semester before the scheduled final-examination period. Unable to convince an unwilling student body, they were successful in "persuading" a frightened administration.

In a search for a semblance of academic sanction for the foregone closing decision, a rump faculty meeting was improvised on a few hours notice on May 7. Neither the faculty senate nor any other known faculty organization was involved. The meeting "passed" a resolution proposed by the academic vice-president to the effect that the university suspend classes indefinitely, thus acceding to the "student" demand for an abrupt end to the semester. In a memorandum the following day, the academic vice-president informed the campus of the closing decision with the following preamble: "Resolutions passed Wednesday night and Thursday at the meetings of the Main Campus Faculty and of the Undergraduate Student Senate are being implemented as rapidly as possible. . . ." The wording was significant. The administration, in which all the decision-making power in the university is vested (under the supervision of the board of directors), suddenly demoted itself to a mere executive arm of the faculty and students.

I will not go into more detail except to mention that, after having witnessed this travesty of the way in which essential university decisions should be made, the faculty got together and prepared a resolution with one hundred twenty-three sponsors. It was aimed at preventing similar closings and suspensions of classes in the future except in a clear instance of actual physical emergency, in which the university president must obviously have immediate emergency powers. But in any other situation the university could not suspend classes or final examinations without a two-thirds majority concurrence of the academic faculty voting in referendum. The resolution carried by a 21 to 14 vote in the faculty senate (with seven of the fourteen negative votes cast by ex officio members of the administration) and was ratified by a 303 to 128 vote in a general faculty referendum by secret ballot.

This experience confirmed the need for a firmly structured faculty role in the university governance. The academic faculty must have the power of preliminary advice and ultimate consent in all academic policy decisions and supporting budget allocations. As an institution of higher learning, the university cannot be managed by the unilateral principles and practices that characterize business administration.

By the same token, it is also necessary to dispel recent confusion about the academic governance of a university and the role of political democracy in the society at large. Higher education cannot be governed by the general democratic principles of one person, one vote, majority rule, and protection of minority rights. Proper functioning of a university requires principles of governance that stem from the nature of its specific function. A university is a delicately structured enterprise, which requires rules and procedures that will safeguard the development and transmission of advanced knowledge. A rationally justifiable methodology is of the essence in the performance of this function. It is therefore misleading to characterize the university as a "free marketplace of ideas." There is no place in the curricular structure of the university for cooked experiments or deliberately falsified assertions.

This is not to say that there is no scope or room for idealistic causes or political activities on campus. What it does mean is that such interests and concerns belong among extracurricular activities that do not interfere with the curricular schedules and reflective nature of the university's educational function.

On a different plane, there are problems concerning the growing pressures for faculty unionization, which also may lead to the intrusion of nonacademic practices into the academic structure of the university. But only if the faculty is duly integrated into the university governance does it become clear that faculty unionization is not the proper answer to the material problems and concerns of the academic faculty.

Imposition of faculty or student quotas for extraneous reasons and under nonacademic criteria can also be effectively resisted only through proper faculty influence in the university governance.

Thus, it seems to me, that the proper faculty role in the governance of today's university must be the key item on the agenda for all of us. This concern must be pursued systematically, and the University Centers for Rational Alternatives can play a decisive role in this effort.

Who Is the Enemy?

Seymour M. Lipset
Harvard University

The source of many of the problems that have been discussed so far at this symposium rests in our own behavior. For years we have been concerned with the students. I must confess that I have published a book, *Rebellion in the University* (1972), dealing with politics in academe, which focuses on the behavior of students much more than on the principal actors, the intellectuals and the faculty. The problem of politicization has essentially been the problem of ourselves. If we want to look for the villain in the piece, we must look in the mirror. Much of academe is not really committed to academic freedom. Many are not truly committed to civil liberties. Some are not really committed to democratic rights, except in principle. And this is the reason we are having a problem with the Department of Health, Education, and Welfare.

I was in Washington recently and was taken by an assistant secretary to visit another high member of the administration. I discussed HEW's policies with him and gave him my version of the same kinds of facts that Paul Seabury and Sidney Hook have given us. He said he agreed. He assured me that his colleagues also agreed and were indeed very sympathetic. He then told me that the administration was not going to touch this problem, because those who were concerned about the imposition of quotas did not constitute a sizable constituency. HEW will not touch the problem of reverse discrimination because the constituency and the pressure involve politically weak groups in terms of votes they can affect on the issue. When more pressure comes from one direction than from another, any good politician knows how to behave. And they are behaving that way in Washington.

When the president of a university tries to defend meritocracy, he is attacked by the student newspaper and student activist groups, and no faculty member (or almost none) rises to his defense. Why then should the administrator do anything? The question is why faculties behave as they do.

I think one has to recognize a phenomenon that is particularly characteristic of American faculties, though one also finds this in France and some other countries. It is a pattern of judgment and action that implies that there are no enemies on the Left. Faculties and intellectuals in this country, particularly in major institutions and particularly among more serious scholars (I am speaking statistically, not taking into account the role of "deviants," such as are represented at this symposium) are predisposed to sympathize with every left-wing cause. They are "ritualistic liberals"—to use a phrase that I think Professor Hook coined many years ago. Press a button, and one knows how they will react to national, political, and social issues. John Searle talked about the fear of being thought reactionary. For example, at the height of the McCarthy era, a national study of social scientists showed that it was much more unpopular to be a defender of McCarthy on campuses than to be a Communist, in view of the general attitudes and values held by faculty members. I think this was true, even though a few Communists and people accused of being Communists were actually fired.

I am not sure that we can deal with our concern about politicization without recognizing the phenomenon for what it is. American society predisposes the best and most creative intellectuals toward the Left. Professor F. A. Hayek published an article in the University of Chicago *Law Review* in 1949 long before anybody collected statistics on intellectuals and politics. He said that the American academy was predisposed toward socialism and then went on to say that it is the most competent, the best professors who are socialists. He explained this in terms of selective moving into one's occupation; that is, that bright young people on the Left become academics, while bright young conservatives go into business or the professions.

In this context, a pattern occurred on campus after campus when student groups raised issues that much of the faculty on major campuses were sympathetic to. The faculty's initial reaction was to say, "We disagree with the means you use, but we agree with your ends." But this is no way to argue, because if the ends are moral, the fact that the means are not is something you cannot object to strongly. On campus after campus, from Berkeley to Columbia, Harvard, and other places where these crises occurred, the initial reaction of faculties was to vote with the student protestors against the administration, against any effort to maintain order and academic standards. That happened in the first faculty elections at Berkeley and at Harvard. It is also true that at Berkeley, Harvard, Cornell, and many other places the more conservative or moderate caucuses won the second, third, or fourth faculty elections, because when the faculty began to realize that the student activists wanted to make militancy a way of life, they found this against their interests. Faculty who are extremely liberal on extramural issues are often narrowly self-interested on intramural ones. In many universities faculties used the opportunity of the protests to cut their teaching load. In school after school this was the biggest single consequence of the student revolution. The teaching load is lower at Berkeley; it is lower at Columbia. And although it has not been lowered at Harvard, that is because it was pretty low to start with.

Still, liberal faculty-student activist tension emerged, caused by the self-interest of the faculty, concerned with maintaining its research facilities, a light teaching load, and high salaries. When students started interfering and their protests affected such matters, then the faculty turned on them. But it did not turn on them to protect academic freedom and acceptance of ideas, but only because the unrest had become a threat to research facilities, funding, peaceful relations, and the like. On such points, we find a lot of faculty, including some very radical faculty, defending traditions.

Noam Chomsky, for example, is a strong critic of the federal government, especially Defense Department policies. For many years he was also a beneficiary of government grants. He is honest and consistent in his position on the matter. He says that all money is dirty, so why not take it from the Defense Department. Essentially, Professor Chomsky has a point. The Ford Foundation, for example, gets its money from the same dirty sources, so he finds nothing morally superior in Ford Foundation money.

The period of intense politicization has ended, though this may not necessarily be permanent. The political cycle has turned, because periods of turmoil become self-exhausting. In this period the best we can do is the typical job of the academic and intellectual: to analyze why and write, so that hopefully the next time around we will be somewhat better prepared to deal with a crisis. (Frankly, I am not very hopeful; I suspect that when another crisis of a political nature hits the country it will again find its mass base in the university.)

Although it is a fact that students have been the protest center of society, I do not think the problem of the American university and the faculty is bad teaching in our educational institutions. As is fairly obvious, the better institutions became centers of unrest. I also do not think that institutions can lessen *political* protest by doing something about teaching.

A distinguished colleague of mine was the author of a report after the Columbia events, in which he has suggested that nothing would happen at Harvard because Harvard did not have the bad governance procedures that Columbia did. A year later Harvard had its troubles. Frankly, I did not anticipate what happened at Harvard, but I thought the analysis of the Columbia situation was wrong. Our distinguished colleague did not understand that what happened at Columbia was a political event that could happen at Harvard or any other institution, no matter how good it was or how able the administrators and the faculty were; it was not the consequence of a bad educational system. I disagree also with those who believe that increasing faculty involvement in the governance of the university would avoid intramural tensions. There is no university in this country in which faculty is as much involved in governance as the University of California at Berkeley. They have much power vis-à-vis the administration; they deal with the budget and everything else. And yet we know what happened at Berkeley. Increased faculty power, in itself, will not lessen the tendency to confuse scholarly judgments with political ones.

The Torment of Tenure

Nathan Glazer
Harvard University

Tenure is now subject to a number of very different kinds of attacks and is being studied by various groups from the point of view of whether it can be defended. On the one hand, tenure is attacked by critics, who say it is not used to defend academic freedom—its principal justification—but simply to defend professional privilege and jobs. It is the same issue as whether the American Medical Association defends the integrity of the medical profession or the economic interests of medical practitioners. Part of the attack comes from legislatures outraged by the enormous costs of higher education. Part of the attack comes from right-wing critics of radical faculty protected by tenure. (Though the best-known cases—for example, Angela Davis—did not have tenure.) On the other hand, tenure is attacked by critics of education, who believe that education can be made less boring and more relevant, if there is greater freedom to hire and fire.

Despite the critics, tenure not only remains strong, but it is, to my mind, for good or bad, impregnable. There are two main reasons for this. First, all public workers become increasingly impregnable to dismissal—whether sanitation men in New York or teachers anywhere. Indeed, studies show that the highest percentage of tenured staff in higher education is to be found in community colleges, not in the elite universities, private or public, or the elite colleges. Community colleges have such high proportions on tenure because they have the same personnel rules as public elementary and secondary schools, where tenure is more rapidly and universally achieved than in higher education. The second reason for the impregnability of tenure is the rapid rise of collective bargaining for teachers in higher education. This will add, to the professional defense of tenure, the union defense of jobholding. The decline of college enrollments and the financial crisis in higher education may lead to dismissals, but whether this is done under tenure rules or seniority rules will not affect the dominant position of tenure.

Would modifications of tenure improve colleges and universities? In the light of the facts, this is beside the point—it won't happen. It is also true, however, that it is hard to see that most proposals to change tenure would improve teaching and research. Proposals tend to come from two directions. First is frequent review of permanent staff from the point of view of their adequacy. Would this really lead to dismissals? It is hard to see that it would. Rather, through a system of logrolling (the reviewers would inevitably become the reviewed next time around), all jobs would simply be confirmed. It would be a more expensive and costly way of getting the present situation.

Proposals also come from another direction: "instant" or, at any rate, more rapid achievement of tenure. It is pointed out that, in addition to the strain among nontenured faculty caused by the need to produce and compete, they are constrained to conformity and caution by the need to stay in the good graces of senior faculty and administrators. I believe that Japanese universities operate with "instant" tenure with no ill effects. (It should be pointed out that Japanese industry operates the same way, and strangely enough, despite American views as to the importance of insecurity for competition and achievement, it does very well.) The impact of collective bargaining must be to achieve easier and earlier tenure. It is not clear that this has to be disastrous.

One change that I would consider to be very healthy is a "president's privilege"—the right to retire and to add faculty, independently of regular procedures, up to perhaps 2 to 4 per cent of the faculty.

I would like to raise one issue concerning tenure that will be of special interest to University Centers for Rational Alternatives. That is the use of tenure to protect faculty members who are devoted publicly to the destruction of the university and its values, including academic freedom. The issue has been raised very sharply in the case of Professor Bruce Franklin at Stanford University.

Franklin, an English professor and an authority on Herman Melville, has moved from an antiwar position to a pro-Maoist position in recent years. He is a leader of a group called Venceremos, one of whose emblems is a machine gun, which encourages all its members to acquire and become proficient in firearms, and which is committed to violent revolution. The group is organized on the basis of democratic centralism. Franklin publicly asserts that he is under the orders of the group. For example, part of his defense to the charges I will list was that he could not have done what he was charged with doing because the group had determined he was more valuable to it as a member of the Stanford faculty than off it, and he was under orders not to risk his tenure. Franklin is an admirer of Stalin as well as Mao. The defense table at his hearing was decked out with portraits of Lenin, Marx, Stalin, and Mao.

The administration suspended him with pay on the basis of incitement of students to violence in February 1971; it also got an injunction denying him the right to appear on campus. Four charges against him were finally heard by an elected board of seven full professors in an open hearing in the autumn of 1971. The board recommended his dismissal, a recommendation accepted by the president and trustees. The four charges were: disrupting a public meeting at the university at which Henry Cabot Lodge was to have spoken; preventing him from speaking; urging students to shut down the Computation Center and not disperse when police at the Computation Center ordered them to do so; urging and inciting students to engage in disruptive acts that threatened injury to individuals and property. The majority of the board upheld the administration on the last three charges.

Now some of you may think the case is a victory for the principle that a faculty member may be disciplined for disruption of the university. That is true. But there is a less positive side to the story, and that is the enormous costs that were incurred by Stanford to uphold this principle. There were thirty-three full days of hearings, running each day from one to five or six in the afternoon, and at each hearing all seven professors were present. A law firm from Los Angeles represented the administration; the cost for this was undoubtedly high. A huge transcript was prepared, and thousands of pages of other documents. A lawyer was hired to advise the board. Franklin was not given legal aid by the university, but he remained on full salary, with no teaching duties, until August 30, 1972.

Additional costs were the damage from radical students' protests after the Franklin decision. One building was destroyed by fire at a cost of around fifty thousand dollars; in these disturbances, many other fires were caught early. A bomb set outside the bedroom window of one of the professors on the board failed to go off; the members of the board and other university officials received special police protection. Certainly the cost of firing Franklin—for urging and inciting, with some success, actions regarded by a committee of his peers after due process, as destructive of the university—runs to hundreds of thousands of dollars.

One hears at Stanford the argument that Franklin's dismissal introduces a chill in free expression by other faculty members. I find this comical. But it all too likely introduces a chill in the action of the administration against other faculty members. It is a Pyrrhic victory. Stanford cannot afford another.

If tenure is a problem, as I believe it is, what do we conclude about it? Primarily, we must find a simpler mechanism for a faculty to govern and administer itself. Duties, as well as rights of tenure, should become clearer, and faculties should not hesitate to act on them. (Note that charges against Franklin were not brought by the faculty—though heard by them—but by the administration.) It is a devastating fact that *no faculty has ever moved against a fellow faculty member to take away tenure, for any reason.* Even the American Medical Association and the American Bar Association have a better record than that.

But if Stanford University's faculty has been so divided and passive in the case of a Bruce Franklin, can we really expect any faculty to take the kind of actions that would defend academic freedom on its campus, at the cost of dismissal of the faculty members who threaten it?

A Dangerous Precedent

Jack Hirshleifer
*University of California,
Los Angeles*

To strike a slightly more optimistic note: it has been insufficiently recognized how great a protection is provided by the diversity of American institutions of higher education. We have public and private, religious and secular, elite and mass colleges and universities—all competing, all providing scholarship and places or refuge against abuses. This consideration reduces the weight to be attached to the specific abuses raised in the symposium. I am certainly opposed to institutions reserving places according to race or sex, I am opposed to the youth-city concept of the university, and I view the prospect of unionization with great concern. Nevertheless, the danger is not so extreme so long as there are some universities *not* reserving places by quotas, some inspired by classical rather than youth-city models, and some rejecting the management-versus-labor image of the faculty role. I have confidence that the aberrations that are our concerns would not, in the long run, be able to withstand the competitive pressure—the pressure of the manifest intellectual superiority of those institutions that successfully maintain their integrity.

This consideration suggests that the most evil consequence of the affirmative-action coercion by the Department of Health, Education, and Welfare is not so much the content of the orders being handed down—the numbers-game decrees—as the precedent they establish for homogenization of higher education according to the lights of some Washington agency. Even if the specific HEW demands were truly for nondiscrimination, a principle I wholeheartedly favor, I would be opposed to conceding to HEW the right to monitor university achievements in this regard. There is no reason for, and many reasons against, all institutions being required to follow models of behavior administratively determined in Washington. I would therefore urge that, in our opposition to HEW's coercion, we emphasize, not so much the objectionable content of their orders to the universities, as their very warrant to give orders. I do not mean this in a legal sense. It may be that, under present laws, HEW and even many other federal agencies are fully entitled to insist that all universities buckle under to administrative dictates. But if so, it is up to us to point out the serious threat such laws pose to the independence and diversity of the universities.

Rationalizing the Financing
of Higher Education

Stephen Tonsor
University of Michigan

It has been refreshing to see so many people reexamining rather hardened opinions. I suggest that a great many of the problems we have examined bear, either in a major way or in a minor but significant way, on the method by which higher education is financed. No one has connected the fact of government intrusion and interference in the life of the university with the fact that such a large part of every university budget comes from the federal government. After all, a peasant knows that the man who pays the piper calls the tune. Until the United States has a system of full-cost tuitions paid by every student, we will not have rationality and order in the university world.

There is no reason why the public at large should pay for higher education when these costs should be borne by the student himself. It will immediately be objected that such a program would exclude the poor from post-secondary education. On the contrary, a program of loans to pay full tuition and other educational costs, guaranteed by the federal government and repaid as a tax against future income, will shift the cost of higher education to the consumer and enable even the poorest to procure the best education available. Why should the poor but able student be condemned to spend his first years at a mediocre community college because it is inexpensive state education when, by assuming responsibility for his own education, he might attend the best private school in the land? What, under the present system, happens to all those students who have little interest in and less need for an academic education?

Let us guarantee our sons and daughters truly adult status by making them responsible for their post-secondary education. I believe that such a program is not unfair but will, in fact, produce the widest recruitment and training of talent from all socioeconomic levels of our society. I believe, too, that full-cost tuitions as a source of university funds will introduce accountability, rationality, and order into college and university administration. Both society and the educational institutions themselves must begin to recognize precisely what education costs. There is no magic bottom drawer, from which university administrators get money. I find my colleagues often behaving like cargo-cult Melanesians, believing that some day the great jet planes loaded with cargo will come in and the goodies will be dispensed.

If we rationalize the financing of higher education and make the student responsible, we will introduce institutional order. Beyond that, the way in which students choose their programs and the kinds of commitments their studies represent will be a direct reflection of their willingness to spend their own money, not other people's.

Scholarship and the Humanistic Tradition

Paul Oskar Kristeller
Columbia University

In this examination of the many causes and aspects of the current crisis of the universities, and of education in general, there is one additional factor that has not yet been considered: the complete lack of public understanding of the meaning and significance of scholarship and especially of humanistic scholarship. Many, though by no means all of us, have been convinced that the philosophical, historical, and literary disciplines that we teach and write about are part of a living tradition that ultimately goes back to ancient Greece. Further, we believe that these disciplines are making continuous advances as genuine branches of knowledge, through the critical rethinking of old problems, as well as through the accumulation of new information and the refinement of new methods. We also believe that trained and experienced scholars are best equipped to transmit this knowledge through teaching and that this knowledge is gradually being diffused through schools and publications, and thus it ultimately benefits, in different degrees, all members of our society and society as a whole.

For a long time, a philistine sense of practicality has favored the natural sciences for their technological applications and the social sciences for their glittering promises, and little but lip service has been paid to the humanities, which promise no such tangible advantages. Newspapers and other media have both reflected and perpetuated these attitudes. They have been, at least in this country, notoriously silent on most discussions and achievements in the scholarly community, a significant exception being a somewhat sensational interest in archeological excavations and the art market.

The scholarly world has failed to make itself heard or understood. Most of us simply did not feel strong enough to break the walls of indifference and resistance, and others thought that they could quietly pursue their work in the sheltered atmosphere of their institutes and libraries. Yet in recent years, our situation has become even more precarious. Young and not-so-young radicals have openly and loudly attacked our values and pursuits as irrelevant. We are asked to justify our work in terms of ideologies that are unproven and that try to make up by noise, arrogant claims, and idealistic pose for a complete lack of moral and intellectual foundation. Moreover, the universities are asked to discontinue their traditional work, for which they are well equipped, and to solve instead the grave social and political problems of our time, for which they have never been equipped and for which only political agencies are responsible and effective.

These challenges, in spite of a lack of merit, are very dangerous indeed. The academic community, swollen during recent years of expansion by many persons attracted by the material and social rewards of the profession rather than by its traditional demands and ideals, has failed to take a unified stand on questions touching upon its very survival. The lack of public understanding has made us an easy and defenseless target for journalists and politicians alike—and this at a time when economic crisis and public demands for mass education make us more than ever dependent on public financial support.

The task before us, if we want our ideals to survive, is as clear as it is difficult. We must reaffirm our own principles and thus strengthen our own position, convince our wavering colleagues, encourage and instruct our students and young associates. We must press the newspapers, popular magazines, and other media to listen to our point of view, to which they have traditionally turned a deaf ear. Finally, we may try to bypass the media and reach the general public through lectures and through some of our publications. I hope very much that University Centers for Rational Alternatives will continue to make a valuable contribution along these lines.

The Importance of a Positive Appeal

Louise Rosenblatt
New York University

The reluctance of faculty members to stand up and be counted has been repeatedly mentioned during this symposium. I should like to indicate one reason why, it seems to me, we have often failed to enlist liberals, who share our views on campus disruptions or other matters. They are afraid that they will appear to be supporting the status quo. This becomes a problem particularly in connection with the question of discrimination in reverse. As we have been reminded, there is a very real situation that cries out for correction. There *has been* discrimination in the universities; there *is*, at present, discrimination. In concentrating on a denunciation of the Department of Health, Education, and Welfare, we are open to the accusation of indifference to the discriminatory situation that does exist. Then we have to protest that, of course, we are opposed to all kinds of discrimination. This is a defensive attitude.

This defensiveness, to my mind, has been a problem for University Centers for Rational Alternatives and for liberal faculty members in general throughout this period of turmoil. In order to protect the fundamental things that we value in the university—its academic freedom and its humanistic traditions of intellectual integrity—we have to oppose those who sometimes, no matter how misguidedly, are aroused about matters that do indeed call for reform. Hence, we should not be content simply to say, "We are against discrimination in reverse," because that seems to be a resigned acceptance of the present situation. Nor is it sufficient to protest that we *are* in favor of the goals sought by HEW, that we reject only their way of implementing those aims. It is necessary to go beyond the negative posture and to show that we are concerned positively with eliminating discrimination, without endangering academic standards.

"Rational alternatives"—the affirmative implication in the title of our organization—should be more fully realized. If HEW's crude methods are to be fought, what are the "rational alternatives" to discrimination in reverse? What can be done to insure that those who do meet the highest requirements are recognized, without reference to race, creed, or sex? How can university faculties in all disciplines improve recruitment methods for graduate students and for faculty appointments? By demonstrating involvement in such questions—at the very least, by expressing support for those who seek to develop valid methods of preventing discrimination, or by stimulating efforts to initiate reforms—we can be in a strong position to fight the invalid methods imposed by HEW.

This should also overcome the reluctance of those who fear that they will be seen as accepting the status quo by default. This symposium is evidence that UCRA is moving into this more affirmative phase. To be dedicated to the protection of what is sound in the idea of a university requires readiness also to seek rational paths toward changes when they are needed.

The Challenge of General Education

Theodore de Bary
Columbia University

I think that Professor Searle raised a question that goes to the substance of our problem and to an issue we have to face. We've been
speaking out of both sides of our mouths about it, and we haven't tried
to bring those two sides into a coherent relation with one another.

Professor Searle addressed himself to the importance of general education and the decline or the disintegration of any real, significant
concern over general education. In his definition of the university in
terms, essentially, of an elitist concept, he spoke of the pursuit of specialized scholarship and research. Several essays have emphasized the
importance of upholding academic standards in the pursuit of that
kind of scholarship and scientific research. The problem for us is how
we can maintain those standards, how we can carry on that kind of research, if we do not, at the same time, manifest a concern for what we
call general education.

Clearly, the kind of society that supported and sustained scientific
and scholarly research is undergoing change—change of many kinds.
But certainly, one of the great changes is the decreasing acceptance of
the basic values that have permitted and supported that kind of
scholarly excellence. We ourselves recognize the value of scholarly research, but the means of sustaining it are being steadily eroded. I do
not think that scholarship can be saved unless we face the problem:
What kind of general education, in the country at large, will produce

either the kind of financial support necessary to sustain that scholarship or the kind of political support (or electoral support, or general social support) that sustains the public financing of our institutions? In either case, we have to have an educated population that recognizes the need for these things, that is willing to support the essential values inherent in them, and, in a sense, that is willing to fight for them. If scholars concern themselves only with advanced research on the frontiers of knowledge and pay little attention to general education, our lines of logistical support become overextended. By default, the intellectual formation of our students falls into the hands of anti-intellectuals.

Reinforcing the Challenge

Arthur Bestor
University of Washington

I would like to reinforce something that Professor de Bary has raised about general education. We have said various things about standards. Standards may be slipping in some fields; it is difficult to imagine, however, that standards in the professional schools will slip very far— or those in graduate schools or for majors in undergraduate fields. It seems to me that the complete collapse has occurred in general education. The great projects at Columbia and later of the post-World War II era have somehow become trivialized. They were originally conceived to explore the whole of Western culture or even world cultures; then they are turned into textbooks and are assigned to assistant professors or teaching assistants. Finally, they become an ad hoc set of courses with no content at all, produced basically by students with some kind of special interest, which may be totally unintellectual. The University of Washington runs what is called a Free University, which does not give credit. Anybody can offer a course, and the result is a mélange of courses of the most incredible and fantastic variety. This shows what will happen if this trend is not checked.

The concept of relevance has also been trivialized. Relevance, like beauty, is in the eye of the beholder. I think the reason that we, as scholars, are pursuing esoteric subjects is that we see relevance in them that others do not see. Our job, as teachers, is to communicate our sense of relevance about the things we are doing. However, relevance often takes another form. Recently, our student paper announced on the front page that a professor of geography, who had a blind student in his class, asked the whole class to go around the university and put Braille signs on all the elevators. The paper editorialized: "At last they are making university education relevant." I think that nothing could more effectively demonstrate the irrelevance of university training to those concerned in that affair.

I would also like to reinforce what Professor Searle said about the relationship between one's own research and undergraduate courses. I think part of the reason for trivialization is the feeling that all courses for undergraduates should follow a form that does not allow much time for the professor's own interests. This seems to me to be a false conception of what education has been. Coverage of material is one thing. That can be handled in various ways. But the actuality of what the scholar or scientist does can be communicated, it seems to me, only if the student is brought into some direct relationship with what the scholar is in fact doing and with what is occupying his mind.

In Defense of Quotas

Harold Chase
University of Minnesota

The case for quotas is not getting a fair consideration. I think all of us are familiar with the basic ideas behind the demand. As a matter of fact, some people at this symposium first made the case for quotas. What people have discovered is that when the military was told, for example, "Get some Black officers," and when the government went to the Ford Motor Company and said, "You should get some employees in the executive ranks who are Black," the answer was always the same: "You know we've got standards; we can't do it." Consequently, forced quotas were thought to be the only way, during this transitional period, to make a change. If people are forced to accept quotas and if they also have standards, they will see to it that those employees brought in under quotas are brought up to the level of their standards. And it *does* work. It worked in the military, it worked in industry, and it can work at the university too. In short, quotas ensure that creative energy will be employed to end invidious discrimination.

The Need for Coalition and Proper Strategy

Isadore Blumen
Cornell University

I want to make just three brief points. I was asked, "What are you doing at this symposium? You are not a philosopher!" I think this is one of the problems we have: to some extent, the positions one finds here are those of people affiliated with liberal-arts colleges and whose primary concern is with the legitimate problems of liberal education. I think, however, that we have many allies, many people who have worked with us very well in times of trouble. It was the horse doctors at Cornell who fired the first shot in behalf of academic freedom. They were very much aware that, in the past, the drug industry and other groups had placed a great deal of pressure on them to restrict their research and teaching. We should not forget that we have allies from a broad spectrum. They certainly include scientists, some of whom have forgotten about the Scopes trial and others who may have some sense of history. I think we want to keep them as allies.

Furthermore, I want to stress another matter, which can probably be described as "world-healer" politics. It is true that many administrations have collapsed or shown no leadership. Those of us at Cornell are very much aware of this. But there have been administrations that have not collapsed, that need support and help. They deserve it. There are faculties that have collapsed, but there are faculties that have not collapsed. We have to bring them together and not simply throw up our hands. Maybe some of them are not collapsing now because they remember the old saying: "There is nothing that clarifies the mind so much as the approach of the hangman's noose." I would like to urge, therefore, that we all take advantage of these political things.

The other matter I would like to address myself to is a real danger inherent in Professor Chase's view of benign quotas. He spoke of the value this had been in the armed services, but I must ask the question: How many generals today are Negroes? The answer is "very few," because it takes a long time to produce a general. What we have to do is address ourselves to the question of how we bring Negroes and women, given the physical, social, and economic circumstances, into membership in the university community. I do not think that it can be accomplished at this stage by quotas at the faculty level. We have made some steps forward: a large number of our Black population have achieved a high-school education. We now have to take the next step, which is to bring a large number *through* the universities. The step after that will be to bring a large number through graduate school, and then we take the next step up the ladder. We do it whenever we can and by whatever means. If we emphasize this positively, we shall be doing a good thing. But we cannot, we must not, do the thing that led us down the primrose path during the period of disorders: we cannot promise instant justice.

Counsel for the Future

Samuel Lubell
American University

I want to pass on a few thoughts that may be helpful on questions that have arisen on the role of the Department of Health, Education, and Welfare. You might want to consider the difference between laws passed by Congress and executive orders. This happens to be a very big issue, developing across the whole spectrum of our government. Although Congress has been very loosely delegating powers to the executive branch, there may be attempts at tightening these powers.

There are a couple of other thoughts I would like to share with you. Though I am not an expert on education, I do know about the political climate that we are dealing with.

A lot of people at this symposium have talked in terms of the politicalization of this and that—of all kinds of things. The general thought has been: Why can't we push this out of politics and make education nonpolitical?

I want to caution you about this. Is it possible in our times? We are in a great crisis of transition. One conflict in the country is to define what is political and what is not. You may want to ask yourselves whether desiring to make something nonpolitical is not a political action in itself. Look at it in the larger context that Daniel P. Moynihan mentioned—that the educational process has to yield a certain attachment to a stable society. (And this, of course, is tied to financing considerations.)

I believe Professor Moynihan's notion is true, with one large qualification: we do not now have a stable society. The question of what will make society stable in the future is still very much at issue. This again is something we ought to keep in mind: that we are thinking about and adjusting to an unstable society.

Two other things may help define what the educational needs of this society are and to what extent and how the university can best meet those needs—though not necessarily in one package.

This is your greatest strength. If society changes in any direction—left or right—and if the university can meet those needs, it is then performing a function and should move toward a certain reconciliation with those demanding some relationship to public service.

The other thing is this: I do not believe you can get very far with your deliberations unless you gather some facts. You cannot reconcile and deal with any of these problems in words and philosophy alone. You need to gather facts, find out what is going on, who is working, where and how.

Let me give you one note of encouragement; this is in reference to Professor Bunzel's excellent essay on the whole trade-union question. I was one of the agitators for a newspaper guild in Washington. I faced the same concern: I did not want the newspaper guild to affect the intellectual integrity of the writing of journalism, but I *did* want to improve working standards and the financial side of the profession. Very much so. I was the lowest-paid columnist in Washington, writing a daily column for thirty-five dollars a week. Looking back—and this may be of some value to you—I think that you should not make the mistake of assuming that what you do in improving the financial side will necessarily either help or hurt you in preserving professional integrity.

Generally, improvement in the financial picture for journalists has increased newspaper costs. It has raised the question of the survival of newspapers, and of how many outlets there are.

On the intellectual side, the main changes and the main problems in newspaper writing have come from changes in the society. The basic problem was the failures of newspapers. They have not failed as badly as many people think—nor do I think the universities have failed as badly as many people say. But the main failure has been that journalism did not develop new reporting techniques to deal with societal changes.

You, too, have a financial problem, but the question of intellectual integrity is tied to your ability to develop educational techniques that meet the needs of society.

The Scholar–News-Media Gap and Public Education

Leonard R. Sussman
Executive Director,
Freedom House

"If the country is to be governed with the consent of the governed," Walter Lippmann has written, "then the government must arrive at opinions about what their governors want them to consent to."[1] Yet Mr. Lippmann elsewhere declared that "as social truth is organized today, the press is not constituted to furnish from one edition to the next the amount of knowledge that the democratic theory of public opinion demands."[2] Most newsmen would readily agree with both assertions. Men of the press—newspapers, news magazines, and radio and television news departments—generally believe that they play a major role in the transmitting of opinion once it has been formed. But many newsmen bridle at the suggestion that the press is the primary force in educating the public to form useful opinions on current issues. This dichotomy is illustrated by the voluminous documentation that the advertising and promotion departments of the news media present to potential advertisers to prove that a particular television channel or newspaper can move a viewer or reader to buy a product, and by the equally persuasive statistics compiled particularly by television networks to demonstrate that television viewing neither inspires acts of violence nor generates radical change. In one instance, television can "sell"; in another, it cannot.

To be sure, there are limitations within each of the modes of mass communication. A picture on TV carries a strong, often emotional charge, but it may be deficient in conveying the substance of an event or idea in sufficient context to inspire continuing reflection by the viewer. A picture may also critically distort the meaning of an event; the test of truth, therefore, is not whether what was shown actually happened but whether it conveys a total message that is true. "The media should be expected to show more concern for the accuracy of the message received," emphasized a staff report of the National Commission on the Causes and Prevention of Violence.[3]

There are also limitations within the audience. Exposure to the mass media has been shown to be highly selective. Readers and viewers tend to read or watch selectively, depending in large measure on their predispositions.[4] Yet the media *do* affect the audience. Ingenuity is therefore required to combine the visual and auditory arts—in both print and broadcast media—so that the public is encouraged to watch, and ultimately to *think*. To generate thought in the mass-media audience is perhaps the hardest task. Newsmen are not all universally committed to that task. Consequently, Mr. Lippmann, one of America's most resourceful and insightful journalists, could state categorically that "the press is not constituted to furnish . . . the amount of knowledge that the democratic theory of public opinion demands." If the press is not so constituted, why isn't it? And if it were, what would it have to do differently?

Since the schools on all levels must take note of the educational influence of the press and public media—sometimes counteracting it, sometimes reinforcing it—the relevance of our question to the issues discussed at this symposium is obvious.

Let me state at the outset that I believe the news media in all the varied forms are the last great hope of a free, technotronic society. Upon the media, whether they or their audiences would have it so, rests the vital role of informing two hundred million citizens about diverse events, trends, and intrinsic implications within this highly complex society, within nations far removed in space but posing imminent or long-term policy choices for us—and about the ceaseless interaction between foreign and domestic issues. The situation with respect to social knowledge is quite different from the layman's ability to differentiate the aorta from the cerebellum, as Marvin Bressler points out. "The layman's views [of social issues] become part of the 'effective public opinion' with all the action consequences . . . "[5] The time has long passed when a well-educated elite could spend years leisurely moving through preparatory school and universities before assuming leadership roles in the society. Today, not even the elite who will make it through college and into their societal roles can fully keep pace with the changes in our society and in our international relationships. Yet today, more than ever before, an increasingly larger segment of our citizenry is expected to develop opinions and help select policies and political leaders. Even if the issues themselves were not more complex than ever—the tally of legations at the United Nations alone suggests the diversity of interests and policies now affecting international relationships—the quantum jump in communications technology would in itself create a serious information explosion.

Given the complexity of factual situations, their magnification through the news media, and the need to sort out meanings if one is to play a citizen's role—how can this informational need be met? To put it bluntly, since it is impossible for the mass of Americans to return to high school or college for continuing education, the mass news media should reconsider its responsibility to a free society.

WHAT IS NEWS?

The question "What is news?" lies at the heart of the controversy over whether the press accepts an educative function. Traditionally, newsmen have defined "news" schematically (it is the who-what-where-when of an event) or ontologically (it is what you read in your newspapers or see on television—in effect, what newsmen *say* it is) or subjectively (the reporter's judgment, based upon his assumption of the audience's interest in conflict, immediacy, human interest, impact, saliency, or proximity). Most of the criteria for newsworthiness suggest a short time lag between the event and the report of it; the subject may be frivolous, but if it happened today it stands a good chance of appearing on prime-time TV news. If it is cataclysmic to hundreds of thousands of persons but happened yesterday, it may get crowded out; or, even if it took place today but occurred six thousand miles away, it may suffer oblivion on tonight's TV news show. It stands a somewhat better chance of being reported in the few serious daily newspapers, though the *New York Times*, over the past ten years, has reduced by 25 per cent the wordage devoted to international affairs. And these were years of major, dramatic changes on the foreign scene.

What appears in print or is broadcast, then, depends largely upon how the media determine what is news. It should be understood that I am not suggesting that any authority but responsible editors of the media should determine the principles under which the press operates or its daily functioning under those principles. I do not accept, however, the dictum of one network-news president that no one but an active newsman has the background, or indeed the right, to criticize news coverage or programming. The processing of news is too important an aspect of American life to be left solely to any one professional or commercial body. In point of fact, "news" of considerable moment may be found imbedded deep in the labors of scores of professions and occupations, not the least of which is the realm of the scholar and the educator.

THE SCHOLAR CAN REDEFINE NEWS

There should indeed be a link between the scholar and the news media in the interest of enhancing public understanding of events near and distant (in both space and time). A now-classic example of the failure of TV news departments to recognize the need to blend scholarship with "newsmanship" to produce a higher level of mass education was the handling of President Nixon's visit to China in 1972. The newsmen who accompanied the President were nearly all Washington-based political reporters or TV generalists. Virtually no China specialists were sent by the networks, who knew that Americans would spend hours watching satellite-relayed reports from Peking. John Chancellor and Barbara Walters, featured on the NBC network during the "reopening" of China, described in great detail the banquets, the articles on sale in the shops, and Mrs. Nixon's shopping tour. Back in the New York studio, meanwhile, waiting for an occasional moment to interpret the primary diplomatic and political event, sat a China scholar from Columbia University. Far removed from the scene, he could add little to the knowledge of Americans in the brief time available to him. How different might it have been if he had gone to Peking and the Chancellor-Walters team remained in New York to put earnest, laymen's questions to the specialist on the scene?

The Nixon travels abroad promoted an unusual expansion of "hard" news and the opportunity—which newsmen should seek more often—to weave in "soft" news. "Hard" news is the day's fast-breaking event; "soft" news is the background information, the examination of meanings, of trends, of possibilities ahead. Often, today's headlines on "hard" stories fade by tomorrow, but the "soft" story may presage highly significant developments that will affect many of mankind's tomorrows. Admittedly, a segment of the press increasingly seeks the trend story that has broad implications for the future. But often such articles are shaped along preconceived lines determined by traditional press coverage. Generally, the "soft" story, no matter how serious its implications, cannot successfully compete for space or prominence with today's "hard" news. To be sure, one cannot confidently predict very often that a distinguishable trend will materialize as foreseen. But if earnest scholars regard the issue as important, the educative function involved in printing or broadcasting the subject should be deemed a strong factor in its favor.

Let us examine a case in point. Early in 1972 Professors Robert A. Scalapino and Paul Seabury, political scientists at the University of California, Berkeley, prepared a fifteen-thousand-word paper, "Foreign Policy and the 1972 Presidential Campaign."[6] The advisory paper was published in association with six United States senators, three Democrats and three Republicans, headed by Senator Margaret Chase Smith. The senators had met with the scholars and Freedom House officers six months earlier to discuss the professors' working paper, "A Plea for Rational and Measured Dialogue." They had warned that "miscalculations of our intentions by [America's] opponents have played a major role in bringing on the conflicts in which we have been engaged since World War II." The authors observed that "great chasms of disagreement over our role in world politics have been opened at home." They designed the final paper to "elevate the substantive, intellectual content of public dialogue on American foreign policy." The paper dealt with each of the major areas of the United States' interests abroad and urged the candidates and their supporters to discuss substantive foreign-policy issues. The paper did *not* attempt to recommend specific policy decisions, but it did suggest certain myths that have been nurtured in the mass media about some aspects of our foreign policy.

The paper was reported in newspapers around the country, favorably commented upon in editorial columns, and, because of press attention, was used in university seminars and by world-affairs councils during the summer of the 1972 presidential campaign. A discussion of the Scalapino-Seabury paper at the *New York Times* produced the following revealing exchange.

Terence Smith (diplomatic correspondent in the *Times'* Washington bureau): The Scalapino-Seabury paper is important. Its value should not be measured in terms of newspaper clippings. But we cannot report it. I wouldn't know how to write the lead.

Sussman: I agree on its importance, but how else can the value of the analysis be fulfilled if its existence is not known to political and educational leaders and the general public?

Smith: Our problem is that the paper does not fit any conventional definition of news. We therefore have a conceptual problem.

Sussman: You are saying, then, that news is not news if it comes in a *new* package. To be news it must be recognizable.

Smith: Yes, and what is further troubling is that the six senators involved do not form a recognizable group.

Sussman: These men and women were invited to take part precisely because they had the national interest and not party or personal gain in mind.

Smith: But that means they do not possess political clout.

Not a line was published in the *Times,* though the equally astute *Washington Post* reported the story on page two.

The paper was a scholarly exercise. Laymen were regarded as the primary audience. The target was the improvement of the political process. Admittedly, this was not "hard" news sufficient to compete with a bombing raid or an earthquake. But—who knows?—long after the earth heals such wounds, the consequences of today's political process may still be jarring mankind. "Soft" news discussed by Professors Scalapino and Seabury may become tomorrow's "hard" news. Is there no "category" into which such educative news fits today? Or must we always wait until the political dilemmas are upon us, until a new crisis is indeed "news" before we produce a smattering of information for the public? When the crisis arrives, the conceptual problem ceases: a crisis is top "hard" news, recognizable, and yet in a sad and unprofessional way, predictable and not nearly as *immediate* as it seems. For, in truth, today's most critical "hard" news is often composed of yesterday's "soft" news that was never explained to, or understood by, the mass news audience. A writer in the Columbia *Journalism Review* put it well: "When one's business is the unusual, he should not be panicked by the *unusual* unusual." [7]

Significantly, throughout the period of the presidential primaries of 1972, the Japanese ambassador to the United States made more speeches on United States foreign policy than all the American primary candidates together. He received ample press coverage for his labor and, in fact, helped measurably to clarify for many Americans some aspects of international affairs that were not being discussed by American leaders in or out of office. Presumably, it was news when the Japanese ambassador spoke on these issues. While acknowledging that the ambassador generates a certain unusual interest when speaking to Americans about their own policies, it can be assumed that the policies themselves were worthy of examination. The press is often in the position of arousing interest in subjects, prolonging that interest (overextending it sometimes on certain exotic subjects), or certainly casting exploratory light upon it. The press knows how to draw political leaders into discussion of issues and how to generate public reaction to those leaders. But first the "conceptual problem" must be solved. The press must accept its responsiblity to educate the public on issues of fundamental concern to the free society.

THE USES OF SCHOLARSHIP BY THE PRESS

Presidential visits to Peking and Moscow are rare; those lost opportunities may not soon return. American viewers and readers might have received significant political and economic background on the thirty crucial years of East-West conflict just past. But, almost daily, equally substantive developments occur across the Asian continent, within the NATO alliance, in Africa, the Middle East, and India. At home, too, fundamental changes are under way in race relations, economic retooling for peace, and in a dozen other vital areas. Specialists in each of these fields can foresee many broad outlines of things to come, of dilemmas and choices ahead. The general public would profit from having some early warnings; indeed, decision-makers at all levels of government would be helped in the long run by having a more informed constituency. How much better might this country have fared if the people had really understood the decisions that drew us into the Vietnam war, kept us there, and ruled against pay-as-you-go economic adjustments? In this context, I do not regard as sufficient the academics' signing of protest or supportive ads, or participation in one-sided discussions that rarely enlightened the public during crucial stages of Vietnam decision-making. I suggest the regularized application of scholarship to the profession of reporting and interpreting news.

In some departments of daily newspapers specialists have long served as consultants. Locally or nationally known scholars have often appeared in the art sections and on the financial pages of major newspapers. There are just as compelling reasons for having an academic specialist on Germany or world trade sit in an editorial conference when the day's news features events in those fields. On major newspapers such conferences often determine the position to be taken in the editorial column as well as the manner in which an important story is handled in the news columns. How prominently will it be displayed (front page or inside), what is the headline element, and, perhaps most important on a serious newspaper, should there be a supporting article providing background or interpretation that goes beyond the news story itself?

On the most responsible newspapers, part of the editorial page may be given over regularly to a scholar who interprets current developments in greater depth than can be provided correspondents on the scene. That is not to say the academic specialist is a substitute for good reporting from the field; he supplements it, adds historic context, and, with the tools of scholarship, projects ahead. Professor Zbigniew Brzezinski does this regularly for *Newsweek* magazine and Professor

Robert R. Bowie for the *Christian Science Monitor*. Both write as interestingly for the layman as professional newsmen appearing in the respective publications. They add perspective not generally found in the general press. In this fashion the press serves as "honest broker" between the academic community and the varied aspects of American society.

Nearly every daily newspaper in the United States has access to nearby college or university faculties. Not only would the editorial and news pages profit from consultation with specialists, but science and, of course, education departments are other likely candidates for scholarly collaboration.

Journalism schools can help train journalists to use the vast output of the scholarly journals as source material. Seven years ago the Graduate School of Journalism at Columbia University initiated a training and research program in the social sciences. It emphasizes the use of academic materials both for "spot news" stories and as background for writing on current social issues. A feasibility study has been completed by Edward W. Barrett, director of communications of the Academy for Educational Development, Inc., evaluating the creation of a national social-science information center designed to collect, organize, and analyze the latest findings and to assist journalists in interpreting them for the public.

Newspapers and newsmagazines are no longer the major source of information for Americans. Since 1963, television, with all its limitations and impact, has become the primary source of news.[8] The academic community is sorely needed in the newsrooms of both local channels and the three major networks. Television newsmen would not unanimously agree. Some welcome *limited* participation by specialists. When documentaries are planned—with decreasing frequency in network TV these days—scholars in particular fields under examination are often consulted; fewer appear on camera. In some network newsrooms, however, there is the conviction that newsmen in the field or with field experience have sufficient background for the limited purpose permitted by the medium. For, declare TV newsmen, interesting the audience must come first and, they add, scholars are notoriously poor at that. For that reason, broadcast news producers seldom ask scholars to appear before camera on a prime-time news program. Efforts to employ the talents of academic specialists often end in frustration, one TV news producer has said. Scholars do not understand the limitations and mechanics of a daily news program. He agrees that the shows reach tens of millions of viewers every day and most need the expert guidance that an academic specialist can provide. He adds that he cannot protect the pace and continuity of his program if he uses a rambling, repetitious exposition even from the world's most learned expert. This complaint says as much about the inadequacy of TV's mechanics as it does about the scholar's inability to speak in sharp, concise sentences and cram important ideas into a fifty-second format.

Certainly, no teacher worth his salt would defend rambling discourse in the classroom or on television. But the harsh strictures of TV programming represent an insuperable problem for any sustained development of ideas (or even balanced reporting). The half-hour TV news program covers twenty to thirty different news items in about twenty-five minutes and fifteen seconds (the remaining four minutes and forty-five seconds are reserved for commercials). Clearly, sixty or even ninety seconds is insufficient time in which to report a new, major, and often complex development and explain its implications—whether the voice is that of a talented professional newscaster (whose material is written by an equally talented professional writer) or that of an academic specialist capable of enriching the report in breadth and depth. There simply is not enough time. The time strictures must be broken first.

Yet the scholar should also be trained to get quickly to the nub of the development and make his contribution. He must be prepared to go to the studio on very short notice, sometimes at odd hours of the day or evening, and after discussing a new development at length he may discover that he may appear on camera, if at all, for perhaps forty-five seconds. Is it worth the effort? Yes, if meeting the public's need for balanced information in greater perspective is important to the academic specialist. He should become a welcome figure in the TV newsroom. Ultimately, he should be consulted on the assignment of field crews to areas where trends are developing ahead of today's visible events. And that implies a dimension for television that is not now regularly observable. Just as TV carries a built-in stereotype of the televised scholar coming across as boring and slow-witted, so prime-time TV news accepts rigid stereotypes of itself—for example, as boxed in economically by half-hour limitations, since news programs do not generally produce as much income as entertainment shows.

But the television medium is too important a force to permit its educative values to be restricted or distorted. Television deserves the scholar's attention not for what it *is* but for what it might be. At this moment, it is perhaps the most important of the many channels leading into the homes and minds of Americans, particularly young people. It could provide all manner of background information on our society and the world. One day soon, perhaps with the arrival of cable television and its twenty broadband channels potentially competing in every home, we may see a far greater diversity of programs—including ample time for the specialist on and off camera. But that day will come only if federal regulations do not—by design or default—permit the monopolizing of cable TV in ways that restrict the public's choice in the new medium as in the old.

Scholars should prepare for that day by making themselves available now for consultations with radio, television, and newspaper editors.

NOTES

1. Walter Lippmann, "The Job of the Washington Correspondent," *Atlantic*, Jan. 1960, p. 49.

2. Quoted by Robert E. Park, "The Natural History of the Newspaper," in *Mass Communications,* Wilbur Schramm, ed. (Urbana, Ill.: University of Illinois Press, 1960), p. 13.

3. Staff papers, *Mass Media and Violence,* Vol. IX (Washington, D.C.: U.S. Govt. Printing Office), Nov. 1969.

4. Bernard Berelson and Gary A. Steiner, *Human Behavior: An Inventory of Scientific Findings* (New York: Harcourt Brace, 1964), p. 518.

5. Marvin Bressler, "The Potential Public Uses of the Behavior Sciences," in *Behavioral Sciences and the Mass Media* (New York: Russell Sage Foundation, 1968), p. 21.

6. Published in *Freedom At Issue* (Washington, D.C.: Freedom House), Jan.-Feb. 1972.

7. Gladwin Hill, "The Lessons of l'affaire Hughes," *Freedom At Issue,* May-June 1972, p. 46.

8. Roper Organization annual polls.

Concluding Observations

John H. Bunzel
*California State University,
San Jose*

I would like to make one or two points about the move to collective bargaining and some form of unionization in the academic world, by way of extending my earlier comments. We need to be reminded that those of us participating in this symposium are not necessarily representative of those institutions presently facing the most immediate challenges and changes from this newest venture. Most of them are public community colleges and state colleges or universities. We have not seriously examined their problems, but I can assure you they are real and very different from the problems of the more selective and eminent institutions of higher learning in the country, especially those in the private sector of education.

One of my concerns has been the academic consequences of unionization in terms of quality education and high standards. I have stressed the erosion of collegiality and consensus in the academic community as both a cause and consequence of the growth of union sentiment. But a parallel concern is what I perceive to be an implicit, if not explicit, attack on the concept of merit and professionalism, particularly on the part of the newer and younger faculty members coming into our colleges and universities. I worry about an increasingly civil-service attitude and mentality taking root in the academic community. Unionization may become the agent of change in many of our colleges and universities, and it may, among other things, reflect the loss of faculty confidence in the worth of their own work and value as teachers and scholars. The union movement will also be likely to capitalize on the feelings of many people on our faculties who are deeply distrustful of authority and who look instead to a deepening of the momentum toward egalitarianism.

In his comments about the affirmative-action program, Professor Seabury draws attention to a problem that I am sure concerns us all. I refer specifically to the concern for the loss of university autonomy and independence. In the past several years many of our colleagues throughout the country have resisted the attempts to politicize the campuses by ideologues of the Left. Twenty years ago, during the McCarthy era, the same fight was waged against the extremists of the Right. I would hope that in the years to come we would be equally steadfast in defending the principle that intrusion by the government into the internal affairs of our universities is not to be lightly sanctioned in a pluralist society. We can all support—and should support—affirmative efforts to provide genuine equality on a nondiscriminatory basis to everyone in the academic market who is looking for a job. But we must never allow ourselves to give up our fundamental right and responsibility to make judgments about matters of faculty tenure and promotion on the basis of individual achievement and merit.

Agenda for the Future

John R. Searle
University of California,
Berkeley

There are a few concluding points that I would like to make. First, concerning faculty unions. It seems to me the issue is not: "Are faculty unions desirable?" I think they are the wrong model altogether for structuring relationships in an ideal university. The question is: "Will we be clobbered into having to have faculty unions in order to defend our interests?" What we ought to be concerning ourselves with, I believe, is not the question "Is the union part of our ideal university?" but rather the question "How can we defend our interests so that we are not compelled to unionize in order to defend such basic things as our standard of living and our working conditions?"

Secondly, about faculty government. Anybody who has been a fellow of an Oxford College has to smile at the suggestion made earlier that the Berkeley faculty is powerful. I am sure that it is powerful by the standards of many colleges in the United States, but it seems to me that it has precisely the wrong kind of power. It has the power to place itself in an adversary relation with other sources of power in the university. Now I have a very simple—but I am afraid Utopian—proposal to make about university government. Nevertheless, I think it is good to put forward Utopian proposals to have something to compare reality with, as a touchstone in our proceedings.

I believe that the faculty ought to be responsible for the governance of the university. I believe that boards of trustees should be abolished

281

or placed in the role of constitutional monarchs. I believe that the idea of an independent administration contains very serious weaknesses. An independent administration has no natural constituency and tends to find itself in an adversary relation with the faculty. I believe that the university ideally should be a corporation of the faculty, and the administration should be the administrative and executive arm of the faculty government. Now this suggestion does seem paradoxical, coming from somebody who has been criticizing the faculty for their irresponsibility as I have, both in my book and also earlier at this symposium. But I think that the irresponsibility is often structural. The faculty member goes to bed at night in the full knowledge that he does not have to take the rap for the policy decisions made by the administration. He is not responsible for decisions that the president makes about student discipline, or whether or not the president gives in to pressure from the Department of Health, Education, and Welfare. I want to give the faculty the responsibility for government that goes with its present educational responsibility.

The present system of university government in the United States is an ad hoc system that has grown up haphazardly over the years. It does not seem to me to be working out well in practice, and it does not appear to be theoretically justifiable. Often one hears people harking back to a time when we allegedly had "collegial" participation, but I think that, in the history of most American universities, that is a myth In fact, Flexner was probably right in his time when he referred to the American faculties as a "proletariat." I believe also that the era of independent faculty research baronies that grew up in the great federal-grant multiversities was not an adequate method of approaching the problem of faculty government.

Finally, what should University Centers for Rational Alternatives do? What role can we play? We are moving out of the era when our only concern was student unrest, and our problem was how to defend the university against these attacks. There are more interesting and challenging things we can talk about now. There are two things that I would like to see us concentrate on. First, the entire question of faculty government and university government in general, particularly with regard to the question of what role students should play. This subject contains many interesting questions. For example, what kind of contributions should students make to decision-making? I do not think there is much satisfactory literature on this subject, and I would like to see us consider such specific issues in terms of the larger question of the nature of university government.

Secondly, I would like for us to try to articulate a theory of general education and its relationship to specialized education. I am very suspicious of the dichotomy; I don't teach my courses as either general or specialized, and I don't think many good people do. I would like the whole thing to be rethought. Finally, what may seem a rather unimportant point but is important if we are to be at all effective: this organization, in its public stances, in its public output, has been unnecessarily peevish, humorless, and defensive. I enjoy the handouts that come in the familiar envelope, but I often open them with the thought, "Here is another cry from the wounded bears." Then one reads the litany of atrocities. I think, in fact, that the past few years have been, if nothing else, very funny. I think they have been hilarious, although often they have been tragic as well. As a matter of effectiveness, I believe we will be more successful by poking fun at our adversaries than by the stern, defensive, nervous, and peevish scolding that we often come out with. The tone of many of our official stances has been rather that of the old-time, faculty-committee bore. I would like us to abandon that tone.

Contributors

Arthur Bestor   **University of Washington**

Professor Bestor, who has served as Harmsworth professor of American history at Oxford University and as president and director of the Council for Basic Education, is professor of history at the University of Washington, Seattle. He is the author of *Backwoods Utopias* and *The Restoration of Learning*.

Isadore Blumen   **Cornell University**

Dr. Blumen is professor of industrial relations at Cornell University.

John H. Bunzel   **California State University**

President of California State at San Jose, Dr. Bunzel was a member of the California attorney general's Advisory Committee on Equal Rights and a delegate to the Democratic National Convention in 1968. He has written *American Small Businessman* and *Anti-Politics in America*.

Steven M. Cahn   **University of Vermont**

Dr. Cahn, professor of philosophy and chairman of the philosophy department at the University of Vermont, is the author of *Fate, Logic and Time* and *Philosophy of Religion*.

Harold Chase   **University of Minnesota**

Dr. Chase is professor of political science at the University of Minnesota and author of *Federal Judges: The Appointing Process*.

Theodore de Bary   **Columbia University**

Provost and vice-president in charge of academic affairs at Columbia, Dr. de Bary is Horace Carpentier professor of Oriental studies and editor of *The Buddhist Tradition: In India, China and Japan*.

Gray L. Dorsey   Washington University

Dr. Dorsey is Nagel professor of jurisprudence and international law at Washington University, St. Louis. He is the editor of *Constitutional Freedom and the Law*.

Charles Frankel   Columbia University

Dr. Frankel, Old Dominion professor of philosophy and public affairs, Columbia, was chairman of the U.S. delegation to the UNESCO General Conference in 1966 and was assistant U.S. secretary of state for educational and cultural affairs, 1965-67. He is the author of *The Case for Modern Man* and *Pleasures of Philosophy*.

Richard Gambino   City University of New York

Associate professor of educational philosophy at Queens College of City University, Dr. Gambino is on the editorial board of *Freedom At Issue*, published by Freedom House.

Nathan Glazer   Harvard University

Dr. Glazer is professor of education and social structure at Harvard. He is the coauthor with Daniel P. Moynihan of *Beyond the Melting Pot*, and is the author of *Remembering the Answers: Essays on the American Student Revolt* and *American Judaism*.

Oscar Handlin   Harvard University

Recipient of the Pulitzer Prize for History in 1952 for *The Uprooted*, Dr. Handlin is professor of history at Harvard and director of the Charles Warren Center for Studies in American History. He has also written *The Americans* and *American People in the Twentieth Century*.

Jack Hirshleifer   University of California

Dr. Hirshleifer, professor of economics at the University of California at Los Angeles, is the author of *Investment, Interest, and Capital*.

Robert Hoffman   City University of New York

Author of *Language, Minds and Knowledge*, Dr. Hoffman is associate professor of philosophy at York College of City University.

Sidney Hook   New York University

Emeritus professor of philosophy at New York University, Dr. Hook is a fellow of the American Academy of Arts and Sciences and senior research fellow at the Hoover Institute, Stanford University. He is the author of *Political Power and Personal Freedom, Academic Freedom and Academic Anarchy,* and *Education and the Taming of Power.*

Paul Oskar Kristeller   Columbia University

Dr. Kristeller is Frederick Woodbridge professor of philosophy at Columbia. He has been a member of the Institute for Advanced Study at Princeton, and is the author of *Eight Philosophers of the Italian Renaissance.*

Irving Kristol   New York University

Henry R. Luce professor of urban values at New York University, Irving Kristol was managing editor of *Commentary,* cofounder and editor of *Encounter,* editor of *The Reporter,* and coeditor of *The Public Interest.* In 1972 he was appointed by President Nixon to the board of directors of the Corporation for Public Broadcasting. He is the author of *On the Democratic Idea in America.*

Paul Kurtz   State University of New York

Dr. Kurtz, professor of philosophy at the State University of New York at Buffalo and editor of *The Humanist,* is the author of *The Fullness of Life* and *Decision and the Condition of Man.*

Abba Lerner   City University of New York

Distinguished professor of economics at Queens College of City University, Dr. Lerner has served as a consultant to the Rand Corporation, the government of Israel, and the Institute for Mediterranean Affairs. He has written *The Economics of Control* and *Everybody's Business.*

Seymour M. Lipset   Harvard University

Dr. Lipset is the author of *Political Man, Politics and the Social Sciences,* and *Rebellion in the University,* and was awarded the Gunnar Myrdal Prize in 1970 for books of distinction in the study of human behavior. He is professor of government and sociology at Harvard and a member of the executive committee of the Center for International Affairs.

Samuel Lubell   American University

Newspaperman, war correspondent, radio and television political analyst and commentator, Mr. Lubell is a professor of communications at American University. He has written *Revolt of the Moderates* and *The Hidden Crisis in American Politics.*

Fritz Machlup   Princeton University

Dr. Machlup was formerly Walker professor of economics and international finance at Princeton and is visiting professor of economics at New York University. He has served as consultant to the U.S. Department of Labor, the Treasury, and the Board of Governors of the Federal Reserve System. He is the author of *Remaking the International Monetary System* and *The Production and Distribution of Knowledge in the United States*.

Glenn R. Morrow   University of Pennsylvania

Before his death, Dr. Morrow was Adam Seybert professor of moral and intellectual philosophy at the University of Pennsylvania. He wrote *Plato's Cretan City* and *Plato's Epistles*.

Daniel P. Moynihan   Harvard University

Ambassador to India and professor of education and urban politics at the Kennedy School of Government at Harvard, Dr. Moynihan has served Presidents Kennedy, Johnson, and Nixon in various capacities. He coauthored *Beyond the Melting Pot* with Nathan Glazer, and wrote *The Politics of a Guaranteed Income*.

Ernest Nagel   Columbia University

Formerly John Dewey professor of philosophy and now University professor emeritus at Columbia, Dr. Nagel is the author of *Principles of the Theory of Probability* and *The Structure of Science*.

Robert Nisbet   University of Arizona

Professor of sociology and history at the University of Arizona, former vice-chancellor for academic affairs at the University of California at Riverside, Dr. Nisbet was appointed by the New York State Board of Regents to the Albert Schweitzer Chair in the Humanities at Columbia University in 1974. He is the author of *The Quest for Community, The Sociological Tradition,* and *Social Change and History*.

Henry R. Novotny   California State College

Dr. Novotny is associate professor of psychology at California State at Bakersfield.

Louise Rosenblatt   New York University

Dr. Rosenblatt is emeritus professor of education at New York University and the author of *Literature As Exploration*.

Edward J. Rozek   University of Colorado

Dr. Rozek is director of the Institute for the Study of Comparative Politics and Ideologies at the University of Colorado, Boulder. With W. W. Rostow, he prepared the 1967 revised edition of *The Dynamics of Soviet Society*.

Paul Seabury   University of California

Dr. Seabury, professor of government at the University of California, Berkeley, was formerly the provost of the University of California at Santa Cruz. In 1964 he received the Bancroft Prize for his book, *Power, Freedom and Diplomacy*. He has also written *The Rise and Decline of the Cold War*.

John R. Searle   University of California

Dr. Searle is professor of philosophy at the University of California in Berkeley. He was a lecturer at Christ Church, Oxford, and was a visiting professor at Brasenose College, Oxford. Author of *Speech Acts* and *The Campus War*, Dr. Searle served as a consultant to the President's Commission on Student Unrest (the Scranton Commission).

Patrick Suppes   Stanford University

Professor of philosophy and statistics at Stanford, Dr. Suppes is a fellow of the Center for Advanced Study in the Behavioral Sciences and the author of *A Probabilistic Theory of Causality* and *Axiomatic Set Theory*.

Leonard R. Sussman   Freedom House

Mr. Sussman is executive director of Freedom House and a member of the editorial board of *Freedom At Issue*, published by Freedom House.

Miro Todorovich   City University of New York

Dr. Todorovich is associate professor of physics at Bronx Community College, City University, and executive secretary of the University Centers for Rational Alternatives.

Stephen Tonsor   University of Michigan

Dr. Tonsor is professor of history at the University of Michigan.

Ernest van den Haag   New School for Social Research

Ernest van den Haag, lecturer in psychology and sociology at the New School for Social Research, New York, and adjunct professor of social philosophy at

New York University, is also a practicing psychoanalyst. He is the author of *The Jewish Mystique* and *On Political Violence and Civil Disobedience.*

Cyril Zebot   Georgetown University

Dr. Zebot is professor of economics at Georgetown University, Washington, D.C., the author of *The Economics of Competitive Coexistence,* and the editor of *Agenda for Georgetown.*

Marvin Zimmerman   State University of New York

Dr. Zimmerman is professor of philosophy at the State University of New York at Buffalo.